THE REALIST'S GUIDE
TO A
SUCCESSFUL
MUSIC
CAREER

Follow Your
Own Beat, But
Not If You're A Drummer —

Mark

ALSO BY MATT DECOURSEY

Balance Me

Million Dollar Bedroom

JOEL CUMMINS & MATT DeCOURSEY

OF UMPHREY'S McGEE

THE REALIST'S GUIDE TO A SUCCESSFUL MUSIC CAREER

FOREWORD BY
JEFF COFFIN OF DAVE MATTHEWS BAND

R B
Realist Books

R_B
Realist Books

8900 State Line Road, #100, Leawood, KS 66206

ISBN-13: 978-0-578-51760-5
ISBN-10: 0-578-51760-4
Library of Congress Control Number: 2019942799

CONTENTS

SECTION THREE:
THE IMPORTANCE OF YOUR DEMO

SECTION FOUR:
GETTING GIGS

SECTION FIVE:
CREATING MUSIC

SECTION SIX:
RECORDING

SECTION SEVEN:
PREPARING FOR A SHOW OR PERFORMANCE

SECTION EIGHT:
FINDING YOUR SOUND

SECTION NINE:
BUILDING AN AUDIENCE

SECTION TEN:
MARKETING AND MERCH

SECTION ELEVEN:
MANAGEMENT

SECTION TWELVE:
THINGS YOU NEED TO KNOW, OR AT LEAST SHOULD HEAR ONCE

SECTION THIRTEEN:
BEING A GOOD BANDMATE

SECTION FOURTEEN:
GEAR TALK

SECTION FIFTEEN:
CREW

SECTION SIXTEEN:
TIP OF THE ICEBERG

APPENDIX

FOREWORD

These guys aren't joking with the title of their book: *The Realist's Guide to a Successful Music Career.*

It's been said that "The truth shall set you free." If that's the case, you best get ready for some freedom!

My career started in the early 1990s when I moved to Nashville, Tennessee, after graduating from the University of North Texas. I have played some of the worst gigs you can imagine and I have played some of the greatest you could dream up. Starting in 1997, my career changed dramatically when I began touring with the genre-busting Béla Fleck & The Flecktones. I played, wrote, and recorded with them for fourteen years and won three Grammy Awards with the band.

In 2008, I got a call that would further change my life and career. Dave Matthews Band's sax player had been injured in an ATV wreck and I was asked to sub for him for a few months. As many of you likely know, LeRoi Moore passed from those injuries a month and a half into his recovery. The band asked me to stay on, and after talking with Béla and the band, I said yes. Today, I'm writing this foreword from the tour bus lounge on the way to our next Dave Matthews gig in Dallas. I travel the world with my saxophone and I am grateful every day for my career and the people I play and work with. I will reiterate what this book goes into great detail on: That hard work, dedication, passion, working well with others, understanding your role, determination, vision, dedication, perseverance, and many other factors all play a vital part in your success.

Now, on to my boy Joel Cummins! I have known Joel since the early Flecktones days when we had something called The Acoustic Planet Tour. We handpicked up-and-coming groups, one of which was Umphrey's McGee. These were groups we really liked, and we brought them out on the road to tour with us for a few weeks at a time. They would do their own sets, and at the end, the bands would collaborate for a couple tunes. We usually had two other bands out with us. It was youthful and hilarious. Great music was made and lasting friendships occurred for all of us. Those are some great memories!

One of the things I remember about Joel from the very beginning was his quiet determination. He is obviously a brilliant keyboard player and has studied many styles of playing but he is also someone who struck me as a person who had a long-term vision for what he wanted to do as an artist. Many people, not only musicians, are fine to just chew on whatever bone they are thrown, but Joel, and the band, they were all different to me in that regard. It seemed they were somehow putting meat ON the bone rather than chewing it off. They were determined, successful, passionate, friendly, intelligent, funny, full of gratitude, and had a vision. I KNEW these guys had a future in the music world because I KNEW they were doing all the right things!

Since those early days, I've continued our friendship, and every New Year's Eve (since the early 2000s) I play with Umphrey's McGee wherever they are. It's become a tradition, and it's always a joy to catch up with everyone in their musical and personal situations and to witness their ongoing and well-deserved success.

The Realist's Guide to a Successful Music Career bears witness to that success and the process behind it. This honest, bare-bones, black-and-white, no-bullshit approach is more than appreciated! There is no way to sugarcoat that we are in an industry that is, at best, difficult to navigate, and at its worst, can consume you to the point of wanting to leave it. It's good to know these things up front in order to have an idea of what might be in store for you as you move along in your own process. And make no mistake, it IS a process. One that is never ending and all consuming. It's brittle and biting and full of joy and tears and surprises and laughter and ups and downs and gifts that you will share for the rest of your life. Being a musician is one of the greatest *and* one of the most difficult professions to be in. You have to find time to practice, grow, and excel in your craft. You have to play a role and contribute to not only the music, but to the other people you are sharing your life with. It comes down to building relationships, fostering them, and caring about the people you are in contact with and connecting with, not only the musicians, but the crew and all the folks behind the scenes who make it possible for us to do what we do—NO MATTER WHAT LEVEL WE DO IT AT. Success is not some magic wand that you wave and suddenly everything is good. It takes time and effort on your part. Be a great player but strive to be an even better person.

I believe this book, and the information so generously shared within it, has the potential to reach many young players who dream of a career in music that will span their lifetime. A career where you get to make music that reaches people around the world. A career that takes you to greater musical heights than you EVER thought possible. A career that finds you sharing the stage with your heroes and heroines. A career that makes you pinch yourself to be sure you're not dreaming. A career worthy of your passion, dedication, and the countless hours of practice you have put into your instrument. If these dreams are some of your dreams, this book is for YOU!

Do work that is worthy of the greats who came before you. I hope you find yourself inspired to carry on their spirits through your own personal vision. Be the best YOU that there has ever been.

I will end with a part of *The Realist's Guide to a Successful Music Career* that I feel is of utmost importance and contains ideas that inspire me on a daily basis. I believe there isn't a musician alive, or dead, who would disagree with this:

"Expect that a lot of what you produce is going to suck. Hang on to what matters and dump the rest. The most important part of this process is actually to DO IT. Write, create, produce, and capture! If you follow this recipe enough, you might just end up with something that matters."

Listen to these words and take them to heart. The truth will set you free!

Peace and gratitude,
Jeff Coffin

INTRODUCTION

Talk to those who have "made it" as musicians and most will say they knew at a very young age that they loved playing music. Most will NOT tell you that they dreamed at an early age that they would love the overall business aspect of being a musician. In fact, isn't that what true artists are supposed to disavow—the commercial nature of the trade?

If you plan on having a successful career as a musician, or working within the music industry, then you must embrace the career *and* business elements of music. That's where we come in. As the authors of *The Realist's Guide to a Successful Music Career*, we feel it necessary to bring you the stark reality of the music industry. Key on the word "industry." The word itself embodies business. It means "to produce" or "to be involved in an enterprise." That doesn't mean you have to be overwhelmingly consumed with commercialism, money, or commerce. It just seems prudent to start this journey with some REAL definition of what a music career is. Yes, you get to explore your passion for music and entertain groups of various sizes. If you work hard, perfect your craft, and have an effective short- and long-term plan, then you also might get to enjoy and explore things most only dream of.

So who are WE to guide you? At first glance, Joel Cummins appears to be a regular early-forties guy who likely works at a local accounting firm. And then there's Matt DeCoursey. He pretty much fits the same description. What you might not guess is, Joel's a remarkably successful musician by trade. His band, Umphrey's McGee, might be one that you haven't heard on your local pop radio station, but don't let that fool you. Joel and his bandmates are some of the most successful recording and touring musicians out there. Specializing in a genre

5

somewhere between improv rock and progressive rock, Umphrey's McGee has performed more than 2,400 live shows, in twelve countries, for crowds as large as forty thousand people and as small as five, over a twenty-one-year period. While not embracing the moniker of "rock star," let's be realistic. He is certainly that.

Okay, enough Joel already. How about the other guy? Matt DeCoursey loves to embrace the moniker "rock star," but he isn't one in the classic sense of the word. While working in and around the music industry for nearly a decade, Matt is better known by some as a super-entrepreneur. Not sure what that even means? Here is all you will need to know. Using nothing other than an extra bedroom in his home and a credit card with an $8,000 limit, Matt built multiple businesses that ended up generating more than $30 million in revenue. Along the way he became a "rock star" marketer, startup founder, and the author of two top-selling books, *Balance Me* and *Million Dollar Bedroom*. Both titles have reached number one in multiple categories on Amazon.

So with that, you might be wondering, WHY? As in why is this book being written? That's easy. We intend to provide you with a guide to becoming a productive, creative, and professional musician. Joel's input is like no other that you will find in print. There is no substitute for what his longevity and experience as a player can provide. And yes, since we do in fact need to embrace the business side of this life, Matt can and will provide you with insights and experience that come from being an elite entrepreneur.

This book isn't a how-to guide for becoming a rock star. If that is what happens as result, that would be amazing! What we have put together for you is, instead, a realistic and practical guide for becoming who and what you want to be within the music industry. The goal is to provide the best advice possible, not only from the authors, but also from the best contributors we could find who were willing to discuss the successes and failures they have encountered.

WHAT IS A SUCCESSFUL MUSIC CAREER?

Before we get too far along in this process, let's take a few minutes and create a little bit of definition. As defined by most dictionaries, a career is a profession for which one trains and is undertaken as a permanent calling. It is also meant to symbolize something that offers progressive achievement.

With all this "career" stuff, it is also important to know that everyone's definition or expectation of what constitutes success is different. One person reading this book might feel that a regular Friday night gig at a busy or famous tavern is successful, while the next reader considers anything less than a ten-city tour a failure. What success really means is fulfillment, or in a more textbook sense, self-fulfillment. It's doing what you feel you are capable of, or what makes you happy. It's that simple. If you can provide for yourself, feel happy, and at the same time do what you feel you are capable of, then you have a successful career, whether it is as a musician or a bricklayer.

Now that we got that out of the way, let's address something else. There are a whole lot of avenues you can travel down to meet the definition of a music career. Sure, most are going to look first to recording or live performing artists; however, there is a whole lot more out there. Stick around; we will get into that throughout our time together. It just seemed important to let you know that this book isn't just about learning everything you need to know to play to a football stadium full of screaming fans.

WHAT IS THE MUSIC INDUSTRY?

Let's start with a quick thought exercise. Pick a concert out of your mental index of attended shows. What do you remember?

Most likely it's the people onstage doing their thing, right? What you probably don't know is EVERYTHING involved in making that happen. There are obviously those onstage, but also those behind the stage, above the stage, fifty feet into the crowd away from the stage, and then the people that have to take everything off the stage and move it to the next show. But wait, there's more! There are people in offices, tour-bus drivers, managers, agents, producers, promoters, people selling merch . . . Dizzy yet? That's a lot of people. Well, every single one of them is part of the music industry. Many are operating well within, or past, our previous definition of success. During our limited time together, the goal is to give you some idea about what those people do, how they got where they are, and what it takes to stay there. As you move forward with your career in the music industry, keeping yourself educated and aware of the many avenues available is beneficial. In fact, being an expert on the industry that you intend to make a living within should be something you insist upon.

CAN I GET ONE OF THOSE NOW AND LATERS?

Before we truly get started, one last thing. Everything in this book is intended to help you find success not only now, but also later! Getting where you most likely want to be is a sprint, a marathon, and in some cases a triathlon, all occurring at the same time. But don't worry, we will push you, or sometimes pull you, when needed.

Since this is a realist's guide, here's your first shot of realism!

NONE OF THIS IS EASY. It takes hard work, dedication, drive, discomfort, and the ability to follow your passion down the roads that can be safely traveled.

If your expectation is to immediately become the next quadruple-platinum-selling world-tour-killing rock star, then do yourself and us a favor and put the book back on the shelf. You're going to be disappointed. For 99.9999 percent of people—however talented—it just doesn't work that way.

If we haven't scared you off yet, then all this may in fact be for you. However, it's important to do a little soul searching and goal setting before you begin any worthwhile project, so let's go ahead and do that.

SECTION ONE:

IS THIS FOR ME?

E very holiday season, thousands of hopeful parents make the trek to their local music store—each with grand dreams of what their young child might accomplish with a musical instrument. Some come for guitars, others pianos, many for violins, and the bravest of the brave . . . for drum sets. Each supportive parent is positive their excited child will find a lifetime time of joy.

What happens over the coming months is very predictable. Only a tiny percentage of the recipients continue playing their new musical instruments. Why only a sliver of the aspiring musicians? It's simple. Because people too often get frustrated that they aren't good at something right away. *Why can't I play that song? Why does this sound like crap?* The results are quitting and untouched instruments doomed to basement storage.

With that, YOU are most likely the kid that *doesn't* quit. It didn't take a crystal ball to figure that out; you are probably reading this book for a reason. So now the next question is, what particular action is required to get better, for you to keep advancing your skill or ability to play music? PRACTICE! Regardless of your natural talent for whatever it is that you do musically, you get a hell of a lot of practice.

Why are we talking about practice? Because that is exactly what you need to have a successful career in both the short and long term. You need to practice in the same way that you learned scales, chords, or theory that hopefully turned into something far more interesting. You should also practice playing other people's songs and solos, practice improvisation, and, lastly, try songwriting. Often the act of practice simply means doing. So just do it.

You might be thinking, *How am I supposed to practice having a successful music career?* The first step is setting some realistic and reasonable expectations for yourself. Much like your first attempts at playing your chosen instrument, you are likely to make some dumb—or to be nicer, *inexperienced*—decisions. What is important is that after striking that foul note, you don't quit, but instead come back for another pass.

WHAT ARE YOU TRYING TO ACCOMPLISH?

Do you have an idea of what you are trying to accomplish musically? Have you considered what is YOUR definition of success as a musician or someone involved in the music industry?

If you haven't, stop right now and give it some thought. Next, find the nearest pencil or pen and answer these three questions:

As a musician, I aspire to:
1)
2)
3)

When it comes to music, I am passionate about:
1)
2)
3)

I believe that I have the ability and desire to have a career in the music industry.
YES or NO

(If you just answered NO to the final question, then you have a lot to consider when it comes to what you might be chasing.)

Congratulations! You just accomplished what 97 percent of people, and that isn't just musicians, will never do. You created goals and then mapped out what might make you happy. You also just increased your likelihood of getting there. Seriously! Those that write down their goals, even in as simple a form as you just did, are significantly more likely of achieving them. SO, WAY TO GO!

AN EIGHTH NOTE OF REALISM

Now let's take a quick look at what you just wrote down in that last exercise. Is at least one item from what you aspire to do or become in the music industry reasonably attainable within three to five years, if not sooner? If no, then you probably aren't being realistic with the set of expectations that you just defined. Why is this important? If your mind can't truly and realistically wrap itself around your ability to achieve something, then you aren't likely to get where you want to be.

There is an easy fix to this. You need to reverse engineer your path to success. Take that goal or dream that you have and break it down into a whole lot of bite-size pieces. The mistake that many make when it comes to achieving goals is viewing them as a singular task, when in fact goals are an entire *series* of smaller tasks or achievements stacked on top of one another. You didn't learn advanced music theory on that first day of playing guitar, did you? So why should your immediate goals and path be complicated or advanced right away?

In our own minds, most of us perform flawlessly to droves of adoring fans. In reality, that isn't how it is going to be for anyone, nor is the path there a smooth one. So, with that, some basic consideration needs to be given to whether or not the lifestyle and demands of life in the music industry are for you.

Do you have a tough time speaking to a group of people? While this isn't the case for everyone, that is one of the first indicators that you might have to overcome some stage fright or performance anxiety.

If you want to be a touring musician, are you ready for the

travel demands? This means not only embracing the actual act of travel, but also being away from your family, friends, and "regular" everyday lifestyle. Some of you are thinking, *I love traveling.* Well guess what, traveling for leisure and traveling for work are two different animals. And when you are touring as a musician, please understand that it is work. That doesn't mean you can't or won't get to have fun. But, there are going to be a whole host of things you are going to need to do, all which we will discuss soon.

How do you handle criticism or failure? If you find yourself furious every time someone doesn't like what you just did or played, then you have a bumpy road ahead. How do, or will, you feel if your performance flops? Or if no one shows up? There isn't a musician out there that hasn't had to deal with both.

How do you feel about trolls? Not the weird little magical creatures, but those that fill the Internet spouting insensitive, overly critical, and often hateful rhetoric online. Get ready because there is nothing magical about these trolls. The way you handle failure and criticism have *a lot* to do with your ability to make it in the long run.

Before we move on, some of you may already be thinking, *Man, why are you trying to talk me out of my dreams?* That is certainly NOT our intention. This book is *The Realist's Guide,* after all. Our desire is to send you off prepared to find and fight for your dreams. Hopefully most of you are bulletproof and immune to everything forewarned. If not, learn to be.

IN REGARDS TO FAILURE

Thomas Edison failed at making the light bulb countless times before getting it right. Your favorite instrumentalist also failed a whole lot on the way to being the monster of rock that you grew to love. Short-term failure is imminent; it's how you react to, learn from, and handle it that will determine your fate. After all, if everyone was amazing at playing music from the get-go, and if people didn't find it easier to quit, then the world would be jam-packed with world-class musicians. Take a moment and thank those that quit or are about to; they are just making you look that much better.

Going forward, think of failure as getting one more way of NOT getting it right out of the way. Each failure is another step closer to success. Some need more than others. What is important is that you know, understand, and embrace the act of necessary failure. Doing so will make your life easier. In no way does that mean that you should accept failure. Instead, accept that it is part of the process, and that the more of it you get out of the way, the sooner you are likely to achieve your goals.

AM I ANY GOOD AT THIS?

So here we are. Reality once again! At some point you will have to ask yourself, and hopefully be honest, whether or not you have the talent, personality, or other characteristics necessary to get where you want to be. Knowing that we all have a different definition of what success is, this can be tricky. If the be-all and end-all is that you are delivering the world's greatest licks onstage in front of one hundred thousand fans, then guess what, you'd better have some talent and be willing to perfect it.

Unfortunately, many along the way will perish. No, not die, but for many, reality will deliver the verdict. At this point you can choose to try to power through. Some will, most won't. But that doesn't mean that you can't have a successful and fulfilling career involving your passion! For the optimists reading this, it might just be reality steering you toward what you should be doing. That is up to you to decide.

THE PASSION TEST

A concept coined by Matt, this simple test starts by asking: "Am I passionate about what I am doing?" If you aren't, that is a problem. Since the journey to success is littered with obstacles and adversity, those that aren't passionate about whatever they are chasing are likely to quit along the way.

The next part of the passion test is: "Can you see your passion for what you are doing?" If it isn't awesomely obvious and more or less oozing out of you, then how are you supposed to pass that along to others? An inability to do so results in a lack of passion for what you are producing. The outcome is that no one cares.

There is a big difference between popular and passionate! Popular is usually short term and fades; passion, however, can fuel and inspire anything and everything around it.

The bottom-line: If you aren't passionate about music, or what you say you want to do with or around music, then you might need to consider whether your intentions are genuine.

THE TIMES THEY ARE A CHANGIN'

During the just-more-than forty years we have been alive, the music industry has gone through multiple, drastic, and exciting changes. With that, it is important to understand the present and possible future state of the industry.

Depending on your age, you too have seen significant changes. Maybe it was the popular format of CD to the MP3 to Napster and now streaming subscription services. Regardless of when you entered the time line, it is important to have a firm grasp on the evolving industry and how it can, could, and will affect your ability to be heard.

All that being said, we are in the midst of a golden age of connectivity. Never in history have musicians had so many obtainable—and often free—tools allowing for instant connectivity to whomever they want to reach. In fact, what once threatened to kill the recording industry, THE INTERNET, is now its most powerful asset. While it might be hard to convince Metallica or Dr. Dre that this is the case as millions of stolen or pirated files travel through cyberspace, but *you* as a musician can quickly and affordably produce music at a level once only accessible to those chosen to do so, or that had the means to afford it.

Knowing all this, wouldn't it be smart to play to your strengths and use the most accessible assets around you? That was rhetorical because the answer is YES!

With all this accessible technology and ability to publish, a new school of musician and celebrity was born. These new-school stars populate YouTube, Twitter, Facebook, and SoundCloud as we speak—and so can YOU!

Regardless of the ways music is recorded, one thing will likely continue to be the working musician's meal ticket. In fact, it's remained somewhat constant despite being surrounded by high levels of change: the live performance.

I'M NOT HEADED TOWARD A STADIUM GIG SOON. NOW WHAT?

As stated, the numbers are not in your favor if success only exists as a megastar. Whether it is music or anything else in life, the closer you get to the top, the thinner the crowd. That's just the way the math works. For those seeking careers in the music industry, though, that isn't necessarily bad. Those that manage to "make it" are also those that need the help of others.

Careers in the music industry exist in too many positions to list. However, this healthy list of options should give you a few leads:

- Music production
- Music management
- Music marketing

- Music instruction and teaching
- Studio/Session musician
- Promotion
- Positions with musical instrument manufacturers
- Sound engineer
- Stage tech
- Road crew
- Local and regional live performers

While this guide is more musician-specific, there's a wealth of other career opportunities worth exploring in the industry. We understand that you didn't choose this book to learn how to get a job as a stage tech. But the book IS about music careers and ALL these paths certainly qualify. They all exist within a very codependent ecosystem. Meaning, most don't survive without the others—making all very viable, lucrative, and possibly enjoyable options for exploring and making a living through your passion for music.

Also consider that being around success, breeds success. Some of these gigs might be a great fit for you while you work on discovering your own path. Being around what you want to do and seeing others do it successfully is experience you should cherish.

TREATING YOUR MUSIC LIKE A BUSINESS

As we wrap up our preliminary exploration of the industry, your expectations, and the demands of getting there, it's important to quickly address a few business-related things.

If you are serious about a career in music, then you will also need to be serious about the business of your music. This part can be enjoyable, too. Playing a great gig and getting a nice check at the end of the night is fun, rewarding, and providing you with things you need in life. With that, please don't breeze past the parts of this book directly related to keeping track of and keeping up with the business side of your music. Being hasty in this regard will limit your future success, and FAST! A well-rounded approach to your future includes making a plan, considering possible outcomes, and following your sense of passion for what you are doing.

Before we move on, if you made it this far without being scared off, congratulations, you just advanced to the next level! What you are about to learn will not only be fun, but should provide you with the needed tools to avoid costly and time-consuming mistakes. Prepare for a level of clarity and the realist's path to success. In fact, this is probably a great time to start defining that path. Yes, that's right, more decisions. Stick with us. What comes next is not only entertaining, it defines how you see yourself musically, and prepares you for the thrilling spontaneity of creation.

A CONVERSATION WITH TAYLOR HICKS

Ever know someone with an insane amount of talent waiting for the right moment to showcase it to the world? That is a great way to introduce the story of Taylor Hicks. Taylor comes from a colorful background and will be the first to tell you that his difficult childhood led him to blues and soul music. Now known as the Season Five winner of *American Idol*, Hicks was hardly new to music, touring, or recording when he walked into to his now famous audition for the show. Having self-produced two albums and performed at small venues across the south, Taylor is a great example of hard work, preparation, and opportunity crossing paths. Since winning *American Idol*, Taylor has continued performing, recording, and was acknowledged by *Forbes* magazine as one of The Ten Top-Earning American Idols.

JOEL: What's the most important musical decision you made when you were starting in the business?

TAYLOR: I think it starts from an emotional standpoint musically. As a young kid, growing up as a vocalist, I found songs that kind of got to my emotion a little bit. And I kind of keyed in on that because I knew if there was an emotional connection with the music that I was singing and playing, then I felt like it would be more believable.

I mean, so much of music is emotion. It's human connection, right?

It is, and I was kind of going through family situations. Family was going through a divorce and stuff. It was a little bit of a rough childhood. And I felt like musically, if I could connect singing and emotion, then that would ultimately . . . it was therapeutic for me to a certain degree. Luckily for me, I found

Ray Charles at an early age and he was kind of the musical root to my tree, so to speak. The further along that I got into being an entertainer and a musician, I knew that if I'm emotionally connected with the music, then I can emotionally connect with the audience. And ultimately that would be good for business.

Right. It's interesting how those intersect. And you really can't fake it. People will eventually see through that. There's something to be said—and this is certainly true, I think, for Ray Charles—about authenticity.

Yeah, very much so. Finding your own voice is very important. Being around different performers, for instance doing the Broadway thing and being around theatrical majors from all over the world and all over the country, and then putting the toe into the Broadway world and seeing all these singers and vocally and stuff, just from a vocal perspective, in my opinion it's not how much you can run with your vocals, it's the tonality of what you're singing that will make people remember you. And I think a lot of kids these days, they're really into the running, the runs of the voice, when *I* feel like as long as your tone is rememberable, then people will recognize you. That's something that I like to talk about from a vocal perspective, having been around different arenas of the business.

Because *that's* authenticity to me. Tone is authenticity.

That's the thing that no one else can really replicate. It's yours and yours alone.

Exactly.

So you say you were inspired by discovering Ray Charles early on. When you found Ray, did that strike you in a way that you're, like, "Okay, this is my genre, this is what I want to do." Did you start singing right after that and kind of get into the soul vibe?

I just got really obsessive-compulsive about the emotional connection that I made with what he was doing. And then ultimately that kind of blossomed into wanting to pick up instruments, and then that's where the harmonica kind came into play. And then ultimately putting it in guitar form and learning how to play guitar. It's interesting, each instrument that I found and learned on my own kind of replicated what artist or what music that I was listening to at the time. It was almost like Ray was kind of the vocal part. Then once the harmonica came it moved into the blue-eyed soul singers who could play and soul singers that could play harmonica and sing, like Van Morrison. Then as I started learning some chords on guitar and stuff, it moved into Bob Seger, so it was almost like, as my musicality grew into different instruments, I kind of replicated what artist I studied. It went from Ray Charles to Sonny Boy Williamson to Bob Seger to Van, and then I started writing.

I figured if I had harmonica, if I could play a little guitar, if I could sing, then the graduation from that point was to write. And once I put all of those pieces together, I really knew that this was a calling for me, and there was a reason why I was able to learn and emote and write. It was kind of like all signs point to the entertainment business. Now, I tell people, and this is a funny quote, is that I went gray very early on, and I think the reason why I went gray is because I knew that I wanted to be in show business and I knew how hard that was going to be. And then once I realized I had to stay in show business, it all went white.

Wow, that's something else. One of the things I'm hearing, though, is that it seems like it's really important to pick up not just one instrument, but maybe a couple different instruments, because that's going to further help expand what you're able to do.

Yeah. Obviously in this business you have to be really versatile. You have to cover a lot of bases. For me, I knew that success in music, you're going to have to be, not prolific, so to speak, but you've got to be good enough to be able to entertain people and also be able to write. And the more instruments that you learn, the better. And for me, I kind of learned all the instruments on my own. I wish at the time someone would have put me on a musical education path, because I don't have any formal training musically. It's all just feel and play.

Well, neither did Paul McCartney.

Yeah. That always feels good, to know that.

Moving on, what was a really important decision you made on the business side that impacted your career?

Interestingly enough, when I got to college, I got into a band that had some success. At eighteen, I feel like I was in kind of, like, a budding Umphrey's McGee. It was just in the Auburn form. We got an agent out of Nashville. We played a lot of fraternities and sororities. We got a van and started playing clubs around the Southeast and stuff. It was truly a fairy-tale gig at eighteen or nineteen years old in college, because I got to see the world, which was, in my mind, as somebody from Alabama, the world only extends probably not too far past Pascagoula, Mississippi. You know what I mean?

Yeah. Right.

It was so much fun to be able to experience that musically and stuff. I don't really know if this is a mistake. I'll never know the answer to that, but I really don't know if it was a mistake or if it was something that was meant to be, but as our numbers were building and we were doing great business early on, my head grew as well.

My ego grew, and I decided to quit the band. I decided to dismember the band that we had. I don't know if it was something that was kind of a self-saboteur mentality, or something that was in me, but I never will forget it. We played the Supper Club, the War Eagle Supper Club in Auburn, Alabama, when I was younger—and that was a thousand-seat club, a real historic place.

Right.

We used to sell it out. With my band Passing Through, we'd sell it out, and I never will forget it. I dismembered the band and then I decided that I was going to go out on my own, like be this big solo artist.

I never will forget the owner of the club, who I'm still friends with to this day. He kind of looks at me. We have a laugh about it now, but he told me he was going to put me on the sign next. And I went from doing a thousand people in Passing Through to doing fifty with Taylor Hicks.

That was a big sobering lesson in music business for me because I realized, A) I couldn't go back to that point again, but B) I really was going to have to rely on my name and kind of start all over again, so I think it's important when you're starting out young in the business to really know what . . . You make sure that the business and the brand that you're in, which you guys are . . . I mean, you guys are like the perfect example of being able to take care of a brand for a long time in the music business. You got to make sure that you're comfortable with what your brand is from an early starting point so you can really cultivate that brand and ultimately build on it.

The hardest thing I think is, sometimes, it's just hard to know if that's the right thing for you. Like you're saying, how do you know? Obviously, that was a huge decision for you that maybe in the short term was kind of a little bit of a reality check, but now, looking back in the long term to where you are, I would say, "That was a good decision."

Now that I look back on it, yeah. It was really tough. It was really tough starting over and rebuilding from the ground up.

Now, granted I did it when I was twenty-two years old and then I kind of lived and died by my own name and by my own sword, but it's very important if you really want to build a brand, because there's an old saying that I think a lot of people know in the business is that there's music and there's music business, and they are two totally separate, different things. They sound very similar, but they are very different. It is a business, so you have to build your brand from the ground up and you got to know what you're working with as early as possible.

Absolutely. From there, what career pivots did you make that presented themselves to you and how did those happen?

Interestingly enough, how *Idol* happened, I was the last taxi-cab ride in Hurricane Katrina, and I realized very quickly that taxi-cab drivers flee hurricanes too, and so I caught the last cab four or five hours before the storm hit and drove twelve hours in counter-flow traffic with the taxi driver to West Monroe, Louisiana.

From West Monroe, the storm passed, and I rented a car and drove it to Birmingham, so I had a plane ticket that was canceled from Southwest, and I got to Birmingham and, as a broke musician, Southwest gave me a free ticket anywhere in the country, so, as a broke musician with a free ticket anywhere in the country when I was twenty-five years old, the one place that I think a broke musician would go with a free ticket is Las Vegas.

I flew to Vegas on a whim, and I got to Vegas about 12:30, and my brother called me and said, "Man, I know you've been going through a hurricane basically, but *American Idol* tryouts are in three hours at the Convention Center." So I went and I got in line, and I guess the rest is history.

It's crazy how fate and opportunity kind of present themselves sometimes. I always like to say that you have to have your ducks in a row upstairs before you have to have them in a row downstairs. I think my fate kind of intervened at that point in time, and obviously opportunity creates luck.

Right.

For me, I never missed a gig. I always paid my band members even when I didn't have really the money to pay them, and karma, man, you know what I mean? If you want something really big and wonderful to happen in your life, you got to be big and wonderful to people in the same way.

It's so true. It's like all the people that you see on the way up, you're going to see them on the way down, too. If you're a jerk to people, they might not remember your music, but they're going to remember that you were a jerk to them.

That's very wise. If you're smart enough to realize that you can't be . . . The odds of being Tom Cruise and having . . . and Tom Cruise goes through peaks and valleys.

It's just a part of the business where you're going to have to accept that there's going to be a time where you're not going to be the hottest band on the planet. You're not going to be the hottest actor. You're not going to be the hottest musician.

Everybody goes through the peaks and valleys. If you can wrap your head around it and be smart from it, from a financial aspect and from a music business aspect, and pick things that can sustain your career, then, ultimately, you'll have fun with . . . just as much fun as the peak and just as much fun as the valley.

Yep, I think one thing I've told people a bunch is don't let the highs get too high and don't let the lows get too low. It's a very emotion-filled business, and it's tough sometimes to keep a straight head.

Very much so. That's what I love about y'all. I feel like you all kind of share that same mentality. You have such a really great way that you guys ride this thing. I think that's a profound statement.

We try to keep each other in check, too. I think that's the other thing. You got to be able to be close-enough friends with each other to be honest and to say, "Hey, you're wrong," and also to admit and say, "You know what? I was wrong." They're both important.

Totally.

Moving way ahead now, how do you balance a career in TV with live shows, and do you connect with your audience differently in the visual medium rather than live in person?

I guess it just depends on what kind of TV you're doing. For me right now, the food and travel show [*State Plate*] is a little bit more personality based, which is interesting because I think this is kind of the first time that I think people have seen the personality, because when you're on a show like *Idol*, you really only get, like, two and a half minutes to really sing. Then there's only seven seconds that you get to see the personality, it feels like. It's a very short time frame for people to get to know your personality.

I feel like that's something that just kind of has to come in what you're doing. When you're doing the music, you're doing the music shows and you're touring musically and stuff, your personality's kind of dumbed down a little bit, and you're more focused on the music that you can present, because there is kind of a little bit more of an artistic expression that comes from me on touring music, because it's songs that I write. There's a little bit more of an emotional connection there.

Obviously when you're doing television, it's a different thing, because you kind of have to know your role. The last roles that I've done from a television perspective, and even for Broadway, have been more personality based and jovial based, and then obviously the musical side gets a little bit more introspective, I think.

Sure. Do you feel like those two different sides of what you're doing benefit each other? Have you had people discover your music because of the show, or have you had people discover the TV show because of your music?

I think it's a great cross-pollination. What's interesting is that, believe it or not, people kind of discovered me through the medium of television. It's television where they know me from, and then I've had to really shed the light on kind of the artistic expression.

Again, we're talking about the business side of music and how each approach is different for each brand. My brand needs both of them. It needs the TV side and the personality side, and then obviously the TV side and the personality side and the people that watch that, I want them to know that there's also a serious musician and there's a serious artist in there too. For me, I think they kind of go hand in hand with each other.

Yeah, makes sense. What's the best piece of advice you could give to an aspiring musician just getting started?

Opportunity creates luck. Learn as much as you can about the business of music, the business of show, because you're going to have to have the business side as much as you're going to the artistic side. Be good to people, and karma will bite you in the ass if you don't watch it.

What's the worst piece of advice you've ever received about your music career?

"Don't try out for *American Idol*. That show wouldn't be good for you."

Wow. It's funny when those things happen and you reflect back and you're like, "Man, what were they thinking?"

Yeah. You have to use your instincts. Instincts are really good in this business. Instincts and feelings. Instinctual things and sixth sense and feelings about things are really good in this business because you and I both know, you got to throw everything against the wall and hopefully something will stick.

More times than not, it's not going to stick. You have to throw a lot at the wall to hopefully make it stick. I like to tell people from eighteen years old to twenty-eight, for a good ten years, everybody told me . . . I had fifty thousand nos. People told me, "No, not now. We're looking for something different. Your music's too bluesy. Your music's too soulful. You're not good for this," or, "We appreciate it, but not right now." There's so many different ways that I've been told no. I think ultimately if you keep at it, then you're going to get that one yes, and you're going to have to realize that's your opportunity to create a name for yourself and catch your break, and you're off to the races.

Yep. Awesome. Last question here, what do you think it takes to stay on top of your game?

It's a lot of hard work, and you have to live and breathe what you're doing. You have to live and breathe this business. It's not an eight-to-five job.

This job, it's an eight-to-eight job. Wherever you are in your career, artistically, you have to be . . . If something hits you in the middle of the night, you have to have the sense to get up and write about it. Or, if you're not feeling well and you have a lunch meeting with someone that's in the business who might can help you and you're not feeling good, go meet them. What's interesting is that you might not meet him, but he might bring his buddy who might give you an opportunity.

Yeah, or if you show up and he's like, "Wow, so you weren't feeling well and you still came to meet me?" That might be something that people respect and they find impressive.

Yeah.

I think you have to love what you do, and just what you're saying, I think about the musical part of Umphrey's, and even sometimes different business ideas or stuff, all the time. It doesn't turn off. You have to be into it enough, I think, that you're willing to do that.

You have to love what you do. One of my musical gurus on this planet is an artist by the name of Keb' Mo'.

Oh yeah, I know Keb'.

Ever since I was twenty-three or twenty-four, I would always go and see him. I would give him my CD that I was making. I was always letting him know. There were times where I got to the point where I was kind of ready to move on and work at a bank. He would always call, and I would kind of just say, "Hey, I'm ready to get off the merry-go-round." He said, "You really have to love this to be able to be successful at it. You really have to love what you're doing." To be honest with you, I really did. I really do love being able to entertain folks, and I've been very blessed to have that opportunity to still be doing that. You have to love it. I think if you love it, it's not a job.

SECTION TWO:

IMPORTANT DECISIONS TO MAKE

In order to arrive at any destination, you must first have some clue about where you want to go. Sure, you can wander aimlessly and arrive at many destinations along the way, but does that seem like a great plan? Your planning and consideration process has many parallels, but there are some unique differences when it comes to planning your career in music as a solo artist compared to those planning on forming a band/group. Each presents challenges and limitations, but in the end, both are viable options if you have what it takes to make it happen. Regardless of your choice, or perhaps reaction to something that formed organically, you have what could be, at this early stage of your career, an infinite number of choices.

WHY BE A SOLO ARTIST?

Do you have a singular vision? Are you a prodigy on your instrument? Are you willing to be or want to be the only one in the spotlight? Are you prepared to do everything yourself? If so, then a career as a solo act is an option for you. However, you should know that this is a much more difficult path to travel. Why? It's pretty simple. All you can do is all you can do. You won't have the power of numbers on your side. There won't be others to help distribute the work. The upside of all this is that YOU can better control your direction and not have to rely on others to share in your vision, passion, or decision-making process.

As a singer/songwriter solo artist, your performance options are much more diverse. This will force you to take a different approach. For example, there are going to be a lot of venue options that are available to you, or not available, compared to the possibilities a band has. An easy example of this is the coffee house venue; they probably don't have the room for four performers, nor the tolerance for the loud banging of a drum set. On the flip side, many venues, often those can and will pay larger sums for performers, aren't going to be interested in having one person strumming a guitar and singing in favor of a full band or DJ.

Is there a "right" approach? No. Remember, it's your career. It's your music. And it's your happiness that determines what is right.

WHY START A BAND?

Creating and performing music with others brings possibilities not available to the soloist. Those who play together for years can create a musical language that is truly unique and special. As a result, a bond or musical understanding is born. However, none of this is likely if those involved don't share a similar desire or musical vision.

Many reading this guide will, or want to, pursue the "group" option. It in several ways offers the higher upside and an appealing shared risk. At the same time, what is a strength can also be a weakness. You will likely need to make majority or consensus decisions, be reliant on your bandmates' stability and reliability, and on the business side of things, you will need to split your performance fees across multiple pockets versus just your own. Once again, no right or wrong decision here—just a few more moving parts to maintain and consider along your journey.

Another consideration is that bandmates aren't always easy to find. At least ones that share your vision, passion, and common goals. For some, the frustration is constant. In fact, it's very common and predictable when it comes to the following:

- Does everyone have similar objectives?
- Creative input and differences?
- Availability, schedules, or other responsibilities?

- General character and reliability?

While some of this stuff might not seem like a big deal in the beginning, IT IS! Any one of these factors can have a profound impact on your ability to achieve your goals, the longevity of your project, or even getting your first gig. For example, if you have one band member that is never available at the times that the rest are, that makes it hard to practice and perform. Or if you have a band member that can't or won't travel, then you have immediately limited your ability to perform outside your local market. Therefore, if one, or the rest of you have ambitions of touring, well, forget about it. These are all important factors to consider. Not doing so can and will result in frustration, disappointment, and then a lot of wasted time after you break up due to your "differences."

Since all these factors are foreseeable and avoidable, before we move forward they deserve a little more discussion.

DOES EVERYONE HAVE A SIMILAR OBJECTIVE?

This is a pretty easy question to answer. In order to do so, ask yourselves the following questions:

- Do we want to eventually do this full-time, or are we okay with part-time action?
- Is playing original, non-cover music our end goal, or does that matter?
- Is everyone in this for the long term, or are we just passing the time?
- If we grow and build a following, is future travel an option?
- Do we have significant personality differences?
- What things in life (i.e., family, jobs, etc.) are "competing" with the band?

CREATIVE INPUT AND DIFFERENCES

Not being on the same page when it comes to what you are trying to create is tough to overcome. At first everyone might be comfortable performing certain types of music and songs. But in the end, if there isn't any passion or desire to do so, your act is likely to be short-lived. Think about it. To play out, you will need to practice. That means that by the time you are performing for a live audience, you will have already played those songs A LOT, and if you don't like that, or you don't care, IT WILL SHOW. Also, any long-term goals or aspirations will be stalled, slowed, or flat out stopped every time you need to replace any disenfranchised bandmate who quit.

If you are seeking to play original music, the same consideration needs to be given. Meaning, are we, or am *I*, playing the type of music that I'm passionate about creating? If you aren't "into it," your interest in it is likely to fade over time. Another sticking point is related to the role that each member of the band has. Establishing the "creative" roles is sometimes hard or even unnecessary, but it's not a bad idea to give it some early consideration.

WHAT IS YOUR PLAN OR END GAME?

You started this to have fun, right? Well, we hope so too. However, if your goals involve a long-term approach, then this is remarkably relevant! It can affect decisions along your growth path, and more importantly, have a lot to do with who you end up choosing to create and play music with. If you have one member of your band in it for the short term, just know that it will end up being something that becomes a factor, often at times when you least want it to be. If things go the way you hope, then this is something that can present a big, big problem for you.

<u>Here are some common factors that can determine longevity:</u>

- Family
- Income
- Careers
- Level of commitment
- Age and health
- Lifestyle factors

FUTURE TRAVEL AND LIFE ON THE ROAD

If your plans include long-term goals or the pursuit of doing something bigger, then touring is likely coming along too. This applies to both solo artists and bands. Your local market is only going to support you to a certain point, especially for acts performing original music. Bands that play cover music have a slightly different set of rules, as they have a higher likelihood of getting steady or regular work performing at venues or in front of crowds. If this isn't you, and you want to pursue something bigger, that means you are going to have some road life in your future.

Road life is easier for some than others. It's not even an option for some. More specifically, those with family or career obstacles that don't allow for packing up and hitting the road for any amount of time. This is why it is important to establish and consider what *your* future goals are. The approach of "let's see what happens" unfortunately isn't going to override the fact that one of your bandmates is a single parent and simply can't hit the road with three kids in tow.

There are other factors to consider, too, when it comes to life on the road. Like the fact that some just aren't happy traveling, or at least traveling in the manner that you might need to during the early stages of your process. At first, some will say, "I love traveling! Visiting all those places is amazing and fun!" But are you talking about vacationing, or traveling for work? There is a HUGE difference between the two. When you are on the road performing, there is A LOT of work, driving, and cramped conditions—even more so in the early stages of a solo artist's or a band's growth.

Because this is so important, let's play a little game. Picture yourself in a van with everyone you play music with. Now in this van are also your instruments, luggage, and who knows what else. If you are just getting started, it is unlikely that you have more than, or even one other person to help out. So it's up to you to drive, move and set up your gear, coordinate everything, and oh yeah, perform, too! This is the likely scenario you will go through on the way to where you want to be. And this is probably the norm for a while. Sorry, that's just the way it works. If you are someone who could be, or is without a doubt not going to do well under these conditions, then you have a few more things to ponder.

If you're a DJ or one-person act on a small instrument, you might be able to fly to gigs without a van or trailer. Consider the logistics of this as you search for your direction.

PERSONALITY DIFFERENCES

We aren't going to give you a break yet! Another major factor to consider when determining, or assessing the long-term possibilities of your band are your collective personalities. Are you a good fit with one another, or are you already driving one another nuts? If it is the latter, then you have a problem. Let's go back to that crowded van scenario on the way to your upcoming twelve days on the road. There is nowhere to hide or get away. Sure, you can plug some headphones in and attempt to seek solace, but it will be a LONG trip that you won't want to repeat.

The act of performing takes up the smallest part of your time on the road. This only magnifies and increases the effects of the personality differences that might be present. Then on top of it all, you are likely to be a lot more tired, stressed, or worn out in between shows. It's inevitable within a band to find a range of personalities, but they need to be *compatible* with one another if you're going to be team that can work and grow together.

AGE, HEALTH, AND LIFESTYLE

Is it fair to say that what you were comfortable with at one age later changed over time? It's natural. What you are cool with at nineteen isn't likely to be the case at thirty-five. Life changes, and with it our expectations as to what our lifestyles can, should, or could be like—all factors to consider when doing long-term planning. Equally, if you are sixty and the rest of the players in your group are thirty-three, then you aren't likely to be part of a reasonable twenty-year plan, for obvious reasons.

HOW TO FIND A GOOD BANDMATE OR COLLABORATOR

Up to this point of the book we have done a lot to establish that common goals, desires, and personalities are a crucial part of your future success. So why would any of that be different when it comes to finding your future bandmates? After all, it's hard to create a strong plan if everyone is working with a different agenda.

When it comes to your decision as to whom you are going to take on the music business with, it's just about as important of a decision as you will make. Not to take the fun, creativity, and excitement out of the process, but you do need to remember that if you want music to support you then this is a business decision. That being said, successful businesses DO in fact have the best people. If that ingredient is missing, then you might not have much to work with. On the other side of that coin, if you team up with talented people that lack character, you are going to have a completely different set of problems.

FINDING LIKE-MINDED ARTISTS AND CHEMISTRY

What is your personality type? We all have one. To keep it simple, you are either outgoing or not. Those who are outgoing are chatty, often bold, and like things to happen faster. For those who are quieter or introverted, you likely want to think things out, have a plan, and are often bothered and annoyed by people who don't. These are all things to consider when determining if you have the right mix of personalities for the long term.

Why is all this so important? Because you have A LOT of future decisions to make. Your personality and preferences as to how things are done will affect these decisions. In the world outside music, there is an entire industry dedicated to improving the way that people work with others, and it all starts with the personality type.

So how do deal with personality differences? It starts with knowing that they exist and then creating some kind of definition or structure around them. For instance, it is a good idea to have someone in the role of leader. If that isn't the way you want to do it, then create definition and structure as to what decisions should be made as a group, and then how those decisions will be decided.

What you are going to go through in order to create, then maintain, a successful career in music is hard work. Therefore, if you aren't ready for that, or if you're teamed up with others who aren't ready to work hard, then your chances are limited. A lot of this drive should be coming from your passion for what you are doing, as well as who you are doing it with. If this is in question at all, that is a red flag.

A strong work ethic is part of someone's character, meaning, you usually are, or are not a hard worker. That lack of this specific trait is going to only create friction between bandmates who are hard workers and those who might not be. Why? Because it is only natural after a certain amount of time to become frustrated with the fact that you feel like you are doing all the work. This also leads to the feeling that others don't care as much about the project and process. These are all enemies of the passion that is needed to fuel your success.

LIVING NEAR EACH OTHER

When things are easy, well you know . . . you are a lot more likely to do them. Creating music requires practice. Therefore, living near those who you are working with, or having a central practice spot, will increase your desire to practice. This is really important in the beginning, when everyone is more or less trying to figure out if it's going to work. A long drive to band practice after working all day isn't exactly a motivator.

OUTSIDE COMMITMENTS

What is demanding your attention? We all have a finite amount of attention, energy, and more importantly, TIME. Everyone has a different reality when it comes to how much time and energy they can devote to something, as well as when they can do so. This is a key ingredient when it comes to creating a plan for your music. For those of you in the early stages of your career, you might have school or other related commitments. Those who are older often have spouses, kids, or a career that takes precedence over playing music.

Knowing all this, it's a good idea to understand what commitments the other members of your band have. Are they flexible, rigid, or likely to affect the longevity of what you are doing? It's better to acknowledge this up front than to find out later. And what is the best way to figure this out when it comes to new bandmates? ASK! All you need to ask is this simple question: "What is playing music competing with in your life?"

IN THE END, THE PLAN MATTERS

Look, we get it. Not all this stuff is fun. But it is important to have goals and desires that extend past the now. It's even more so if you are a creator hoping to take things to the next level. We guarantee if you talk to performers who many consider as being at the top of the mountain, most if not all will agree with us. You'll find similar levels of passion, drive, and desire.

Let's key in on the "passion" part. It can't be faked, bought, or created on demand. It simply exists or doesn't. Is everyone who you are creating and performing with equally passionate about what you are doing and hope to achieve? Only two answers exist: yes or no.

We can't overstate this advice. Finding those with shared goals is a key ingredient if you seek long-term action or bigger dreams.

RIGHT NOTE: If you have to find a temporary second job to support your career, try to pick something that has to do with music. When my band Umphrey's McGee started in 1998 in South Bend, Indiana, I needed to find a little supplemental income to make ends meet. A friend and his girlfriend worked at nearby St. Anthony Parish directing the kids' choir and accompanying church services on piano. When they graduated from Notre Dame and moved away, they suggested me as their replacement. I started working at $40 an hour, including another $40 an hour for any time that I spent practicing the material each week. At the end of that school year I was told that it would be helpful if I could find someone to either conduct the choir or play piano, as they needed two people to do the job well. Ryan Stasik, our bassist, was traveling to study in Japan that summer and had to find a month-long job to raise a little money for the trip. He had something lined up back at home in Kalamazoo but wanted to stay in South Bend with the rest of the band so we could keep writing and rehearsing. I was able to hire Ryan to conduct the choir. I stayed on for two years as the morning school service accompanist. It worked well for being in a local/regional band. But most importantly, that first summer we were together as Umphrey's McGee, both Ryan and I found local gigs that involved music, paid well, fit into our schedules, and made a positive contribution to the lives of kids.

OKAY, TIME TO MAKE SOME MUSIC!

I bet you thought we would never get to this part. Well, the wait is over and it's time to make some music. Hopefully what you read so far did a lot for you in regard to the creation of a solid foundation. While all that is important, what really matters is the music itself. It's why you are doing all this, right?

Playing and creating music can happen in an infinite number of ways. Maybe you regularly sit down and play with friends. Or meet up to play with other musicians and have a great time! This is a typical catalyst that gets people together repeatedly and then one day, well, you're in a band. Other times you put the pieces together in a more deliberate, planned way, or perhaps decide that you want to play solo. Whatever makes it happen and results in something that feels right, probably is.

ABOUT YOUR FUTURE CREATION . . .

The whole act of creation, being a maker, and then producing what others consider art is a tricky game. Inspiration, art, creativity, vision, and moments of clarity can't be forced. This is one of the most frustrating truths for artists. If you happen to be one of those who can turn it on when you want, congratulations. You are one of few. For the rest, it's often a battle. On top of that, if you are playing with others, you need the magic to happen simultaneously.

Here are a few tips that may help aid the creative process:

- Try to recognize your moments of creativity or inspiration, then make the most of them. The weird thing about these moments is that they often arrive when you aren't expecting them. Sometimes your most creative and inspired moments coincide with mindless tasks, like mowing the lawn, taking a shower, or whatever you want to insert here. Why? You aren't *thinking* about it. There's no urgency or stifling self-critique. Your mind is free to wander and create. See what works *for you*, then recognize and revisit. If it works again, milk it.

- Another way to potentially induce creativity, imagination, or inspiration is to surround yourself with it. This one is hard to specify because we are all inspired by different things. Some might find posters of musicians they admire motivating. Others can be inspired by another's art, or maybe even a setting or place. As long as it's healthy and productive, then it's a good thing.

- Expect that a lot of what you produce is going to suck. Hang on to what matters and dump the rest. The most important part of this process is actually to DO IT. Write, create, produce, and capture! If you follow this recipe enough, you might just end up with something that matters.

IN REGARDS TO PLAYING OTHER PEOPLE'S MUSIC

Determining what kind of, and then more specifically, which songs to play can be difficult. But whether you chose to be a solo act, or just started the next big band, at some point you are going to have to play "covers." Sure, there are maybe three bands in the history of music that never played another's songs, but in the realistic world of performing and growing your project, this is something you need to embrace.

How Do I Choose What Songs to Play?

Determining what cover songs go into your catalog should have a lot to do with whom you think your audience will be. If you see yourself playing after-work sets at the local, blue-collar pub, then coming in hot with the entire Taylor Swift catalog might not work out the way you want. Same goes for the reverse. Performing Steely Dan's or Hall and Oates's greatest hits to a bunch of teenagers or an audience of college kids might not go over well.

While both of the scenarios just described may be far from your next gig's situation, there are a few things that can help you be prepared for any audience or venue:

- Have a variety of tunes prepared.
- Be flexible and adapt to your crowd.
- Consider songs that are known and appeal to broader audiences.

Taking these things into consideration will substantially increase the likelihood of keeping your growing audience happy and boost the likelihood of being asked to return wherever you want to play.

Wait . . . I Don't Have Any Gigs Yet

While it might seem as if we have the cart in front of the horse when discussing cover songs and your live catalog, we don't. This is all needed framework when it comes to getting you ready to pursue live performances. In fact, these are some of the most important building blocks when it comes to creating a stable and lasting ability to get live—and hopefully paying—gigs!

As a reward for all this mundane "business" talk, now we get to do something fun! That's right, all this planning and consideration leads us to something awesome. It's time to record a demo! Yep. If you aren't one already, you are finally about to become a recording artist.

A CONVERSATION WITH HUEY LEWIS

Hugh Anthony Cregg III isn't a name most will recognize; however, Huey Lewis certainly is. One in the same, Huey Lewis and the News as his band is known have dropped hits in the top 10 twelve different times. Starting his career as a founding member of the band Clover, Huey and his band gave us such hits as "The Power of Love," "I Want a New Drug," and "The Heart of Rock and Roll." He also starred on Broadway as the slick lawyer Billy Flynn in the musical *Chicago*. Simply put, the guy is a recording and performing legend.

JOEL: What's one early decision in your career that then impacted you for years forward?

HUEY: Wow, that's very interesting. I'm gonna say management. Meeting my manager was a big important thing.

And how did you find your manager?

I recorded a demo tape at a local studio and the studio owner thought it was good. She sent it to Bob Brown. He managed Pablo Cruise at the time.

Very cool. And then he reached out to you and said what? "I like the sound"?

He did. Bob reached out and said, "Let's take a meeting." And we got on like a house on fire. He's a New Yorker. I have an uncle—also a New Yorker—who was very, very similar. They even looked suspiciously alike. I felt like I'd known this guy a long time and we hit it off right away. He said, "Look, I don't know where we're going here, but if you want a manager, you got one."

Is that in the Clover days?

This is *after* Clover 'cause Clover had just broken up. I was running a little jam session. The local club came to me and asked, "Do you wanta night? Monday nights are always a big night for us." So I said, "Sure, I'll take Monday night."

And then I created an evening called Monday Night Live. We had a Monday Night Live band and we kind of got a local happening. We played like four or five tunes of our own and did other stuff. We invited other bands to play as well, and had comedians, some sketch, and frilly stuff. Kind of patterned it after *Saturday Night Live*.

It got quite popular, so the studio owner tried to come visit and couldn't get into the nightclub. She called me the next day and said, "Wow, man. You got it going on. How would you like a demo day in the studio?"

And I said, "Great. We'll take it." We went into the studio, and for a laugh we cut a disco version of the *Exodus* movie theme that we called, "Exodisco." 'Cause that's what we were doing at Monday Night Live . . . funny stuff, you know.

Got it.

And so we cut that for a joke and weeks later Nick Lowe called me. Nick called to ask me to come to London to play on one of his records, which I did. And he and Dave Edmunds, we cut two . . . I played on two of their records and there was a down moment in the studio and I said, "Hey, you guys wanna hear something funny?" The record company was there and I played them "Exodisco." They loved it. They said, "Man, that's great. Come on in and we'll make you a deal." I said, "Really? Wow."

The next day I asked Jake Riviera, who was soon to become Elvis Costello's manager: "What do I do?"

He says, "Go in, ask them for three thousand pounds and thirteen points, and tell them you need the money now." Okay, great. So I went in, I told them that, and they said, "Well, we need a little more vocal on it."

"No problem," I said. "What do you want?"

"Well, we want you to sing a little more here."

I said, "No sweat. Just give me the money." And they gave me the money. I went back home and announced, "Boys, we got something going here. I just got to sing 'em something from "Exodisco." But I got to put some more vocal on it." I went back to the studio and because it was a demo—a multi-track recording—they had accidentally erased the tape. They had actually wound an aligning machine and erased part of our demo that I just now got a record deal with. And I had to put more vocal in it and they were apoplectic about it, and so I said, "Well, look, I gotta rerecord the thing, so I'm gonna need a whole week of studio time."

They said, "No problem. Whatever it takes." So I took the multi-track. I put the vocals in two tracks of the multi-track, and sang a little bit more and mixed it down to another two-track.

It took me an hour and a half and I spent the rest of the week cutting three other songs. And those three are original songs that we'd written. And those three songs, and that demo tape, was the demo tape that Bob Brown heard when he signed us to a deal.

Amazing. It's important to get paid up front, isn't it, when you're getting started?

Yeah. Well, you need money you know. And back in those days, they owned everything. I mean, you didn't own your masters; you didn't own anything.

I remember when Prince had that slave thing written on the side of his head. I mean, he was actually correct. I don't own my masters. "The Heart of Rock and Roll"—I don't own that.

I mean, that master is owned by Universal Music. And after thirty years, everybody sues it as a reversion, but you don't get it back if you signed as a loan-out corporation, which we did for tax purposes. For now, those masters are not mine. They're owned by them.

Wow. Yeah, that's something you definitely try to avoid now in the music scene. Do you think that it makes sense for most artists to try to stay independent or should they still be going for a major label at this point?

It's really a tough thing, you know. It's a good thing you're doing this book because there used to be one avenue and *only* one avenue to success back in my day. And that was . . . If you imagine the eighties, you know 1980.

First of all, radio . . . *top 40 radio* . . . started with the advent of push-button radio in Fresno, California. And the theory went, as long as people didn't hear something they didn't like, they'd stay on your station. But as soon as they heard something they didn't like, they could push a button and switch stations.

So the idea was, narrow your playlist to the favorites only, and therefore they'll just hear favorites, favorites, favorites, and never switch off of a station. And of course, in the sixties, FM radio came to be, and because they were a new format, not very many people wanted it. They played anything and everything. But then of course everybody got hip to FM radio and all the cars got FM radio and now suddenly FM radio started to program themselves, and by the early eighties, there was only one format that mattered, and it was called CHR (Contemporary Hit Radio). And that was not only top 40 now, that was like top 28.

They would only play, like, twenty-eight songs and it would be a sliding scale so that the top three songs got maybe ten plays a day.

Right, I get ya.

And the number twenty-seven and twenty-eight got one or two plays a day. I'm kind of making this up but it's close. And that was the only format that mattered in the eighties. The theory was—

It was driving everyone to hear the same songs. You know, the big hits.

But it was an editing process that's interesting because when you listen to CHR, if you wanted to hear Huey Lewis and the News, you had to hear Garth Brooks also. And you also listen to the Commodores. It was the only format that mattered. And amongst that format was when MTV first started.

People forget this. When MTV first started, their playlist exactly mirrored a tip sheet called Radio & Records playlist. It was a radio world. It was an audio world. And all that mattered was a hit single on CHR radio.

To that end, everything was truncated. Everything was short. Better get to the hook by thirty seconds or it's over. You got to do this and so consequently that became our hardest challenge, 'cause really, left to our own devices, Huey Lewis and the News was much more like Umphrey's McGee.

You know, we were more like a jam band in a way, so the hardest thing we had to do was truncate everything—abbreviate everything and then have a hit with a voice that didn't sound like radio. In order to have a hit, you needed to be played on every radio station in America at the same time.

Right.

That took a big national distribution network and promotion network to lobby these CHR stations to finally become one of those twenty-eight songs. The only avenue to success was, number one, attract a record company, sign a record deal, now out-compete the other bands on that record label, so that you became their priority, and then release the record that was their priority, have them spend money promoting it, and then of course you had to have a record that was good enough to stick when they played it six times in one day.

And make that money back.

And make that money back. But nowadays, there are a million avenues to success. Through television, through the Internet, *American Idol*, through writing, through . . . I don't know, a million ways. I don't think there's any really one way anymore. You know what I mean?

Right.

It's such a complicated maze of media. You need to just find your way through somehow.

Is it more important now to try to be authentic and to try to be yourself?

I think so, yeah. And in a way it's much better because you don't have to market yourself as much. You don't have to conform as much. In our days, there were absolute formulas that you had to adhere to. I think now, the formulas are much more wide open, to be honest.

To kind of go back to what you were just talking about before this, how do you write a hit? Is there a secret?

I think the secret to writing a hit is to rewrite and rewrite again. Synthesize it down. Because you're making a song that's going to be played all-too-often. You're aiming for a market where they play your song eight to ten times a day, so it had better be pretty perfect. Every little part of it needs to be perfect. What song in the world merits being heard a hundred times? None! But that's the format we were trying to compete in.

Right.

There's no such thing as a hit like that anymore. I mean, a Geico ad is close now, but not even. You know what I'm saying? How do you write that? I think a hit is a good song that's written and rewritten and rewritten and rewritten and rewritten. You just synthesize the shit out of it until you make every little piece of it catchy.

Did you guys have a feeling? Did you know when you'd written something, you said, "This is gonna do it, right here."? Did you know?

Kind of. There was a time when I really felt like I knew what was going on because I had my finger on the pulse, and yeah, kind of. But you never really know what's gonna get up and fly. But again, what's interesting is, when you're working on those

57

things, and in our case we didn't have Pro Tools or that stuff. We didn't have digital. We had analog. We only had twenty-four tracks. But within that, we had to make those songs as perfect as we could within that thing. So the emphasis was on perfection in those days. Now, with Pro Tools, sort of anybody can do it. It's different.

Do you like writing more on your own or collaborating? How did you guys function back then, and is that different now?

No, it's always the same. The hardest part is what is this song about? Songs need to be about something. They really do, even if it's the most trivial little thing. It can be about anything, but it needs to be about something that the singer believes in, that is credible. When the man says, "I'm going to Kansas City, they got some crazy little women, and I'm gonna get me one," you gotta believe he's going to Kansas City, he knows about the crazy little women, and he wants to get him one. And if that's the case, then it works, and the whole thing works. It's gotta be true. When you write, it's gotta come from someplace that's real, true, and people can tell that.

That's pretty cool. I feel like your band in particular has had some of the same people that you've worked with for, I don't know, thirty, forty years. Two questions. What does it take to keep a band together? And secondly, you have your name, Huey Lewis and the News. Tell me a little bit how you guys picked that name and how that impacted anything, as far as band dynamics.

Sure. Well, the way to keep a band together is pay well. [Laughs.] I'm joking. No, it just works. It's one of those things. The thing that breaks bands apart is not the work. It's the other twenty-two hours or the personal stuff and all that shit. If you can travel together long enough, then you can probably stay together. That's the hardest part. It's either organic and it works, or it doesn't. For us, it works pretty good. Plus, nobody wants to switch roles. Nobody covets to be, wants to really be the lead singer but me, and like that. It kind of works that way.

Right, it's kind of important when you're putting together a band to have people that are willing to have these different roles. You can't have three different lead people in the band.

That's it. What was the second part of your question?

I was curious about how you guys chose your name.

American Express was our name, which I thought was the perfect name because that's kind of what we sounded like. Now, when we met our manager Bob Brown, he said, "Man, we gotta make it Huey Lewis and American Express." "Really, why?" "Well, it's more focused. You can do the interviews," and blah, blah, blah. "It's better that way." So everybody said, "All right, cool, whatever the fuck." Really, that's literally how it happened.

Now we were Huey Lewis and American Express. Then when we signed the record deal, and literally on the eve of the release of our first record, Chrysalis Records was worried that American Express would sue us for the name or some shit. We had twenty-four hours to come up with a new name.

And how did you choose the News?

We just thought of a million names, and that was kind of the best we could come up.

Oh man. It's so funny. Isn't it amazing? You have these decisions that have to be made in such a short time, and that's what you have for the next fifty years.

Yeah. I mean, I still like American Express. I still wish we were called American Express.

Another question that I've been asking a lot of the musicians is what is the best advice and what is the worst advice that you've ever been given in the music business?

Let's see. The best advice was probably from Jake Riviera. He meant it sort of facetiously, but I think it's true. His advice was kind of a strategy, kind of a business strategy for rock and roll, which was "Infiltrate, then double-cross." You need to listen to everybody, but take other people's opinions with a grain of salt and ultimately stick to your own core, knowing what you know most about yourself is probably the best advice I've ever gotten.

Stick with what you believe in, you know.

Yeah, just stick with what you think is great. Stick with the songs that you like the most. If other people aren't getting them for some reason, keep working on them. Keep rewriting them. Keep working on them.

Yeah, absolutely. One of the recurring themes I've come across is that some of the biggest successes only happened after hundreds of failures.

Yeah.

It's very rare that somebody hits major success and sustains it right from the beginning.

No question. And it's the slightest little thing. It's almost like a trick. It's like balancing plates. You can't get them, you can't get them, then all of a sudden, bingo. Now I can ride this bike, and it's just a piece of cake. It is funny.

How about the worst advice?

Well, I didn't do a corporate deal. It wasn't anybody's advice. It was my own idea. When Michael Jackson had Pepsi, that was the first time anybody from the rock and roll world had any kind of corporate tie.

It was kind of anathema for a long time.

You're right. Coca-Cola asked to take a meeting with us and said, "You know what a Q quotient is?" I said, "No." "Well, it's a combination of likeability and plausibility and credibility and recognizability and all these ratings. And you have the largest Q quotient of anybody in America right now." I said, "No kidding?" They said, "Yeah, and *that's* Coke-ness."

Anyway, they offered us lots of money for a TV ad featuring "The Heart of Rock and Roll." And I said no.

Artistic integrity.

Yeah, stupid. Here's another story with it. We're in New York, and I'm in a Jewish deli, literally, on the pay phone. This shows how far back it was, before cell phones. I'm on the pay phone, and my manager's telling me we got an opportunity to do this gig or some kind of thing. I think it was an ad or something. Do we want to do it? I said, "I don't know, man. It doesn't sound very credible. I know it's money, but it's *just* money, right? It's not anything. Do we want to do it?"

I hang up the phone, and turn around, and who's sitting there right in the truck stop but Henny Youngman. You know, Henny Youngman, the comedian?

Oh yeah, okay.

He looks at me and goes, "Hey, you're Huey, right? Huey, listen: Take my advice. *Nem di gelt.*" I said, "What?" He said, "*Nem di gelt.* You know what that means?" "No." "Take the money."

Take the money. No doubt. Any other final parting words of advice?

Here's the thing: If you're gonna study it as a business plan, the odds are you're not gonna make it in the music business. I was awarded the Distinguished Alumni medal from my old prep school, and in it they prepared all this stuff on the day I sent it over. And one of my classmates got up and said he did all the math, and the thing is, the odds of being a success in the music business are one in twenty-nine thousand. Something like that, right? In any capacity. That's not just singing—in *any* capacity.

I always tell people this. I say, if you're thinking about it as kind of a business plan, you might as well just forget about it. Unless it's the only thing you want to do. You probably ought to think about something else. But if it is the only thing you want to do, well, then study the hell out of it, figure out how to be a success.

Yeah, if you love making music and creating music, that might be enough for you to be satisfied.

It needs to be, because that's the thing. I have a lot of responsibilities, and I got a family, and I have all this stuff, and I put on these big shows. But I wouldn't have any of it if I hadn't hit it. I would be in a band somewhere playing harmonica. I wouldn't be miserable. I'd be fine. I'd be playing harp somewhere. I knew that. I was willing to do that. That's what I want to do, in any capacity. If that's the case, then power on, read the book, and get 'er done.

SECTION THREE:

THE IMPORTANCE OF YOUR DEMO

Never in the history of music have independent, upcoming, and aspiring musicians had more access to high quality and affordable recording tools. THANK YOU, TECHNOLOGY, for being so awesome. Never has there been a greater ability to easily and affordably record your efforts. In fact, you probably can do so from what's in your pocket right now! Today's smart phones readily possess better recording technology than most professional or aspiring musicians had access to just twenty-five years ago. Is it "studio" quality? No. But that isn't the point.

Now back to your demo. You need one—at least if you have a desire to play anywhere that involves more than just putting your name on a list and waiting for your turn. In the early stage of your music career, your demo, as well as the way it is presented, can have a heck of a lot to do with your future success. The reasoning is simple. Venue owners or those that schedule performers are very much aware of the easy access everyone has to recording tools. So, someone that shows up wanting a booking without any sample or demo available, likely isn't very serious or good in the eyes of the booker.

You need to present yourself as being in the BUSINESS *of playing music if you want to get paying jobs!*

Those you're seeking bookings from are very much into the "business" side of your music. But for different reasons than you. They want to fill up and then keep people inside their establishment. Nothing results in its opposite faster than terrible or poorly chosen live music.

Another thing to strongly consider is you aren't the only one competing for that prime, paid spot. The likely scenario is that there are a *whole lot* of people jockeying for it. On top of that, at most established places there are probably several acts that have regularly occupied the slot you seek. So the real question is, what are you doing to make a favorable impression? How will you stand out or create some reason for that decision maker to pick YOU?

It's all in the music and your profile, all represented within a few select moments of your recording career. That's right, your demo!

CREATING A DEMO

Hopefully we haven't put too much pressure on you regarding the importance of this particular part of your approach. Before we get too far into it, know this: Recording music is HARD! Despite the many tools that exist to make it easier, it's still hard. Why? Because the microphone doesn't lie—well at least not prior to postproduction. In addition, many have "red light syndrome." This is a condition that results in freezing, overthinking everything, and becoming "stiff" when the red light associated with the record button turns on. Luckily, there is a cure. It's knowing that you can redo this as many times as you need to. With that, here are a few tips that will help you approach this science experiment in a way that should produce better results.

BEFORE YOU RECORD

Before you hit the record button, have a plan. This plan should focus on how you are going to capture the attention of the listener, and FAST! Fifteen to thirty seconds—that's all you have, if that. Your demo is not the place to have a long, drawn-out intro. Show what you can do quickly, efficiently, and impressively.

SHOWCASE YOUR SKILLS

If you are a singer/songwriter, then record something that has a vocal track at the top of the song. If you're an instrumentalist, then do something that showcases your strongest skills. Regardless of what you do, it can't just be good. It has to be great and it has to garner a reaction from the listener. Without that last part, why is a booking agent or venue owner going to believe that you will capture and keep the attention of their patrons?

WHAT SHOULD I INCLUDE?

Most demos consist of two to three songs. Try to choose music that will separate you from your competition. It is also important to present a variety of songs if you have them. If you aren't a cover band, but you play a cover that you feel strongly about, it's okay to include it, but as the final track. Regardless of what type of content you include, it should be your strongest material.

THE RECORDING PROCESS

It is called the recording "process" for a reason. Doing it well usually requires certain steps and tools. As previously mentioned, modern technology has made it easier for musicians to record and distribute their work, but your results are likely to improve with the addition of a few, critical things: a quality microphone, a suitable recording environment, and last but not least, a proper platform to produce the music itself.

ALL MICROPHONES ARE NOT CREATED EQUAL

Microphones are built to do a variety of different things. Some are meant to record incoming sound from one direction, others from all directions. Some are made to record instruments and drums, others specifically for the human voice. To make selecting the right one even harder, MICROPHONES CAN BE REALLY FREAKING EXPENSIVE!!! So now what?

Fortunately, for those just getting started, there are a variety of all-purpose mics that can be used to record your instrumentation *and* vocals in a high-quality way. Unfortunately, your smart phone does not do this. Yes, it was mentioned that a smart phone can and could record a demo, and it can. It's just not best way to do so, as the overall quality will reflect in the end results.

A SUITABLE RECORDING ENVIRONMENT

This is pretty straight forward. You need a QUIET space to record. Microphones are sensitive, meant to pick up EVERYTHING. In fact, you probably didn't even know how loud the world was around you until you turned on your new microphone and hit record. That's right, that's the fan running inside your computer, or the cars driving by outside your apartment.

Despite the world's many sounds, there are things you can do to make life easier when recording, and once again tools that can help you find the quietest place possible too! Here are a few tips for finding and creating a suitable place to record:

- Download a free decibel meter on your smart phone and test your space.
- Choose a room with carpet, or "stuff" in it. It all dampens the sound of the room.
- Avoid empty spaces with flooring like hardwood or concrete, which creates too much decay! Also, avoid rooms with lots of glass, which cause unnatural reflections.
- Try to avoid things that move a lot of air. Meaning, fans and vents. This won't matter if you're being really loud, but if recording a solo instrument or vocal track, you might hear all that air movement loud and clear!

- Clap your hands! You will immediately hear whether or not your space is acceptable for recording.

Not to sound like a parrot that is repeating everything, but . . . Technology! Use it! There are SO MANY audio recording platforms available that listing them would be cumbersome, so here are just a few:

Garage Band and Logic Pro X

If you own a Mac desktop or laptop then you most likely have Garage Band. This is Apple's free recording software that is included with most, if not all, of their equipment. There is enough horsepower in Garage Band for any beginner or intermediate user to create a quality demo, or even album. Apple includes this, as they want you to graduate to their paid upgrade, Logic Pro X, which is similar in nature, but has more elements of control.

Pro Tools

While not blessed with the most creative name, Pro Tools is a staple of the modern musician. That being said, there is A LOT to know and understand inside Pro Tools. So much in fact, that novice users are likely to be overwhelmed. However, for those that do in fact know their way around recording, they will use nothing else.

Ableton

Ableton is great for Virtual Instruments, and productions using a lot of looping, effects, or automation. It's also great for making things fit in to different tempos with the warp controls.

Most large-format tracking studios will have all three of these, so you should be able to open your sessions on any of these DAWs in any studio of size. What DAW (Digital Audio Workstation) you choose to work with depends a great deal on what kind of music and workflow you prefer. Ableton is not well-suited for live tracking of real instruments since you can only record one version of a part on one track. In Pro Tools and Logic, you can record as many as you'd like and toggle between them on the same track, ultimately deciding on the best parts of that track and making a final composite version of that track to mix. Logic is great for mixing MIDI (Musical Instrument Digital Interface)/virtual instruments and live instruments since you have the best of both worlds and it's very affordable. In all these DAWs it's best to demo them and see what works the best for you.

ACTUALLY RECORDING SOMETHING!

We told you this was a "process!" Now that you hopefully have the right material selected, a decent microphone, and nice quiet place to record, let's discuss creating an actual recording and the process that goes into doing that. Understanding it properly will not only improve quality, but also reduce the frustration associated with not knowing any better.

SET PROPER LEVELS

As we established already, your microphone is sensitive. Knowing this, it is important to set up proper "levels" within whatever you have chosen to capture your recording. Not doing so will result in "clipping," which will create distortion in the recording. This is done through testing your levels prior to, or with, a few practice runs.

On the opposite end of the distortion spectrum are weak input levels. This is when your input channel isn't "hot" enough. Meaning, it is only sending a fraction of the signal to your recorder that should be sent. This results in a shallow sound, or one that has all the "white noise" sounds of your recording space included.

Please note: If your very first recording sounds amazing, then you are the first person in the history of recording to arrive at this result!

WE ALL HAVE FLAWS, SO CAN YOUR DEMO

Your demo is actually that, a quick demonstration of what the listener can expect when you are there performing. Therefore, it doesn't have to be perfect. Yes, you want to make sure you are hitting notes accurately both vocally and instrumentally, but small imperfections in the recording should not take precedence over a take that captured your true sound, excitement, or passion.

SEPARATE TRACKS

Back to the "process" of recording. This calls for a healthy dose of isolation. Meaning, it is best to record the individual parts of your music apart from one another. This allows for greater control and possible manipulation of each part. For some, this is tough, as you are used to playing songs with all parts included. Just know that if that is the way you choose to record, you will lose an element of control that might be needed to turn something/someone up, down, or even off. That said, if you are confident in your group's performance together, many great recordings have been made with a full band in the same room. How you decide to record is an important first step in the process that will affect many elements down the road.

MIXING

If your demo is the first real recording you've done, you'll likely want to have some help mixing it to get it sounding as professional as possible. Remember, you only get one chance to make a first impression and you don't want the first impression to be: *This person obviously doesn't know what they're doing.* You probably don't need more than a couple hours with an engineer as the demo should be pretty straightforward.

I'M DONE RECORDING AND MIXING. NOW WHAT?

It's perfectly fine to have your demo primarily in the digital format. Whatever you do, don't send links to download, as you will drastically diminish your chances of your demo getting heard. The last thing a prospective talent buyer wants is to take up space on his or her devices with your music. A link to stream is typically the most non-invasive way to share your music these days. You can also feature your track on your website for easy access. If you feel the need to produce a physical product, thumb drives or CDs are okay, but there are many people out there who don't even own a CD player anymore.

CREATING AN ONLINE PRESENCE TO SHOWCASE YOUR DEMO

Coming in a close second to the invaluable demo you just recorded is the need to establish some kind of online presence. As we discussed, you don't actually "drop off" your demo like the musicians that preceded you once did. The new-school approach is lightweight; this means you need to create something that can be referenced online. Don't sweat it; it's A LOT easier than you probably think it is. And better yet, can be done for FREE. Yes, that is right, you can have your webpage for free. How? We are going to give you one!

All you need to do is visit RealistsGuide.com, create an account, and then fill out a few questions regarding your music.

There are other free options available too. We live in a new and exciting online world where all kinds of websites offer what is called "freemium" services. Much like the competition for paying gigs, the online realm is also highly competitive. To get you assimilated into their world, many sites and services offer free levels of service. Yes, the hope and desire of those offering are that you will eventually become a paying user. And there are likely to be limitations or restrictions. But if free is what you can afford, then you certainly have options.

Along with the world of freemium online services are places where you can host your demo tunes. One great option is YouTube. Sure, YouTube is primarily meant for video, but you can certainly upload your audio tracks and use various still shots or other visually appealing offerings while your music plays. If you are able, consider adding any video possible, even if it is just you talking about the song that is about to play. The more YOU that can be delivered during this initial presentation, the better off you are.

In conclusion, there is NO reason why you can't have a demo of reasonable quality, present it through a web page that can be created at no charge, and do all this with the resources that are probably already in your pocket. Hopefully you see why NOT having all this, or at least most of it, will lead to the decision maker at your venue of choice feeling like you don't have what it takes to get that coveted spot.

Be proactive and prove them wrong. *That's* how you bypass the competition and get the gig.

A CONVERSATON WITH JAKE CINNINGER

Jacob Alan Cinninger is the lead guitarist in Umphrey's McGee. Raised in Niles, Michigan and now a resident of South Bend, Indiana, Jake has graced stages in venues big and small. What is not small, however, is Jake's experience, skill, and insight into all aspects of the music industry. Once a member of the country band Avalanche, Jake was destined for stardom only to see his path change for reasons he couldn't control, but all of those stories are probably best told by him.

MATT: You started as a drummer.

JAKE: Yeah, I started at three on drums. Got the Sears, Roebuck silver edition and beat it all to hell.

One of the most crucial points was when I realized that I had really good time. I think when you really get down to it, even Ginger Baker said, "The reason why I played with Eric Clapton is 'cause he had perfect time."

Having perfect time, or somewhat close, was solidified by my parents' killer record collection, I would find a great time-keeping record like Fleetwood Mac's *Rumours*. It got my clock to where I wasn't rushing forward or dragging. I started to really feel the center of the groove.

So that helped you as a guitarist? You've mentioned to me in the past that you'll often think, "I need to put a rhythm in here."

Yeah, always.

So, you're thinking percussively.

I think of it like a stick.

Do you think it's helped you as a recording artist, too, like in your studio?

Oh yeah, big time.

Do you have a click track going in your head?

I can play really well with a click track or not. It's something that you definitely have to work on, especially if you're a drummer. Slow tempos and click tracks are just nightmares for some drummers in the studio. It's like they're constantly waning in and out of the click. What I like to do is, if it's a slow tempo, is a sixteenth note click track, instead of click, click, click, click. If you're gonna miss a beat, you're *really* gonna feel it with a pulse like this. I'm feeling micro-division time. It's actually like double-time, but we're playing a half-time groove. Little things like that—just knowing what to do in those situations, learning from experience, and from mistakes.

I never knew this about you earlier, but Joel told me you were in a band called Avalanche that was on the verge of country stardom?

Yeah, big time. We had an investor who sort of harvested a bunch of area musicians. I was playing the Million Dollar Saloon one night and two guys in trench coats walk in, sit down at the bar, and watch me play. I'm like, *This is kinda weird. Who are those guys?* Then they come up to me and say, "Hey, we're investors in this project we wanna get together. Here's the lead singer and songwriter." Then we ended up using half the band that I was playing with to become Avalanche. They were all my buddies.

What happened?

We were using Nashville's biggest producers, biggest studios, everything. Sony Records was involved. The red-carpet treatment was happening. The sign-on bonuses were kicking in. Then one of the singers got into a car wreck and killed someone.

Oh man.

Yeah.

That's how it ended?

That's what happened.

So if that hadn't happened, you might be on the Country Music Awards.

Yeah, I would've been wearing a ten-gallon hat and a bolo.

You would've looked good. But I get it. Would you have turquoise bolo, or something different?

Oh, I had a turquoise shirt, bro.

What kind of country was it? Because I think modern country is more like rock 'n' roll. Was it like outlaw country, like Waylon Jennings?

No, it was slicker. Imagine Eagles, Crosby, Stills & Nash, mixed with top 10 country.

So, country. I don't feel like that is what you're passionate about. I feel like you like what you play now.

Totally. There is a cookie-cutter sort of thing with a Sony brought-up band. They harvest the producer and everything starts . . . It's gotta sound a certain way.

How common do you think that is? I think most people don't think about bands as having investors.

It was kind of crazy. That's why I was like, *Whoa.*

But that's more common than people know.

Yeah, it is.

Just to cover actually promoting, actual real recording.

Yeah, they would send us out to this ashram in Calabasas, California, so we could get tighter as a band and go through all this super spiritual healing with crazy gurus—

They're sending a country band to a mind retreat?

Pretty much. Man, once that happened with Avalanche, I had a really bad taste in my mouth about record companies and the way music is perceived by the masses and all that.

Did that contribute to you wanting to have your own label with Umphrey's?

Not only that, but now stylistically, I'm gonna take all that I've learned and put it into a ball, and we're gonna try to make this all work. From bluegrass to metal to funk to reggae, and play it all stylistically proper. Now let's make a band. Let's do a Frank Zappa meets Pearl Jam. Great songs, but then technical bliss. With this kind of ethos you can set up a band for longevity, because it's fun. You're getting to go out there and just play like John Coltrane every night, and sort of scratch all those itches. That in itself keeps the artistic wheel going, just because every style's happening in the books. There's no time to get lazy. 'Cause artists are inherently lazy.

I think people are, yeah. I think it's just natural. The natural choice is always the easiest.

Okay. You went from Avalanche. Was Ali Baba's next?

Yeah. That's when I basically kinda went back home and was like, "I wanna form a group that can exceed my expectations."

So you started that group, or was it already there?

It was started with me and Steve Krojniewski, and then we found Karl Engelmann. It was just a perfect, crazy three-piece. We didn't sound like anyone. It was cool.

And then you go to Umphrey's, and the question here is, what's your advice for someone who's gonna join a band that's already doing something?

Yeah, that's a good question.

On any level. 'Cause here's the thing. It's not really the greatest plan to just come in and play whoever was there before you's notes for notes.

You wanna melt in slowly. I would say ego is the one thing you leave at the door. You're joining some other tribe that has all these little quirks and things that you don't know about. You don't really know these people that well yet on a personal level—just on a musical level. So yeah, it takes time to morph in. Or say you'd like to make suggestions—

You show up as a better listener in the beginning.

Yeah, like the classic saying of having big ears is the best thing you could have as a musician. Then you're also making eye contact with people, not staying inside your own artistic bubble.

That's one thing we do a lot onstage—use eye contact, where other bands try to use that ESP thing.

So how do you handle that? How do you handle screwing up onstage? 'Cause everyone does it.

Victor Wooten once said, "Oh man, I make mistakes all the time. It's just, I make the mistake sound right." You play a mistake with confidence, it's like jazz, man.

I think 90 percent of the things that I say, I don't know what the fuck I'm talking about. I just deliver them with a lot of confidence.

It's a feeling. Gut impulse is everything. Like a fighter, karate guru.

What's the worst career advice anyone ever gave you? The first thing that just popped in your head is probably the right answer.

I would definitely say, "You should try to add some politics to your music." That's just the worst thing you could ever do. I do not wanna hear Eddie Vedder rant. I didn't pay for that.

Yeah. Less talk, more rock.

Musicians are not politicians.

No, I agree. Politics, religion, and sex are three things that you almost always come out of a conversation about in worse position with the person you're talking to.

That's true.

So just don't. Don't.

What's some of the best advice someone's given you?

Probably, "Whatever you do, do not sound like your idols. But take as much as you can from them and spin it upside down, kind of, in a way." I think that's some of the most important things you can do. It can shoot yourself in the foot. Like everyone who sounds like Trey; they're not gonna have a job. They might be great at being Trey.

Yeah. But they're not.

But they spend too much time inside of a bubble that they can't get out.

SECTION FOUR:

GETTING GIGS

N ow that you've got your band or solo act going, it's time to start finding some gigs. This the fastest way to provide yourself with the cash flow needed not only provide for the members but also to provide opportunity! That last term is pretty broad, largely because there is A LOT of opportunity out there for growth if you have the funds. Cash is needed to record an album, upgrade equipment, improve travel, or add members to your crew so you don't have to do everything. However, in order to find and book a gig, you need to look like you are in the business. Here are few simple tips for doing so.

YOUR PAID GIG PREPARATION CHECKLIST

HAVE A BASIC WEBSITE

One of the most common errors that new acts make is convincing themselves that they don't need a website. There really isn't a reason that you shouldn't, can't, or don't have one. Websites are so easy to create these days, not having one is really inexcusable.

On your website you'll want to include examples of music, a calendar of your upcoming appearances, a short bio and explanation of your music, merchandise and other items for sale, your management and/or booking contact, and links to your social media presence. You may also want to have some photos or videos so people can make a visual connection to your work.

Ok, you get its importance, but what if you have absolutely no experience building a website? Well, that is an easy answer. Popular site builders are everywhere online. Platforms like Wix.com offer free and easy to customize templates that can have you online and looking credible within an hour. On top of the ease of use, the cost of keeping your site online is minimal. As in less than $20 a month, if there is even a subscription at all.

Here are additional tips for creating a website that conveys YOUR message:

Make It Obvious!

Don't make the visitor have to figure out what kind of music you play. This can easily be done with a simple line of text such as "An Enjoyable Night of Popular Cover Tunes" or "Grand Rapids's #1 Metal Band!" Regardless of what does it for you, get right to the point. Venue owners and booking agents know what they are looking for. If you make them have to figure it out, they are more likely to just leave your site than solve the mystery.

Use Interactive Media If You Have It

If you have video or other media—more specifically, demo tracks—then embed or include them! Sites like SoundCloud and YouTube make this easy, and so will your simple site builder platform. The best way to sell the "experience" you and your band provide is to let your website visitor experience it too. That being said, if your video shows your band playing in a basement for an audience of three, you might want to reconsider, but having quality content and not including it would be a strategic error.

Make Contacting You Easy and Obvious

How to contact you or what is needed to schedule a show should not be hard to find. This is as simple as adding a "Contact" or "Booking" page. If the way to inquire about bookings is a simple contact form, be sure to test it, and that it's sent to an inbox that gets checked daily.

Include a List of Songs You Play, or Can Play

This detail is really important for cover-heavy bands, or performers that play at events like weddings, parties, and places that are likely to want to hear popular music over and above your original material. If you play multiple songs from multiple artists then you might just list "Playing Popular Cover Songs by These Artists . . ." We get into some more specifics about this in a minute.

Create a Promo Pack

This next part is the "intermediate" to "advanced" level of play. If you want to gain the attention of club owners or booking professionals, having something that can be viewed on the Internet, or downloaded and printed out, is a plus. This is a one-pager, meaning fit it all on one page. Sure, you can use the back of that page too. Just remember, no one wants to read your twelve-page document, so think of this like you would a leaflet or a flyer that details your "services." Basically what you are doing is making it easy for anyone who books talent to deliver your presentation the way you want it to be sent to any interested party. For example, a couple is booking a wedding band at Venue X and the talent booker sends them three to five promo packs for possible bands. Do you really want to be the band that didn't have something to send?

Establish a Basic Cover Tunes List

Having an established list of original and cover material to play is important. It will help you appeal to—and hopefully book shows at—a wider variety of venues. Learning songs from various genres that people will recognize helps keep the audience's attention and interest when you weave in your originals. This is a straightforward and important way to help expand your fan base and to get people more familiar with what you do.

SELECTING AND TARGETING VENUES

Who do you want to be heard by? Then, where are they found? These are essential questions to answer when trying to build your audience. Many venues offer a wide array of performance genres and many have a very defined audience type. Does your act fit into any that meet the more specific end of that? If you are a solo act who plays folk music, then the local punk rock dive isn't a good place to focus your efforts. In fact, it's probably a great way to make zero progress.

Some venues will have what's referred to as a "built-in crowd." That means there are regulars who will come check out new music. This is an important question to ask early: *Is there a built-in crowd or is show attendance entirely draw-based?* Draw-based means if your act doesn't draw a crowd, you're not going to get help elsewhere. Some places fill themselves simply because they are popular places to drink, hang out, or have fun. Early on, if you can find gigs like that, you are in pretty good shape. The opposite side of that leaves you as the promoter too. Meaning, you are going to need to hype your own shows. Of course, doing that anyway is a must, but *depending* on it is risky.

Overall, you most likely have an idea about where you potential listeners are located. If not, it shouldn't be too hard to figure out. Who knows, you might even have a little fun finding the answer.

THE DAY OF THE WEEK MATTERS!

Let's get right to point on this one. Play concerts on Saturdays, ᵈays, and Thursdays in that prioritized order. Occasionally a ⱽ or Thursday may be better in a college town, but *typically* ay will be your best night of the week to perform. If you ore a prime night, that's not always a terrible thing— when starting out. Sometimes venues will have monthly residencies during slower nights of the week, which can be a good way to build your audience and take some chances developing your sound.

RIGHT NOTE: The prioritization of days is mostly true for cities in the United States. Keep in mind it's not necessarily true for Europe, South America, or Asia.

"GOOD" NIGHTS AND "BAD" NIGHTS

Before you confirm a show, always ask the promoter if he or she thinks it's a good night to play. You never know what you might be competing with, from a college sporting event to a popular fraternity night on campus. Bottom line: Establish a relationship with your promoter and set yourself up for the best chance of success.

IF YOU CAN'T BEAT THEM, "TRY" TO JOIN THEM

Booking yourself in the same market as a much larger or well-known act within your perceived genre may backfire. Your potential listeners can only go to one show, and if this is the case, it probably won't be yours. One clever solution is to see if you can be the opening act for this other show. This approach can actually give you, your fans, *and* the promoter the most potential upside.

In the event you do end up competing against a larger act, consider moving your show time to the afterparty slot, and then market your show as exactly that! A fair amount of people at the earlier show will be looking to keep the party going, so why not help them out?

NEGOTIATING GIG OFFERS

At this point, hopefully you feel comfortable with some of the basic strategy behind your shows. In fact, so much that you are getting offers for potential gigs! Now what? Let's take a few moments to discuss opportunity versus risk, and all the possible variables that come along too.

DOOR DEAL OR GUARANTEE?

As an unknown, you are a risky dice roll to many promoters. Your first visit to a market is likely to come with minimal guarantees at best. At worst, a percentage of the door deal. Before you know what you're worth, asking for a small guarantee with a "versus deal" may be the best choice. A versus deal gives the artist a percentage of the door *after* the deduction of all expenses. That way you'll make something, *plus* have an opportunity to make more if the show goes well. This is a potential win-win for both the venue and yourself. If you fill the house the venue wins for multiple reasons, and having incentive to fill the house is likely to make you try even harder to do so.

MAXIMIZING PROFITABILITY

You are worth what you can gross. Well, kind of . . . You'll have a better idea of what you're worth (aka, show's gross) after the first few plays in a market. It's all just math coupled with proven statistics. Being able to say that you grossed X in three prior visits, likely means your guarantee is worth Y. But if you want to maximize your ability to profit, you may wish to take a different approach. Ask for something called a "zero-dollar guarantee" accompanied by a scaling percentage of the door. You'll make the most money possible because you gave the promoter minimal risk. Of course, this means more risk for you, so you had better know people will show up!

Here's an example of how a scaling percentage works: At one hundred people paid, you would take 60 percent of the door. At one hundred fifty people, you would take 65 percent of the door. At two hundred people, 70 percent of the door. If the show sold out at two hundred fifty paid, you would make 75 percent of the door. Depending on the venue specs, the above numbers will vary, so it's a good idea to get to know what the venue's "nut," or breakeven point, is for a show. This is the lowest number the venue has for putting on a show. It includes a lot of factors past what you get paid, so keep that in mind. Venues have to pay people, but more importantly, might weigh "Opportunity Cost," which takes into consideration whether or not YOU are even the best opportunity for them that given night.

CONTRACTS AND ADVANCING A SHOW

Well-defined agreements are in the best interest of everyone taking part in said agreements. So, before booking any show, you will need a general show contract. No matter what size the venue is or how far out or soon the show might be, this is a must.

Make sure that everything you agree on is written down and signed by both parties. This can and will eventually protect you financially, especially in a situation where the show could be taken away from you. Don't do handshake deals or verbal agreements, and if there is a debate about anything, do it over e-mail so there is a paper trail if needed later on.

A good contract covers both "Sunny" and "Rainy Day" situations. Make the settlement procedure very cut and dry at the end of the night, meaning, how and when do you get paid? As an example, after a gig you'll likely be tired and don't want to have to nitpick over expenses and details when you're trying to leave the venue, so this settlement procedure establishes all that ahead of time.

Your basic agreement should cover the following:

1)   Terms of payment/money deal
2)   When will you play and for how long?
3)   Are there other artists on the bill and, if so, how many?
4)   Load in/out times and curfew times
5)   Is there a house sound engineer or does artist provide?

There is likely other language you will want, or might feel you need, to include, Just don't put yourself into a situation where you haven't answered the questions listed above. In the end, it's just good business to do so.

MANAGING RISK AND EXPECTATIONS

Sometimes your ideas will work, sometimes they won't. There may be a logical explanation for why something went well or why it didn't. But a lot of time the music business will defy logic. Persistence and ingenuity will both be invaluable as you create the business associated with your music. It's important not to let the highs get too high, or the lows get too low. Be realistic in your goals, and that will help keep those expectations managed. In the end, sometimes the best made plans fail, and sometimes the worst plans succeed. Just try to learn from failure, and pay attention to success. You grow and get better from both.

RIGHT NOTE: Running a profitable business is about having more revenue than expenses. Therefore, ALWAYS overestimate spending, and then on top of that add an "Oh Shit" line. What's that? It the line where you assume that at some point you are going to have to say, "Oh shit! We didn't really plan for that!" You will find yourself and your pockets much happier when you come in below an overestimated budget as opposed to way over a poorly estimated one.

Amongst the many hats you need to wear, you should add the promoter one too. Getting involved with the planning and advertising of your show is in your best interest. If people don't know you're playing, they're most likely not showing up. Promoters will take all the help they can get! Ask what you can do to work together. Do you have a street team of local people that will talk about your music and show? Will a local college radio station play your songs on the air? Is there a music store that you can partner with and do a free in-store performance? Will a college newspaper run a preview/interview or commit to a review of your show in exchange for press passes? Reviews and previews of your shows also serve the purpose of being endorsements for *future* gigs, adding another layer of legitimacy to anyone considering working with you.

Starting Local

It's okay to play mostly local gigs for the first year or so when you're getting started. You're going to be honing your live sound and will want the ability to try things out that may or may not work. You only get one chance to make a big national splash, so being extra confident in your sound is a smart decision. By the time you're hitting the road and playing more shows in important markets, you want to be able to play a strong live set. You have to be ready to make an impression. The other practical element of starting local is that once you begin touring nationally, you'll want to go back to all the markets you hit the first time. Having a solid fan base at home before you tour nationally is helpful both artistically and financially.

A CONVERSATION WITH PETE SHAPIRO

Entrepreneur, promoter, filmmaker, publisher, and venue owner are each great ways to describe someone, so it's truly amazing when one person's title includes all. That's Pete Shapiro. The owner/publisher of *Relix* magazine, Shapiro has since done some amazing stuff, such as promoting and organizing the Grateful Dead's 50th Anniversary shows, which filled Chicago's massive Soldier Field not once, but thrice. Taking ownership of a venue at the age of twenty-three was just the start for what has become one of the music industry's most well-rounded, experienced, and successful entrepreneurs.

JOEL: Pete, I think you're one of the more interesting people in the music business because you've crossed a lot of interesting different lines of being both a concert promoter and then also having Relix *magazine as something that you've produced as well. Is there anything that stands out in your mind that was an important decision you made that's impacted your entire career?*

PETE: I'm a big believer in one thing leads to another. For me, it has to do with an experience I had in March 1993, when I was a student at Northwestern University. I went to a Grateful Dead concert, and that event changed my life. You know, it led to then going on the road that summer to make a film. I was a film student capturing the whole Dead scene, which then led me to meeting the guy who owned Wetlands, a great rock club in New York, that I took over from him in 1996. Owning Wetlands led to my relationships with a lot of the bands, including meeting you. It led to doing the Jammys, and then Brooklyn Bowl, and the Capitol Theater, my movie, and things like *Relix*. I can trace my path directly to that night in March of '93.

And Fare Thee Well, then, too, which was obviously a huge thing.

Yeah, it's become my thing. I live it every day. I made a documentary about that whole Dead Head scene because I went to that show in March. It was snowing. It was in a parking lot. I saw these kids just like me, same age, but they weren't going back to Northwestern or home. They were on the road searching for something. So I went a couple months later on the road, made a documentary with another student living together in a van, about all these people on the road with the band, the Dead Heads. And the irony is I could not get the band even in my documentary. They wouldn't do it.

But then twenty-two years later, I ended up putting together their 50th Anniversary shows, which was pretty ironic. I got to show some of the videos in between sets on the video screens at the stadiums. We ran some of the footage from my original film when I was on the road.

Amazing. So what do you think is the secret to having a relationship with artists? Or even just being in the music industry and meeting people? How do you meet the right people?

Gary Player once said, "You know, it's funny. The more I practice, the luckier I get." And so the more, I think, you put yourself out to meet people, the better chance you're gonna have to meet the right people. It doesn't always work, you know? But the odds of you going out and meeting someone who could be meaningful to you in whatever way, they go up the more you do it. You've got to put yourself in a position to get lucky.

Yeah. It's interesting because Taylor Hicks said, "Opportunity creates luck," and that kind of sounds like what you're saying there.

Effort. I'm a big believer in the whole ten thousand hours thing, which is Malcolm Gladwell's perspective of achieving mastery at something. You need to do it for ten thousand hours. You need to do it a lot. And I believe in that. I've gotten good at what I do. You've gotten good at what you do. We've both done it for twenty years. You know, I put on a show in New York every night for the last twenty years. You can hear it in my voice a little bit. I've gotten pretty good at it because I've done it a lot.

Absolutely. Yeah, that's a great lesson.

Yeah, so that's big stuff. You want to make something happen, you got to go try and make it happen. It's not guaranteed that you'll have the lucky break, the big thing will happen. That doesn't happen for everyone. It doesn't happen for me every time. But it won't happen unless you try, and you have to try a bunch.

Yeah. I think you're gonna get told no a lot, and you've just got to figure out where those yeses are and, when they happen, to figure out what to do with them.

Exactly.

Let's step back a little bit, and go back to your days at the Wetlands, which was a very famous small venue in New York, where many, many artists kind of got their start. Tell me, what are some of things a new band or artist can do?

Turn out your friends. Turn out your family. Call in favors. Be in a band with other friends, with other people. I meet young people, sometimes they're like, "I'm not gonna go to college. I'm gonna be a musician," or, "Leaving college to be a musician." I'm like, "Ah. What you should do is go to college, and be in a band at college." Sound familiar? You did that. Because it gives you time without the pressure of making money and stuff. College is like free time, in a way, to gig, play with people, be in an environment where you're being social. Part of your job, almost, in college, is meeting people, talking to people. And you can build a bit of a base.

If a band comes and can draw, we'll book them. It's just true. You need to be good, too. People won't come again if you're not good. Everyone's gotta be good. But it's not enough to just be good. I've met people like, "I'm so good. I play great." We still see bands come, and they want to play and have people just show up. But it's a lot of work, even just being a musician. To really be successful you can't just be the musician, you gotta work on the other stuff. You know, early on with you guys, and you still deal with the issues related to the management of the band, and your fan base, and the economics, and all types of stuff. Just it's a lot that goes around it.

Same with me. The fun part is when the band's onstage crushing it. When it's easy, it's easy. When it's hard, it's hard. When it's hard, it's *really* hard. Part of everything, the non-sexy part, is a lot of hard work. One frustrating thing is when I get a huge show, like I'm just doing this . . . I don't know if you saw, but I got Bobby [Weir] and Phil [Lesh], where Phil has to do a duo show. And it's giant. Sold out in minutes. Six shows: Radio City, Chicago Theater, the Wang, and Boston. And it's awesome, but I know when that happens . . . like, the show part—that's pretty easy and simple. It's everything *around it* that comes with a big show: the guest list stuff and logistics. There's a lot that comes with the good, the big. So that was even more work, you know? When I get something good and big, I'm kind of, like, sometimes, "Oh shit. I'm gonna have to do more work 'cause I'm gonna be getting more requests, more e-mails, more questions." When it's not that big, and the show's not that hot, and it's not sold out, there aren't as many requests. It's easier.

Right.

I'll give you one other rule where it's like an oxymoron. It's harder when you're little. It's harder when you're indie. It's harder when you're alone. That what's such an advantage to be these big companies. The big companies have in-house lawyers, they have no cash flow issue, they can do bigger marketing, have bigger e-mail lists, bigger social platforms. They own twenty venues, fifty venues.

It's ironic, though. When you're alone and the indie guy trying to make more on your own, you've a lot more things stacked up against you versus this big guy.

Yeah.

It's easier to be the big guy, and that's why the big guys get bigger.

Interesting. I want to go back to when we were talking about a band getting started. I think one of the things is—it actually might be kind of an advantage, like you're saying—to have the time to work on your sound and to do it where you're not being scrutinized on a national level. I think one of the most intense things is, once you make that commitment to turn nationally, you really only have one chance to make that first impression.

Yeah. Exactly.

And so, for Umphrey's McGee, we did have that time when we were in South Bend, Indiana, where it mattered on a small scale. Okay, can we get people to actually come to our show here. But as far as like a big national picture, we had about two years of working on our sound, and working on writing music, before we tried to play New York, and Colorado. And we had about a year before Chicago. And so, do you feel like that there's more pressure than ever for young bands to kind of get out there, and to be felt on a national presence?

Yeah. I mean, in this current world that we're in, just going to be on the edge of 2018. It's easier, if a one is a baby band, and a ten is Springsteen. There are a lot more fours and fives. It's easier to go in a van to St. Louis, for a Boston-based band, and have like sixty or seventy people show up with the Internet and technology. But it's a lot harder to break through and get to arenas and stuff, because there's no big advances for the label, the album, which helps support a band to just be a band, and not have to get other jobs.

But like in the old days, you'd have to get in a van and play St. Louis to have anyone show up. They couldn't be hearing your music really. I mean, there are exceptions, you know and radio breakthrough. But you couldn't hear a new band in St. Louis in 1996, the same way you can today. Right? With digital music.

That's so true.

So, it's easier, kind of starting, I think. It was harder for you. Now, it's easier for me to pop up a show tomorrow. And we've done the Brooklyn Bowl. Robert Plant, Guns N' Roses, Jane's Addiction. We're like, Robert Plant's going to play Brooklyn Bowl tomorrow, and tickets are going to go on sale tonight at 8:00 p.m. We just put a scent, and it'll sell out in a minute at 8:00 p.m. today.

Back in 1996, we couldn't do that, because we'd have to go make fliers, call the radio stations. Couldn't pop up a show in twenty-four hours. That's the difference between now and before. And the same is that, true, it's harder to break through. The economics, the music selling. You know, selling albums are challenging. Touring's probably easier, because your awareness is easier.

The awareness is easier, but it's harder to gain traction, because there are so many people trying to do it.

Well, yeah. There are also more bands now because it's easier to be in a band, make an album at home without the studio. Just make it and get on the road. Share your music. There's more clutter. There are more bands. It's hard. It's easier, but in ways, more challenging. It's weird, right? There's more clutter. More bands than ever, I think. It's easier for them to hear you in St. Louis.

It seems like it might be easier to get people through the door one time, but that relationship between the musicians and the fans is probably more important than ever.

Yeah.

In creating a more diehard fan out of a casual fan—I think people are looking for that personal connection.

You see these kind of breakthroughs, but those are the exception to the rule. There are people who become giant quickly. You've got to work hard, like you guys have, take time to develop that relationship. Fans want it. They expect it. They've had it before. The cream rises. There's a relationship.

So, new bands, that's where I go back to the college thing. It takes time. There are exceptions that pop out, that just become giant in six months. But typically, you really got to work it still. It's still hand-to-hand combat. Blue collar, get in the van. The easier part is when you get to St. Louis, The Bluebird. You're from Boston, you play at this show. There's sixty people, not two. They've heard your music, because they can hear it on SoundCloud or Spotify. I don't even know if you're on Spotify, if you're talking about baby bands. It is easier for them to know your music, but you've still got to go play and be there to develop that relationship. And that's one reason I think the bands are seeing the jam scene, because it was always touring focused. It was never album focused. It was always a touring culture.

The jam bands didn't take as much of a hit when the physical album sales fell off in this entry to the digital era, because they'd never really sold many albums anyways. They were better prepared for this 2017 music economy, which is about touring, and not recording, revenue.

It's really interesting how the wide scene has gotten more and more important to people's general musical experiences.

Yeah, especially in the age of these phones, and computers. When you want to escape a little bit, it's just sitting there all day. And it's actually when we built Brooklyn Bowl, part of it is that experiential thing. The visual, the screens. It's not really about the Bowl, but what we're able to do with the screens because of the physical layout of the Bowl. We give it that IMAX or Epcot kind of visual experience.

I love it.

Which is key to the whole thing. It's really key.

All right. Let's go the opposite direction now. What's one way an artist can ruin their chances of ever playing a gig at one of your venues? Or not get invited back?

You've got to be polite. Manners matter still.

Yeah.

Social etiquette. If we get feedback that a band—it does not happen a lot, but it's happened—left the green room dirty, or wasn't cool to a staff member, I'm checking. Our culture in various ways, behavior matters, to paraphrase all of that.

I have a good story, which is Hootie and the Blowfish. They weren't the best band of all time, but what they did for twenty years is they got in their van and they drove around. They are famous for, like . . . and this is the era where there were more albums, and radio was big. They would hang out and party and have fun and go out with their local record label rep or the rep from the local radio station. And they would go out and become buddies with them. They had a lot of people rooting for them. That helped them.

If you have people rooting for you, and again, it's why you start. You want to build a base of fans. Like in college, they're your friends, and people rooting for you. And Hootie sold twenty million records that year, because they had a lot of support at all the radio stations.

Because they went and did all these radio things, and then they hung out with the people. So the guy who worked at the radio station in Des Moines, Iowa was rooting for Hootie and played him an extra time.

That's amazing.

When they came through, they hung out and went for beers.

Good will and karma, and just being nice to people make a difference.
Yeah, that's definitely kind of a common theme that I've had talking to
people too. One more question for you. What do you think artists should
be focusing on with their time, if they want to have a long career?

Have a long plan. It could be short term, medium term, and
long term. If you want to have a long-term plan, it's helpful and
smart to think that way. You can't just skip to the long term.

You almost need to have a plan for all three. Don't you?

Right. I was going to say you need three plans. Just have a
vision, but you've got to do the right short-term steps to get to
the medium, to get to the long. They're all related. You've got
to keep that in mind. You have to be smart, and it helps to be
nice.

You've got to put yourself in a position to get lucky. Luck
doesn't just show up. People are always like, "How did you do
so much shit?" I'm like, "Well, you don't even know about the
shit I tried that didn't happen." So you've got to try a lot.
You've got to believe. Partner a lot. I'm big on partnering with
people. A lot of times if you try and do shit alone, it's a lot
harder. Even looking back to college, and making that first film
stuff I did, it was with people. If you try it alone, it's harder. It's
not guaranteed.

SECTION FIVE:

CREATING MUSIC

The more people that hear your music, the more likely someone will come out to a concert of yours. The goal is always to get them into the show and deliver an enjoyable night. When record labels ruled the music industry, live concerts promoted album sales. That was the general point of even touring at all. However, since recorded music has now become available in non-physical formats, its monetary value has shrunk to almost nothing. Now the tables have turned, and recorded music promotes live performances, which is where most artists make money in today's music business. It's absolutely essential you can put on a compelling live performance or it will be next to impossible to build an audience over time.

RIGHT NOTE: If you think there is some crossover appeal between your music and someone else's, suggest collaborating. It's always a smart idea to try to expand the social circles. That said, go after people who are more likely going to be fans. If your music sounds like Norah Jones, it wouldn't make sense for you to collaborate with or share a bill with a band that sounds like Metallica.

BOTTOM LINE: IT'S THE MUSIC!

There are many ways to connect with potential fans, but the hardest thing is to get anyone to listen to your music and want to come back to it. What does this mean? It means your music has to be great for any of the marketing or publicity advice to take hold. Nothing else you do will make up for having average or even just good music. Your music has to be *great*.

You also need to have original material recorded for both audio and video to help you land gigs and other opportunities. As you work on creating your sound, uniqueness or accessibility is one of the most important questions that you will face as you begin to create.

STUDIO VS. LIVE

The studio approach can be different from the live approach. Are you going to do things in the studio you can replicate live or will your work involve things that need to be used as backing tracks? Backing tracks are prerecorded music that will accompany you if there's more going on than you can play live. Do you want your studio material to sound similar to what you do live or will you play live with different arrangements? These are all important questions to think about as you're going into the studio to create.

SONGWRITING CREDIT

One of the questions that will come up as you're writing original material is how does one establish songwriting credit? First off, there are no set rules about how to handle songwriting credit, but there are a few precedents. The typical way to decide whether or not someone deserves songwriting credit is by asking, "If another artist covered the song, is the part that the person's playing important enough to be included in the cover version?" If the part is important enough to be included in a cover, it probably deserves songwriting credit. Another way to go with credit is to simply share credit regardless of who wrote what. The most famous example of this in rock 'n' roll is probably the arrangement John Lennon and Paul McCartney had, splitting everything fifty-fifty no matter who wrote which parts. You can make these decisions on a song-by-song basis or establish a norm.

A CONVERSATION WITH CHRIS GELBUDA

Writing hits isn't easy. Well, at least it's not easy for most people that aren't Chris Gelbuda. He's likely to still say it isn't easy. Originally from Ottawa, Illinois, Chris Gelbuda now calls Nashville, Tennessee home. As a versatile songwriter and producer for Big Yellow Dog Music, the list of talent that he has written or produced for includes John Legend, Meghan Trainor, The Revivalists, and Robert Randolph. He even adds performance credits as a musician for Phil Lesh and Friends. What does it take to make it as a songwriter and producer? Let's find out.

JOEL: What was it that motivated you to get in the music business? Did you want to be a musician? Were you interested in songwriting from the beginning?

CHRIS: Well, I think I got into music because it seemed like it made a lot more sense to play a couple gigs on the weekend and make enough to live, than to do something every day for eight to ten hours. I didn't want to work, without realizing that it was *a lot more* work in the long run than just showing up at a regular job every day.

I actually started as a classical pianist, using the Suzuki method, which is like the ear-training method.

I'm super right-brain, and I learned so much by ear that by the time I got older I couldn't take the professional route—like go join an orchestra—because I only pretended to read music the whole time. I could memorize it all. But I realized I could still play in, like, a rock band and stuff, so I picked up a guitar and started playing Sublime covers, and now here we are.

Did you play keyboards in the bands, or did you just do guitar and singing?

I did keys for a little bit, but I mostly liked guitar because I just thought it looked cooler.

Is that true? Is the guitar cooler?

I mean, I don't know. I see the drummers getting all the action in my experience.

They have to work so hard though.

Eric Wilson, the bass player of Sublime, told me that his dad was an amazing drummer. But his dad didn't want his son to have to drag around a drum kit for the rest of his life, so he taught him how to play bass, and then he taught his good buddy Bud Gaugh how to play the drums. And that's the Sublime rhythm section.

That's pretty amazing. It is something to consider as you're picking your instrument. How mobile are you prepared to be?

Yeah, and how simple or complex. I know some guys that are so excited to get their MIDI-controllers, and their MacBooks, and have this whole temple of sound options. And then I know guys that just show up with a Nord and get the job done.

And it's okay to have both. There are just different ways of achieving creativity.

You now live in Nashville, Tennessee, but you grew up outside of Chicago in Illinois. Did you move to Los Angeles from there?

Well first I went to University of Iowa in Iowa City. I was in a bunch of bands, and when I felt like I was good enough, I just dropped out and moved to Chicago. I played with a bunch of bands in Chicago, and eventually joined Eufórquestra. They still play, actually. They're like an Afrobeat funk ensemble.

And that's kind of when I got the bug to be a songwriter.

In college I was playing with all these cool bands who were funk, hip-hop, and jazz fusion—stuff I thought was cool, like bossa nova. But while I was doing all this exploration, there was a local kid named Jason Reeves, who was bringing three hundred people into the Yacht Club in Iowa City. On weeknights.

He would show up on a Tuesday and have three hundred girls show up, and then a bunch of dudes, too. And they'd all pay ten bucks, and I'm thinking, "This kid's making three Gs a night, like just hanging out in his hometown." And then he got this hit with Colbie Caillat, "Bubbly." He wrote that. He had a bunch of hits, and all of a sudden he was just living in LA on the beach, and I was just like, "This is crazy. The kid made a million dollars just writing songs." So I kind of quit Eufórquestra, and decided I would go figure this thing out.

What's the secret to good collaboration?

Oh man.

Or maybe there's not one but many.

Well, there's a lot. But first of all, I think showing up is a huge. It sounds so stupid, but all the days when I'm hungover or not feeling artistic or unmotivated, *those* are the days when you show up with people that you normally wouldn't even approach, and you have the best day with these people. And more often than not, when I really want to work with somebody, like if I got to sit down with Trey Anastasio and try to write a song, it's not going to be very good. I can tell.

Why is that?

Because I think I have all this stuff in common with them, but it doesn't mean you're supposed to collaborate necessarily. There are all kinds of factors that make a good collaboration, but I think it always helps to just either be willing to fight for an idea, or be willing to go with the flow. If you get kind of stuck in the middle, you can kind of naysay shit all the time. And if you're too positive, you're going to find yourself just letting a shitty song get written, when with a little bit of effort, it doesn't have to suck.

And it's, like, everything is so black and white though. It's, like, don't overwrite the damn thing to death. But at the same time, don't waste your time being too flippant about the whole thing because you have to have an intention. What are you trying to do? What are you actually trying to say?

Now, in my case, I either make people want to drink, dance, or get laid. That's my job. Because that's what radio is. You guys sell a ton of concert tickets, so I don't think you have to operate within radio confines when you're writing a song. You're thinking about how people react to the crowd, and like the synergy of giving back and forth between the people. And there's still a place for that in pop music and stuff.

It's more about the specific songs to me, in pop music. And it's more about the vibe for something like an Umphrey's concert.

Right. Radio is not just an entity meant to bring good music to the masses. It is the business of selling advertisements, and music is what's meant to bring people to hear the ads. It's really good stuff when you think of it that way, but that's literally what it is. I wouldn't say XM Radio is like that or something, but terrestrial radio is like that.

Share a couple examples of songs that you've cowritten with people, because I know you have a bunch of different things you've done that have found some success.

My biggest thing I'm known for is just producing some Meghan Trainor tracks, because I was part of her getting discovered and signed. I produced her song "Like I'm Gonna Lose You." I think it's up to five times platinum now. That was her duet with John Legend. And I did a couple of other tracks for her.

I've written songs for a lot of country people: Billy Currington, Frankie Ballard, Lee Brice, Love and Theft, Wheeler Walker Jr. In Germany, I actually had a number one last year by an artist named Alle Farben, and that was kind of weird because it was my voice on the track.

What was the style of the song?

It was German deep house pop music, but in English. It's kind of like dance music with acoustic guitars and actually good vocalists. That's what they do out there. And they love it. It's awesome.

The best part is that the artist was playing at Lollapalooza in Berlin. He's a DJ, okay? So you know, I wrote the song, coproduced the song, sang the track, played all the instruments, and then he goes out and just does it with a laptop. I didn't even know there was a Lollapalooza in Berlin, but I was out there working, as I'm out there a couple months out of the year.

I go out there and I'm like, "Hi, I'd like to buy a day pass." And they all laugh at me. They're like, "Oh well, you can't buy a day pass. It's been sold out. You can't get in." So, I call up a couple people from the record labels. I call up the drummer of Kings of Leon, who's a buddy of mine, when I saw he was playing. He's like, "Dude, I got a wristband but I'm on a flight to London. I can't help you."

I said, screw it. I ended up getting drunk in the Soviet War Memorial and hearing my song played for, like, a hundred thousand people, and I can't even get into the fuckin' show.

My god, that's how it is sometimes. It's funny because most musicians will watch the movie This Is Spinal Tap *at some point, and then over the course of their careers all these things that were in the movie actually happen. That's a perfect example.*

It's just absurd. I just thought maybe someday I'll tell this in an interview, and here I am doing it.

Okay, so now, do you have your own studio in Nashville?

Well, I'm a partner with Greg Magers, who does you guys's records. But we don't track with them necessarily there. But yeah, I have, like, a B room there, and then I have a studio at my house, and then my publisher's office has a studio. Because everything I do is, like, in the box, for the most part. I'm playing guitar or singing; I'm just like a MIDI master, so I don't need a ton of space to get stuff done.

I mean, there's probably literally a thousand studios in Nashville. You can't even keep up if you don't have one. There is no more songwriter for a living in Nashville. That's what I came there to do, to go play writer's rounds and maybe get a hit every couple of years, and have a kid and do my thing. But the whole thing changed. There are no writers anymore. There are people who write and also perform . . . and also are artists or producers or videographers.

You've got to be able to do different things, huh?

It's just like kids who go to college. Before our generation, maybe one generation before, you'd go to get a leisure studies degree and make a hundred grand a year as a pharmaceutical sales rep or something. Those days are over. You have to be multifaceted and more skilled or you're just not going to be competing with the same people in the job market. It's the same with the music industry. If you write great songs and you sing great, that's awesome. But if you can record them and produce them yourself, that's even better. And it doesn't even put you ahead of the curve. It puts you pretty much at level.

Because these young kids that grew up with iPhones, they can't even really play. They can just throw together tracks that are better than anything I've ever done, in fifteen minutes. I mean, Kendrick Lamar's last record, the kid did it on an iPhone. Did you know that?

Wow, I did not know that.

They run off studios and he plugs an eight-inch cable into an iPhone in a $2,500 a day studio—Windmark in Santa Monica.

Jimmy Jam's place. And he plugs in a thing and sits there, and does it on an iPhone. Not even an iPad—he doesn't even want the space. There's a mantra worth mentioning: If it works, it works. And don't necessarily overthink it.

Yeah.

You don't need to go buy the best universal audio preamp for $2,500, because that's the one that you liked at your buddy's studio. I made that Meghan Trainor record with an Apogee Duet USB, and an AKG C414, on a Mac Mini, which is basically a $1,200 rig. It was all done in a spare bedroom. It doesn't really matter that much.

I think another lesson you're saying is the power of frequency and trying to be as prolific as possible. You're just going to have more to choose from.

Yeah, and I don't think you need to think of it as: "I need to write thirty songs in thirty days." It's kind of like going underwater for a minute—sometimes you just dive in and go as long, as hard as you can, and then you get burned out and you step out of it for two weeks, and that's kind of like why I'm on Phish tour now. This is my fountain of youth. Now that I'm finally in my mid-thirties, I do it a little more responsibly and it doesn't have to take me down a couple pegs every time I do it. Been eating salads and drinking water, and walking into the shows level-headed, and it's been really great.

But, I tend to go hard for about forty-five days at a time. I just go. And you probably do too, with your touring and stuff. You guys go out for long periods of time, and then you have intermittent times to . . . not at much as you should have, but . . .

Well, we're getting down to about eighty to eighty-five shows now. At one point we played a hundred sixty in a year, which was way too much.

That's insane. That's every other day.

But yeah, we found a good balance, and that's important, too. You've got to figure out what should your music and then other stuff life balance be, because you can be very motivated to work, or you can get too loose with it. It can go either way.

Well that's why I still have a Sublime cover band with good Chicago guys, Jonathan Marks of Hey Champ, and Graham Czach. I started that band because I was like, "Look, we can go sell out a room in a town three nights in a row that we've never been to, just because people want to see the music done right. And then we can go back and we can make the music we actually want to make the rest of the month." And it was actually really valuable.

It made me enough where I could afford to be a songwriter. A really tough thing about Nashville is there's so many dreamers there, there's not a lot of jobs. And so, I mean getting a waiting job, like waiting tables is probably the best job you could possibly get, because you're going to make real money.

Right. Well, and the big thing now is that you have to be better than just good, because there are more people than ever trying to do it. And the way the industry is set up, more people can break through in different ways. I think there's a lot of value to talking about practicing now, and playing as much as you can now, because the other thing is that once you get on the road, if you're a musician, it's harder to find that practice time.

Well, not only that. When you start focusing on things like production and lyricists and these other 3-D aspects, you're not as focused on your actual physical craft of what you're doing.

And I'm so glad I spent time learning to actually be a good player because it makes life so much easier than having to sit there and strum the dang thing like a tennis racket, like a lot of songwriters do.

Well, yes, and being able to communicate. Music really, when you get to a certain level, becomes just like speaking English. You and I having a conversation. You feel like, "Oh, this is a language." And it's one of those things that takes a long time. For instance, you being able to play Suzuki piano by ear. You worked on that enough where ear training can come more naturally for some than others. But you understood it as a musical conversation. By the time you sat down to play, you really knew it.

Yeah, it's a wonderful method. But you've got to make sure the kids are actually reading it sometimes too. I remember I was teaching guitar lessons and the kid's saying, "What does it mean when the note is all the way, multiple things below the staff?" And I'd be like, "I'm going to tell you, Johnny, after this bathroom break." And I'm in the bathroom on my iPhone like, "What is that note?" I was so bad, I couldn't do it.

Well, music communicates to people in different ways. There are some people that can read music and play something very well by sight-reading it, but if you took the music away from them, they'd struggle to create something.

Let's talk a little bit about you moving to LA.

It was great because it was good to be humbled and get your ass kicked, which is really the best thing that could happen to you over and over and over again. And get used to it if you want to get in the music business. But it was great because it's one of the few towns left where you can see someone playing in a coffee shop one week and then being a star, or relatively successful, a couple of months later. It's just a crazy place to see careers launch, and it attracts a cool energy. Chicago is a really cool town too, but it's kind of more gig oriented, and not so much career-building oriented.

But don't get me wrong; LA is tough, too. It's just where you see it happening more. I like that a lot. There are lot of people here that care about the format, and they understand what they're doing.

Writing a song doesn't have to be about what's in your heart and your soul, and what's inspiring. It can really be a science where you find a melody that you just think is cool, and you find a way to put it on a slamming track. That's your workday every day. It was just cool to see people do it, but it still took me, like, ten years to even figure out how to do it like they did it.

What led you to working with Meghan Trainor?

There's this thing called the Durango Songwriters Expo, and it's like a three-day event twice a year. They do one in Denver, and basically, it's crash A&R courses on what's happening right now—what music supervisors are liking, and what they're not liking, and how to submit stuff without pissing people off.

And you showcase for these people and then you go into A&R meetings and you play the top and the bottom of a song, and then they tell you why they liked you or didn't like it. Meghan was there. I was there with this guy, Al Anderson. He was the guy, the leader of NRBQ.

We were sitting down and saw Meghan play. Al was like, "That chick is a star." And he walked her CD up to this publisher that he was working for. He's like, "You've got to sign this girl." And she signed her, and the rest is history.

Meghan was sixteen. She asked, "Yo, you think I should go to college?" I responded, "I don't know. I think education is really important, but I also think you're really talented. What's the worst that could happen? You might just start college a year or two later than your friends. I don't think it's the end of the world if you've got all these people that want to work with you. You're talented. Just go for it." And now she's on TV with Puff Daddy every day. It's just, like, so weird.

No, that's interesting. Everybody kind of has a bunch of different potential roads, depending on what their strength is. I think that was probably good advice. You should say, "You should eventually," right? Show something that you like, but you don't need to do it right now.

I'm the opposite. I picked my college based on the music scene, because Iowa City had this place, The Green Room, and the Yacht Club, and all these places that were kind of clubbing places and it's like I wanted to go a college where I could play club gigs.

We played Iowa City quite a bit at one point. We were all living in Chicago, so we were trying to find places where we could develop a fan base that were within a six or seven-hour drive so we could get there on the day of a show and not have to have an extra day to pay for hotel rooms on the road. Or, we would end a tour there because we'd be able to get back to Chicago after that gig and get home.

It's important to think about college markets. On the East Coast, it's much easier to travel between cities. In the Midwest, it's not bad. It takes a little strategy. But living on the West Coast and trying to start a band is much harder because the cities are so much further apart and there aren't as many people out here.

Yeah, but it's so dang beautiful.

Oh, it is.

I think you guys, back in the Iowa City days, were on Christina Aguilera's old bus at one point, weren't you?

Yes, that's true. It had some hot-pink couches, mirrors everywhere. Yeah, it was pretty solid.

An interesting thing to think about is that the traditional "going to a coffee shop and getting discovered" shit is over. It's probably not going to happen for you, if you look at how people are consuming media. That's where you need be looking toward. There's a reason lots of bands are now streaming concerts, because A) fans are getting older and more haggard, and B) you're just going to generate a ton more revenue because people have no problem plopping a laptop into a TV and watching a concert with their friends at their house.

Find a way. You are probably going to reach more people putting on a live streaming Stageit concert, or a Facebook Live concert, than people are going to show up to your show in Boise if you don't know anybody in Boise and you're not popular in Boise. You have to be creative about creating content and not be ashamed of it. People kind of treat streaming like people looked at online dating ten years ago, but it's almost normal now.

On the other hand, I think it's important to be cautious about what you put of yourself out there. That shit never goes away. It's forever.

Exactly. You've got to think about future generations, children, grandchildren. Who knows who's going to see this?

Cool. I think part of what you're saying is being out here, you're just going to meet more people in the business if you're in LA or New York or Nashville than if you're anywhere else.

You're going to meet more people and you're going to see success happening all around you. You're going to be trying to figure out what they're doing that you're not doing. It's not super important to compare yourself to others at all times, but if you're playing with a bunch of bad golfers, you're going to play bad golf that day. If you're playing with a bunch of good golfers, you're probably going to play better golf because they're pushing you, they're driving you. It's Darwinism, you know?

Yeah, right.

And this is the hot bed of Darwinism out here, because there's twelve million people who are all trying to make it, and a couple hundred of them probably are. It's competitive. You're not going to get pushed to get better by sticking around a two-horse town.

But I also say that you don't necessarily have to live in LA to reap the benefits. A lot of people come to Nashville, New York, and LA, and they just plan focus trips for a week or two. They save money by crashing, and then sometimes they'll pepper in a hotel room just to get a little privacy for a couple of days and regroup. But you don't have to move your whole life to these towns.

You can go there and really bust your ass and come out and probably get more work done than people who are used to living in Nashville.

Right.

Like, if I wasn't so hungry to make it right now, I could still kind of settle down and chill a little bit. But I can get lazy sometimes and maybe write five or six songs in a month. I'll watch people's careers literally pass me by from one month of laziness, while people are coming to Nashville for a week and they'll write twenty-five songs. It's crazy.

Is there any shortcut, or what's the secret to writing the hit?

I think the secret to writing a hit is not being afraid to write something that would work for radio. I like good music. I like The Allman Brothers and the Fillmore East. I'd never walk up to Greg Allman and show him my latest pop gem I just wrote. It would be so embarrassing for me to show him that.

Like, when I ran into Gillian Welch and stuff, she's like, "What kind of music do you make?" It's like, "Uh, don't worry about it." But I've realized that I'm not ashamed of it anymore. I'm doing something different. I'm not doing what they're doing.

I think it's realizing what radio is, have an intention, and just have fun with it. If it's not fun for you to listen to, it's not going to be fun for anybody else. If you hear it, and you're not completely overwhelmed with joy and excitement, then nobody else is going to be. It just pretty simple.

Oh, that's interesting.

And art has to shock you. If you're not going to write something that is weird or off-putting, it has to be something that's shockingly good. That's it. Like you were saying, you can't just be great anymore. You have to be *so great*. You can't just be a great singer. You've got to do all this stuff. You've got to learn it, and you've got to compete, and you've got to learn to have fun with it and not take it too seriously, either, because it is music in the end.

That's been my biggest breakthrough just in the last six months. I'm going to have fun, even if I'm going to sit in a dark writer's room every day for the rest of my life. I'm trying to make music that makes people happy, and makes them dance around and want to whatever.

Yeah. Dig it, man. Anything stand out to you as the best advice you've ever gotten or heard?

Well I think the best advice I ever got was: "There's only four country songs you can write." And then he holds up five fingers. He says, "I wish I was fucking you. It's great to be fucking you. It was great fucking you. And fuck you." I thought that was pretty good. At the end, only the middle finger remains.

Once I asked my publisher why another guy at my company was doing so much better than me when I felt I was working harder and writing better songs. She basically told me what I was saying about understanding the format. She said, "Don't write from the heart when you're trying to write a hit song." I got kind of pissed off at first, because it's a weird thing to hear. She's like, "I'm not saying don't write from the heart, but listen to what I'm saying. I understand what we're trying to do here. We're trying to take an artist who has a certain vibe, and we're trying to take this torch for this artist to hold and say this is the best way for me to represent myself. And that makes it a lot easier than just going into some track and trying to make something cool. Because that's just throwing a random dart every time. You can still get bull's-eyes throwing random darts, but if you actually aim for it, you'd be surprised."

So, I wouldn't say don't write from the heart is the best advice, but it's saying understand the format.

Understand what you're writing about, and what your goal is in whatever you are writing.

Yeah, and my own addendum to that is also understand that you could still do that and go home and write a song that you personally love for yourself at a different time. Just because you're writing stuff for Katy Perry or something, it doesn't disqualify from you. It doesn't have to eat up all your time. You can have a multifaceted career. It's just a thing you can do.

There probably are people who have multiple names out there depending on whatever the project is.

Sure, just call it something else. Absolutely.

That's totally legit. It's fine.

Yeah, put your name out. You can just keep coming up with new monikers and doing it.

Okay, what's the worst advice anyone's ever given you?

I think the worst advice I've heard is that we have to fight streaming and have to fight, basically, technology in order to preserve music being a good thing. I think we need to learn that it's not up to us.

The technology's going to continually change.

A guy was basically telling me, "I will never put my stuff on streaming. You shouldn't either. We should all boycott it. We should only sell our CDs, and if people want to hear it, they should understand what it's like to open up a CD and read the liner notes."

I get that. I like buying vinyl.

Here's the thing, it's cool for the people who already want to do it. Give them that option. Stream it, put it out on vinyl. Make CDs. Let people digest it however they want to, but you can't control the conversation of what the best formats are. You should always try to use that to your advantage.

But it's like a lazy river. It's not going to carry you away. You can still have a good time in a lazy river, but you've got to adapt to it a little bit, you know?

Yeah, yeah.

You just kind of go with the flow a little bit. I wish I made more money than I make, but I'm also glad that I can show up every day and crunch granola bars and write songs and get a decent salary. It's free dough, so I'm not complaining.

SECTION SIX:

RECORDING

R ecording music is one of the best ways to invest in yourself. It's what represents you outside of the concert experience and the way that most people will hear your music for the first time. Recordings will also be necessary to stream your content, sell it, or promote yourself. Invest wisely in recorded music, as it IS your art.

Recorded music is your art's time capsule, so always document what you create, whether at home or in the studio. You never know when an idea will happen and if you don't press record, you risk losing that idea into the ether forever. Putting yourself under the pressure of recording should also give you some incentive to play your music as precisely as possible, which is always good practice.

HOME STUDIOS VS. PRO STUDIOS

Let's look at recording at home versus recording professionally. With the technology now available you can get great demos at home. However, only someone who understands how to achieve sonic quality will be able to manipulate home recordings enough to get them to the same standard, or even close to the same level, as a pro studio recording. Using a professional recording studio means using all their high-quality equipment, including sound consoles, processing, and effects. It is challenging to achieve the same level of audio greatness with just a computer at home. This does not necessarily hold true for EDM or for pure vocal guitar music, which can be created in a somewhat similar fashion at home in a simpler way using either Pro Tools or Ableton.

LISTENING TO YOUR STUDIO RECORDINGS

If you're doing any recording or listening at home, get yourself a pair of good speakers in addition to having a great set of headphones and computer speakers—basically whatever you can find. Your music will hopefully be listened to on *all* these mediums, so make sure they all sound good when you are listening back to what you've recorded. Listening to a recording in your car is also smart since that's a place where people will listen to lots of music.

RIGHT NOTE: If you can only afford to have a day or two in the studio, do your preproduction and arranging before you hit the studio to maximize your paid time. This also means getting your performance down so that you know you can play something near perfect once you hit the record button. You don't want to have to waste time doing take after take because you don't know how to play your songs.

PREPRODUCTION

Preproduction is the time when you work out the arrangement of the songs and get all your parts together. A good preproduction session will leave you with more material than you need for your upcoming recording session at a professional studio. Have the songs ready to perform when you get to the studio. Better yet, play the songs you're going to record before you record. You'll have a much better idea of what's working and what's not.

If you've recorded demos of the songs, listen back to them with a critical ear and decide: "Is this going to work? Is there room for improvement? Are all the sections working together?" It's a lot better to figure these things out when you're not paying for time in the studio. If you're working with a producer or engineer, send them early versions of what you're planning to do, so they're familiar with the material before you hit the studio.

STUDIO EFFICIENCY

Once you're setting up professional studio time, always ask the engineer what they think works best in their studio, as there's a significant difference between a live gig and a studio gig. Studio engineers are generally pretty good at what they do. They know how to get the best out of their rooms and are often both engineers and producers. How are you going to record if you're a band? Are you going to do it in a room together at the same time or piece by piece starting with drums and bass and adding each instrument? You can record many ways but some are more affordable, and some are more time consuming. Consider this as you make a plan.

BUILD YOUR HOUSE ON A ROCK

Recording in the studio starts with the drummer. It's beneficial if your drummer can play along with a click track. What's a click track? It's your song's metronome, and will lay out the song on an editable grid. If you can record to a click, it will be easier to edit or even replay sections later. If the song's tempo fluctuates you won't be able to use a click, and that's okay too. Sometimes that's right, but you'll have to get a take playing the song together at the same time. Whether or not you're going to play a song with a click track is an important decision. With every new song that you want to record, you always start getting sounds for drums.

RIGHT NOTE: If your sound involves a full drum kit, have your drummer show up at least an hour before the rest of the band. That way the bedrock of your sound can be established and your general session doesn't start with everyone sitting around waiting for the first hour. If your drum tones don't sound good, it's going to be very challenging to make the recording as a whole sound good.

ORIGINS OF RECORDED MUSIC

When music was first recorded, it was monophonic, meaning there was only one channel. As technology improved, tuners and radio supported stereo mixes. Then recording consoles expanded from two to four to eight tracks, eventually ending up with some desks featuring sixty-four channels of possible inputs. These tracks would then be recorded to tape, and if there was editing to be done, sections of tape would be cut with a razor. Your favorite albums from the fifties to the early eighties were all mixed live, most likely by more than one set of hands. But once digital recording became possible, this all changed, and the possibilities of what could be recorded became virtually endless.

DIGITAL VS. ANALOG

As many musicians and studios switched from analog to digital, many audiophiles realized that recording to tape would still have a purpose in the recording industry. Digital production resulted in incredibly crisp high end, but the low end lacked warmth. Many artists today record the drums and bass to two-inch tape while also running a digital recording program to capture the results. This best-of-both-worlds approach gives you the flexibility of editing with digital methods while benefiting from the analog warmth of two-inch tape. You don't need to record all the instruments to tape; it's mainly just your rhythm section.

RECORDING SOFTWARE

There are many software packages for recording, but most engineers and studios currently use some form of Pro Tools, while EDM artists tend to prefer Ableton. It would be wise to familiarize yourself with Pro Tools or Ableton depending on your needs. With some knowledge of the software, transferring files and recordings from your demos or home recordings can be completely seamless.

Many professional studios also have a half-inch tape machine, which engineers use to bounce stems to so there is a bit of analog sound to all the tracks. As you're searching for the right studio and engineer, always ask what analog gear they have. This will help inform what you need and what you can achieve.

BEFORE YOU LEAVE YOUR SESSION

Unless it's a very simple recording, don't expect to walk out of the studio with anything to listen to, as there is usually lots of postproduction work to be done. Ask the engineer what will happen with your files and who is going to send you rough mixes of the recordings you just made. Establish a general time line so expectations about your mixes will be understood from all parties.

ROUGH MIXES

If you're finished recording all your parts, the next step is mixing the recordings. The first process will be editing with hopes of choosing the strongest performance of any instrument or take that you recorded. These initial mixes are called rough mixes, and you will want to review them to make sure the performances are at the level of quality you desire. Once you've approved rough mixes, then you move on to creating a final mix.

FINAL MIXES

Think of creating a final mix as a malleable fine-tuning of all the details within the song. Do you have a good enough ear to do the mixing yourself? That's one option, but you may want to consider paying the engineer who recorded you to assist in the mixing, as he or she likely has a good grasp of where everything should be. You'll likely need a few stages of mixing to achieve what you want as a final mix, so pay attention to all the details as you make changes, and be patient as you update the mixes.

CHOOSING AN ENGINEER TO MIX

Different engineers are comfortable with various genres. That's something you want to keep in mind as you choose whoever will help you with the mixing. Remember, not all mixes are created equally. There are also preferences depending on the style of music you're producing. To help communicate your ideas regarding tone and mixes, talk to the engineer about the sonic qualities you're working for and share songs that exemplify a sound you're trying to achieve.

Let's say you're producing a dance tune with club potential. You might mix the bass differently than if you're focusing on a vocal with only acoustic guitar accompaniment. Likewise, if you're recording polyphonic vocal music you may want significantly less bass. The sonic qualities of your song should be informed by the instrumentation of the song as well as the intended audience.

MASTERING

Once you've finished mixing, the final step of your recording will be mastering it. Mastering is one of the more intangible but crucial elements of a good audio recording. Most listeners only notice mastering when they hear a bad mastering job. The overall goal of mastering is to balance everything in a stereo mix along with ensuring that playback across multiple formats is uniform and consistent. Audio mastering is a very subtle art, especially now that music is heard in so many different formats.

MASTERING COSTS

Mastering can also be done via many software programs these days if you want to go to for a more affordable route. That said, the best mastering engineers out there focus solely on mastering. No matter what you choose to do, make sure you master your song or songs one way or another, or they won't measure up to other recordings in quality, volume, and sonic width. It's a good idea to compare the sonic qualities of your mastered recording to other recordings you think sound best and see for yourself how they stack up.

A CONVERSATION WITH SUSAN TEDESCHI

Grammy-award–winning singer, guitarist, and songwriter Susan Tedeschi is most well known as the coleader of Tedeschi Trucks Band, a title she shares with her husband Derek Trucks. Before starting TTB, she achieved world-wide acclaim as a bandleader, and shared the stage with artists such as the Rolling Stones, B.B. King, Willie Nelson, and Bob Dylan. Her soul driven, soaring vocals and impassioned, bluesy guitar work have earned her respect and adulation from fellow musicians and fans alike. Susan's genre-defying musicianship and style finds its influences in R&B, gospel, blues, and jazz, but the sound she creates is distinctly her own. Equally adept onstage as in the studio, Susan has also figured out how to balance touring life with raising a family on the road with Derek while playing more than one hundred concert dates annually. With numerous additional Grammy nominated releases achieving both critical mass and commercial success, it's safe to say Susan's music has made a positive impact on the world.

JOEL: I want to go back to the early days of your career. First of all, what was an important musical decision you made early on that impacted a lot of your career?

SUSAN: Well, for one, really around the decision to go into music, because for me, it's hard to pick a direction. I wanted to do a lot of different things. But I realized I needed to focus on one thing. So, when I was in high school going into college, I was trying to figure out if I was going to be in musical theater, or just do music, and not do acting anymore, and all that kind of stuff. That was a big decision. And I decided to just do music. I went to Brooklyn College of Music at seventeen. Every decision is hard. What do you focus on? What do you pick for school? And for me, I wanted to learn some of the business. I also wanted to be a performer. So, I would base some of my classes around that.

Early on, I wanted to be an arranger, so I had arranging classes, and things like that. But the best thing to do is try a bunch of different stuff. But always keep working at trying to focus on what it is that you wanna do. There are a lot of aspects of the music industry, of course. But for me, I always was a singer, and I always wrote songs. So, I think it's important to always keep writing, and do what you love to do.

I was in different bands. I'd be in groups with other people, just getting out there. I even did wedding bands to make money to get through the early college years. Graduated college at twenty. I really didn't start my own band until after I was twenty-one.

I didn't really do that whole scene until I was a little bit older. I legally couldn't get in. It was hard when you're underage. But there was this one place, Johnny D's, and they would have good shit on Sundays, and you could go and sit in and play. And you could be a young kid, and get up and play, and you'd have your parents there with you. And it was Sunday brunch. Around five o'clock, they'd have come and sit in, so that was always a good opportunity. Just getting out and meeting people.

Starting my own band was a big, big decision.

When you started your own band, what were you looking for in people to play music with? What kind of personalities worked well with what you were trying to do?

One of the things that got me excited to do my own band was I met some people that had similar interests. And I met Adrienne Hayes, a young girl who played guitar from Gloucester, Massachusetts. And I remember she knew people like Brad Delp from Boston, and all these different musicians I didn't know. But she knew a lot of blues, which I really like. We had a lot of similar people that we liked.

And then we got together with Annie Raines, who at the time had a duo with Paula Rischell. They had their own little group. And Annie was littler older than us. We were all hovering right around our early twenties. And we started a band. Putting that band together—my first real band—we learned blues tunes, because we really wanted to do a blues band. And we all had common interests. Annie played harmonica, and she really was instrumental in almost teaching us how to play rhythm parts. She would do harmonica parts while I would sing, and then I started playing guitar.

The band didn't really play electric until about that time. That's why I started learning electric and playing out in public. I really would just play rhythm for the first couple of years. I didn't really solo or anything right away. That was a huge step. And then we got a rhythm section with us. We had this guy we'd met, Jim Lamonde, who was a bass player, and a kid that I was going to college with at the time, Mike Aiello. That was the first kind of concoction of that band.

One of the important things was having something, a product. Making an album. And, basically worked our way up. That band was together for a couple of years before we ever made a record. And I think we really started in late '92, early '93, and then we were doing things like the Boston Musical. We saw they had a blues competition, so we did that, and we came in first. We got to go to Memphis. We drove down there, performed, and then came in second. That opportunity got us all these festivals and got our name out there. People liked the idea of three young girls starting a blues band or sharing a stage at the top. And, just playing all different types of stuff. Playing little clubs, playing the private parties, just getting your name out there, and getting the word out there.

It really does seem like you've gotta kinda keep at it, and keep playing, and putting yourselves in front of people. And you never know what opportunity is gonna lead to other opportunities.

Exactly. And that's really one of the biggest things you can learn, is just going out and doing it and meeting people is everything. And there's no right way to do anything, and there's no one style music, or any of that. But I do suggest that whatever it is you guys are into, it's good to do coverage, but it's also good to write your own stuff. Always to keep fresh and keep learning. And to mixing it up. We're always working on it.

How did you balance working on being singer, guitarist, and songwriter, and playing live concerts early on?

Well, early on, I was the bandleader, so I was also the one who did all the phone calls and booking the dates. I didn't have a manager. I didn't have an agent. I was all of that.

I did that for Umphrey's McGee, too. That's funny.

Yeah, somebody's gotta take that role, and so I did. And, I was the one who got paid, and I was the one that booked the dates, and I would also have the van, and I would drive. But everybody would take turns driving. I would book the hotels. I would make sure that we were there first sound check, and get set up. You gotta make sure you're prepared for everything. Make sure that you have a contract. And I would just do a little standard contract with the clubs. And whether it was 75 percent of the door or whatever, I guarantee you seven hundred bucks. That kind of stuff.

Always save receipts—like hotel receipts, gas receipts, etc. Just simple stuff like that. And then, for women, our clothing and makeup. How much are you spending? And just try to budget, because you're not going to have any money. A lot of times you'll lose money at first. You never play music to make money. It's just not a good idea.

Yeah, you have to do it because it's something that you love.

Exactly.

And, if that's not why you're in it, eventually people will see through that.

So, juggling all that stuff, it was hard, but you just kinda pace yourself, and you know what you could do and what you could handle.

It's a balancing act.

It is. It is a balancing act. And obviously early on, it wasn't so hard, doing all that stuff. You stay on it, and I was really motivated, and I didn't drink or do drugs or anything, so I was pretty focused. That really helped. But then later on, it became a lot harder, once you become a mom. That's a whole different ball game. Being pregnant and making a record. Things like that. Everything changes. You get hormonal, or you start singing, and the baby kicking. So, you have all these different things you're feeling. And then raising kids on the road, taking kids on a tour bus. I didn't have the van at that point, so we had moved up in the world. So, constantly building and working toward something. At first you work out of your car, and then you get a van, and then you get a van with a trailer. And a couple of years down the road, you make enough money, you could maybe get a bus. And then, you rent a bus, but Derek bought a bus, which I knew to be cheaper in the long run, if you're touring all the time, 'cause they charge so much for buses.

As long as you have someone who knows how to fix it.

Yeah, well, the trick is getting a really great driver.

Right.

Eventually having management and agents that can do a lot of stuff free for you, and try to keep up. And one of the things is trying to not burn yourself out. Because it's pretty easy to burn yourself out if you don't pace yourself.

Yep.

One of the things I do because I'm fair is I don't like to perform more than three shows in a row. And I still kinda hold true to that. We're doing three in a row here in Chicago Theater, but we're on tour. We played Asheville last weekend, and we played Ames, Iowa this week, and then we played Chicago Theater three nights. But I always make sure that I have a day off after two or three in a row, and then doing work. And then, have another day off. You have to have rest time.

You've gotta listen to your body, and you can't change those things.

A lot of the boys, or other musicians that aren't singing, they can work every night. To them, it's different. It's just more of a physical thing, but not like using their body in a way where they have to have a certain amount of rest. Being the singer, it's important for you to be the one that says how much you work.

Don't just do gigs, 'cause there's always other big gigs, and it's amazing. And they're important or whatever. You have to pace yourself. I think that's really important.

Yeah, absolutely. I'd like to talk a little bit about being a woman in the music business, and what some of the challenges are, and then, are there benefits and advantages, too?

Yeah, benefits. For one, there aren't a lot of women in the music industry. There really aren't. There are more and more nowadays, but growing up, there really weren't a lot of women. So that in the way was an advantage, 'cause it was kinda giddy. Also, when you're going and sitting in at places, it's always great if you're a singer, because everybody always needs singers. They always need people that know words, and that can just hop up and do stuff.

Right.

So, there's benefits if you're a woman, and you're not just an instrumental. You're actually a singer. Also, for me, it didn't hurt being a woman, 'cause it got me in talking with other artists, especially men. They just feel comfortable around the women. I don't think they feel intimidated or anything, so it's kind of easier to be friendly and talk with them. And some of the old blues guys just kinda love women. In a way, it was a benefit for me. I got to know B.B. King really well and toured with him. And knew Willie Nelson, got to do a tour with him, and do Farm Aid and record with him. They were very friendly to me. They were very supportive. I don't know if it was because I was a woman, or 'cause of how I sing. I really don't know. But I feel like being a woman definitely has its benefits, in a certain way, just for communicating.

Well, I think it definitely had something to do with your talent as well.

Sure, it doesn't hurt. But it can be a disadvantage, too. It can be bad because people don't always take you seriously, or maybe have club owners that try and pull a fast one on you, because you're a woman. Maybe they don't pay you what you're supposed to be paid. Honestly, being a woman, you need to be aware of that as well. Just because you don't want people to take advantage of you.

So, that can be scary. Also, you want to make sure you always have somebody with you. You don't want to be on your own a lot. Even though I'm all over, I don't do a lot of stuff on my own. It's important to be aware of your surroundings, that's what I think. And all that stuff really comes into play.

Gotcha. I'm curious, anything come to mind about the best advice that you ever received?

Some of the best advice was to stay humble. There's always more to learn. You never know everything. Like that.

That's so true. I think that, especially as a musician, one of the ways to keep expanding your repertoire as a player and as a composer is to keep your learning head on and continue to do that throughout your life.

Absolutely. And get dressed up for your shows. There's no show not good enough to get dressed up for.

I like that. We have a rule that no shorts onstage unless it's over 90 degrees.

Take your job seriously. And people will take you more seriously.

This is true.

Some other good advice: Play music like music, man; don't do it for money.

Yeah, that's all good advice. When I was talking to Huey Lewis about that, he said, "Yeah, you know I'm happy that I've had a successful career, but if I'd never had a hit, I'd be just as happy playing harmonica in some blues bar somewhere that nobody knew who I was." And I think that really speaks to why you should get into making music.

Anything come to mind as some of the worst advice you've gotten?

Playing shows outside in the winter. It's twenty degrees out.

Not the best vocalist's weather.

We played Copper Mountain, and they have heat for your hands, but not your feet, and you can't move. That's not good.

Yeah, that's not fun as a keyboardist either. I've had that one.

Right. You know what I'm talking about. Don't play outdoors when it's not warm enough.

Other stuff. Don't trust anybody. People say, "Trust me, trust me. I'll take care of this and that." No. Just be smart.

Yep. Absolutely.

If it makes sense to you, then yeah, it's probably right.

SECTION SEVEN:

PREPARING FOR A SHOW OR PERFORMANCE

Even if you've had discussions leading up to the gig, make sure and contact the promoter or the venue a few days before to confirm times and any other details that may have slipped through the cracks. If you're a singer/songwriter with just an acoustic guitar and a vocal mic, your needs are going to be a lot less than if you have a five- or six-piece band with twenty-four channels. If it's an out-of-town gig or you're on tour, double check things like time zones and travel time so you have enough hours built into the day to stay on schedule. It is a good idea to leave small buffers in your schedule as well, as it's likely things will end up taking longer than you expect. Doing this leads to a much more forgiving time line, instead of one where you are constantly rushing and feeling behind schedule.

Tech Specs

Before you play a venue for the first time always ask for tech specs. These will include stage dimensions and whatever in-house gear the venue has and will help you determine what you need to bring. This is particularly useful at gigs where the sound engineer doesn't know much about you. Many venues include tech specs on their websites. Check first before booking the gig to see if the venue is appropriate for your needs. If all else fails, ask the talent buyer or promoter to get you the needed info. Don't be shy. It is truly a better situation for *all* if these needs are defined and you know that you won't be missing, or in need of, something important hours, or possibly minutes, before you are supposed to be onstage.

RIGHT NOTE: When you're touring, one thing you'll always want to have on hand is extra instrument cables. They will occasionally break or go intermittent, but don't fret or throw them out unless it's from extreme wear and tear, or they got wet.

A little soldering is usually all it takes to repair a faulty instrument cable.

CHOOSING WHICH SONGS TO PERFORM

You've done everything to make the gig happen and now you're finally headed onstage. First, how do you choose what music or songs to play? This mostly depends on who your audience is, as there are subtle things that you can do with your music that will make it more appropriate for an audience. For instance, if you're playing at an outdoor street festival and people are having fun, you're going to want to play a little more of a lively set to fit the vibe. Or if you're playing in a theater where everyone is seated and no one is talking, that gives you the opportunity to be a little more dynamic. Maybe you choose to do a quieter piece of material.

ORIGINALS AND COVERS

You'll likely want to have a cover or two mixed in with your set of originals. Familiarity can help lock in listeners' focus if the rest of your set is new music to their ears. While you don't want to become too cover dependent, consider playing covers that will complement your original music.

PACING

Do you want to create an overall arc for the show? Are you more interested in just letting the songs stand on their own? Are there ways to integrate the songs that might make the flow of the show more natural? These are all great questions to ask as you're developing the set list for a show.

It's always a good idea to start and finish with your strongest material. When creating your set list, think of those two pieces as your bookends, then fill in the middle.

PERFORMANCE DAY

BE ON TIME. In fact, give yourself *extra* time as you plan your show day. Showing up late will immediately earn the local staff's ire. These are the folks that are there to help you have a great show and experience; don't piss them off. Once again, *be respectful of everyone else's time* and communicate what your time lines and schedule are as well. If you're clear, communicative, friendly, and focused when you arrive at the gig, things will go MUCH smoother.

RIGHT NOTE: No matter who you interact with at your gig, follow the Golden Rule: *Treat people the way you would like to be treated.* Years from now, you may see the same person on the way down that you saw on the way up. If you're a jerk to the local sound guy, that person may go out of their way to make you sound terrible. Maybe not just this time but five years down the road too. You won't remember who they are, but they *will* remember you.

THE SOUND CHECK—LOVE 'EM, HATE 'EM, JUST DO 'EM

If you have a good crew, or are playing at a venue with one, these folks want to be prepared. They have to answer to others too, as well as try to avoid the worst-case scenario of shrieking feedback occurring with a full house! So, as a precaution, we have the sound check. This word can become a nightmare if you don't approach it properly. Sound check is your dedicated time pre-show onstage to make sure everything is functioning properly and that you and your fellow musicians can hear everything well-enough onstage to deliver a great performance. It's important to go into sound check and be as efficient as possible. Huey Lewis once said, "I have an infinite amount of gigs in me but I have a finite amount of sound checks left."

Sound checks are a necessary thing, but are always going to seem like they are at the wrong time of the day. To make the most of your sound check, try to be efficient but thorough. Here are additional tips for getting the best possible sound in any venue.

WHAT SHOULD YOU ASK FOR IN YOUR STAGE MIX?

The smaller the stage that you're playing, the less you should have in your monitor mix. It's also important to ask for only what you need. If your music features more than three musicians, you may be sharing a mix with other musicians, so consider your needs to figure out the right configuration. Your sound engineer will build your mixes from the drums upward starting with kick drum, snare, high hat, etc. on up to the melody instruments. One easy way to keep the process straightforward is to have everyone onstage have a finger in the air indicating if you want more of a particular instrument. You then make a fist when you're good with the level. Also, depending on the size of the stage, you or your fellow musicians may need to adjust your stage volume accordingly. The smaller the venue, the less stage volume you should need.

PLAY A SONG

After establishing levels, collectively play a song and see how it sounds out front and onstage. Realize that if you have your monitor wedges and amplifiers too loud onstage, you're going to adversely affect the sound out in the audience. Every stage and room will sound slightly different, so consider where you place microphones and stage amps when you're setting up and make adjustments if necessary. For instance, if you set up your lead vocal right in front of the drummer, you're going to get drums in the vocal mix. Not ideal.

This seems obvious, but many shows have been ruined by out of tune instruments. Your show's going to sound awful no matter how you perform if you're not in tune. Make sure everyone knows how to tune their instruments and develops an ear for what being in tune sounds like. Stringed instrument players should have a tuner onstage, preferably in their pedal chain for easy use during the show. As a keyboardist, Joel even has a tuner on his MiniMoog Voyager. Why you ask? It's a voltage-oriented keyboard that will heat up the longer it's on and that will affect the fine-tuning. He constantly makes minor adjustments during a show to stay in tune. He can also bend notes very accurately since the tuner shows a visual representation of being exactly in tune—a good trick for keyboardists who work with analog synths to know. This is not to comment on the more creative aspect of bending notes or *intentionally* playing slightly out if you have a developed ear.

RIGHT NOTE: Try to learn the names of a venue's staff and then personally thank them for their help. You never know when you're going to need the guy working the door to help you out. Or the bar manager may eventually become the talent buyer. Courtesy paired with personalizing the experience will only make the process easier.

THE UNEXPECTED AND MISTAKES

Play your music with intention no matter the instrument. If you play or sing something that you perceive as a mistake, own it— even consider repeating it. You might come up with something that's a more unique sound. But in the end, it's all about how that note or notes are perceived by the audience. If you make a mistake and it's obvious by *your* reaction, it will likely make everyone in the room uncomfortable. When something unexpected happens, follow the improv comic's rule: *Say yes.* Go along with whatever happened and react positively to it. If you can, take it a step further. This especially goes with improvisation. Embracing this attitude going into the night is important. You can't control some things that will happen but you can control your response.

Perhaps the guitarist breaks a string. Can you create something in the moment to cover the time needed to change strings or guitars? The stage power could go out. Will you think to look at the drummer and call for a drum solo, or better yet, get the entire band to play percussion if the musicians are talented enough? Will someone jump up onstage and start dancing with you? Be ready for the unexpected. Say yes and roll with it. Spontaneity can be your friend.

Have Fun and Entertain

Enjoy yourself and show it while you're onstage unless the type of music you're playing calls for a very intimidating personality. The audience probably doesn't want to see someone feeling miserable unless you're singing songs about heartbreak. Show that you're interested in what you're doing. Most likely people paid money to watch you perform. Share your joy.

If you're part of a band, interact with one another, and if the stage is big enough, move around a bit. Live music magic happens as the result of human interaction, so encourage it. Respect your audience. Always make an effort to perform at your best and the audience will notice. If you can't muster the energy to show interest in your own music, you probably shouldn't be onstage.

Audience Interaction

Between songs, or sometimes even during songs, you have an opportunity to connect with your audience. At the very least greet the audience and thank them for attending. If you have a sense of humor, use it. Make people smile. If there's more than one vocalist in the band, little conversations between songs can also be fun.

TAKE YOUR MUSIC SERIOUSLY, BUT DON'T TAKE YOURSELF TOO SERIOUSLY

It warrants repeating: You're a musician and an entertainer, not a neurosurgeon. Music is usually best when the ego is left behind.

LOAD OUT

The gig is done. Hopefully you've had a great show and now it's time to load out and get all your stuff off the stage. First, you'll want to decide as a group whether to immediately pack everything up or to take five to ten minutes to decompress before doing so. If there's another act after you, you may not even want to walk offstage before you begin packing your gear. But whatever you decide, agree on this as a group.

When it comes to clearing the stage and packing up everything for the next gig, everybody should be participating. Whether you're the singer in the band or the trumpet player, try to help out and do other things beyond your own responsibilities. Wrap cables, push gear back and forth between the trailer and the venue, or communicate with the person packing the trailer to get things in the correct order. Do more than what's expected of you and you will encourage others and bring the best out in everyone.

EFFICIENCY

There's nothing more frustrating than some people working and others not. It will likely create resentment and definitely slow down the entire process. Always do your part and try to stay focused as you're packing up and moving out to make it as quick as possible. That way everyone can spend more time socializing or sleeping after the gig.

SAFETY

During load out keeping your gear safe is very important. This applies to both inside and outside the venue. Think about where you're putting your gear and never leave anything expensive visible through a car window because that is just asking for it to be stolen. If you're traveling from show to show, as soon as you can afford some combination of Sprinter or van/trailer—whether it's renting or buying—you'll want to do that. When your gear is locked up safely and out of sight in a Sprinter or trailer, you simply improve your chances of gear remaining that way. There's nothing worse than realizing your music and/or show is on hold because gear was stolen.

WRONG NOTE: It's extremely unsafe for someone who is inebriated to be loading your gear out. Gear will be dropped or broken or, even worse, people will suffer injuries or injure others. Don't be that guy or gal who's too wasted to load out.

Well, you're doing it. Congratulations on that. Keeping it going can often times be a lot harder than getting everything moving. Things change, and change is the only constant that all of you are guaranteed to experience. So are you ready to talk about how to keep this whole thing together for the better, and sometimes through the worse?

A CONVERSATION WITH IVAN NEVILLE

Born into New Orleans soul music greatness, Ivan is the son of singer Aaron Neville of The Neville Brothers band. Playing often with his father and uncle's band well into his teen years, Ivan has since made quite the name for himself as a multi-instrumentalist, singer, and songwriter, putting multiple songs in the Billboard Hot 100 list over the course of his career. In addition to having released four solo albums, Ivan has contributed to the albums of other industry legends, such as The Rolling Stones's *Voodoo Lounge*. Now regularly performing with Dumpstaphunk, a band that also includes his cousin/son of Art Neville, you won't find Ivan at the bar after the show. The now-sober Neville is a voice of support for musicians struggling with substance abuse issues. As living proof that sobriety and the rock 'n' roll lifestyle can go together, let's hear what advice Ivan has for us.

JOEL: Growing up with a musical family, was keyboard the instrument you gravitated most toward?

IVAN: Eventually. The first thing I picked up was a guitar when I was, maybe, eleven. I saw this group on *The Ed Sullivan Show* called The Jackson 5.

Yeah, I think I've heard of those guys.

I was totally blown away, as was everybody in the entire music listening universe. Anybody that had access to anything to do with entertainment, you saw that. The mid to late sixties to early seventies was my favorite period of music. In fact, a lot of stuff that's been sampled over the years, a lot of music you see coming out now, is based on that era.

Look at Childish Gambino—it's retro. This era influenced me to pick up the guitars. I saw bands like Sly & The Family Stone and The Jackson 5 and I wanted to learn a couple of guitar lines.

Basically, we played a lot of bass lines on the guitar. I didn't go the route of trying to practice at home; I just wanted to play a few lines. Looking back, I wish I would have shed it back then on the guitar.

You're a good guitarist now. You know what you're doing up there.

You know what, I wish I would have played more then. Because I would be much better at it now. I can play a little bit. That being said, I picked the guitar up to play songs like The Jackson 5's "ABC," "I Want You Back"—you know those lines that are like bass lines, guitar lines, doubles and shit like that. That kind of stuff. There was one song in particular by Sly & The Family Stone called "Sing a Simple Song." It had a signature line that I learned. This is at, maybe, nine years old.

I'm guessing there were probably people in your family both playing instruments and listening to music around the house?

We had records and what not, and we were always listening to music. My dad was a singer, my uncle was an organ player, and my other two uncles were also musicians. I knew that there was something going on, that music was a special thing in our family. There was always a piano around as well. It was an upright piano in my grandmother's house that was my mom's. She had it as a child. Eventually that piano was in our house, and at fifteen years old I sat down and decided that I wanted to learn how to play the piano.

You were playing mostly by ear at that point?

I was playing by ear. My dad showed me two or three songs on the piano. One of them was "Cabbage Alley" by The Meters. Another was "Such a Night" by Dr. John. I never really totally mastered that one, but I kind of punched around with it. And there was a guy by the name of James Booker—probably one of the most amazing piano players that I've ever heard in my entire life. He was a close friend of my family's and he'd pop by probably a couple of times a year. My mom would definitely have to sit down at the piano. He showed me a couple of little things and I was fascinated by watching him.

Music took on a new meaning to me when I started learning by ear. I started listening to records and the radio, learning songs. Pretty early on I made up a song, too. I started writing right away.

I think writing is such an important thing to just start doing when you're young.

Yeah. If you hear something and you learn a couple of chords, then you've got an idea of what it is. Because you've been listening and learning from what you've been hearing, you come up with your own little take on a few chord changes and, who knows, that could become a song. That's kind of what I did. Then I gradually started writing a lot more. I was always listening and trying to learn off of the radio, because obviously being in a band during that time, you had to play the music that was playing on the radio and I learned a lot from that stuff. But I spent a lot of time just trying to make up and write songs.

Very early in your career you had a couple of top 40 hits and songs that were in seminal films, like Pump Up the Volume *and* Skin Deep. *How did those happen? And looking back, how do you write a hit?*

I was playing with my dad (Aaron) and The Neville Brothers, honing my skills with them. That was my first school of music, playing with The Neville Brothers as a teenager.

You were playing keys at that point.

I was playing keys with The Neville Brothers, and then I got a road gig with Bonnie Raitt, and moved to California. That was a big deal and helped hone what I was trying to do—learning how to play with others and to be a part of the music. Then I started writing a few songs on a grand scale. I had a place, and I would come up with stuff and I was influenced by music that I had heard and different songwriters that I thought were really saying something. I wanted to make songs that I thought were catchy but also had some depth to them.

I really don't know what a formula is for writing a hit song but I know simplicity is very important. You want to make it simple enough to where someone who's not extremely musically inclined can get it and engage and relate to it. The songs that I wrote that are in films, that was by chance but being around in the right situation, and some of the people that I encountered and relationships that I started developing all mattered, which is a totally different thing. When you meet people, always try to be nice and polite because you never know who's the one that might need a song for a film or something.

Half of the work is just being a nice person and being easy to get along with.

That's half the battle. You've got to schmooze and let it be known that you're out there. Because out of sight, out of mind. My first charted song was called "Not Just Another Girl" and it was from my first album, *If My Ancestors Could See Me Now*. The song "Not Just Another Girl" made it to, like, top 100, maybe number 27.

That's amazing.

It was maybe a top 10 adult rock hit at the time—there were many different charts and ways of categorizing music back then. But the song was accessible and it had some likability. It was pretty simple. It had a verse, a decent chorus that was building on the verse, and it had a bridge. That was pretty much the formula for a complete song. That song, "Not Just Another Girl," was in a film called *My Stepmother Was an Alien,* which was a very cool thing just to get that kind of exposure.

Then I had a song that was in *Skin Deep* and that song, "Falling Out of Love," which wasn't a high-charted song, but it did become the backdrop for this whole film. The theme of that song became part of the score.

That's so cool.

Well, I should have gotten paid a whole lot more money for my song being in this movie. Because after the fact, I realized that they used one of the main chord progressions in my song throughout the film.

That's interesting.

It was the theme, but I didn't get credit for the score. I only got credit for writing and performing the song that was used.

I think we got to go find that guy and get your money, man.

You know what I'm saying. You really got to be involved with every aspect of when someone uses your music. Nowadays that is the way for us to really make money. The most secure and consistent way for us musicians, us songwriters, to make any money is for your songs to be in a film or TV. Because now where the music industry's gone the streaming avenue and everything else is online stuff. It's not as profitable selling records. Your records for the most part, unless you're selling a humongous amount, are just basically a means for people to know who you are.

Yeah, the albums are promoting the live show more than anything.

The albums are promoting your live show, promoting you as an artist and your brand. But if you can get songs in films in television, that is the way to go now. And by the way, some of those movies that had my songs . . . you know the movie called *Pump up the Volume*, which was another cult classic, it was a major film. When I was asked to be part of it, I thought maybe it will be a major film, success-wise, but it wasn't. It was kind of a cult movement. I did a song in there called "I Cannot Fall in Love," which I didn't write. I would have written that one but another guy wrote that song and I was just asked to perform it and to produce the song for the film.

Those few songs that were in those films over the years, I probably make the most money consistently from publishing stuff like that. Those films are still in some kind of circulation, whether it be cable TV or wherever they play in Europe and all over the world.

And that's almost thirty years ago for some of these tunes, right?

They're all bringing in a couple of dollars here and there. Not major paydays, but something.

If you're trying to write a good song, but not necessarily a hit, do you think about song writing any differently?

Right now, I still try to think about simplicity. I'm a musician at heart, so it's hard for me to think along those terms. I'm going to write this great song or I'm going to write what I think is a hit. Sometimes it just comes accidentally. It just comes as "Oh wow, this is a catchy little thing."

Yeah, you really can't control it when the muse strikes you.

The goal is to write as many songs as you can. Putting it down and getting to where you can play the song, that's the trick to keep doing it. You may write some songs that may not be very good. But you may write ten songs and one of them may be spectacular.

I've found sometimes when I'm writing music, I might bring three or four ideas to my band and almost always the one that I think is best is not the one that everybody else thinks is the best, you know?

Exactly. And when you're collaborating with others, you have to keep an open mind that all of your ideas might not be loved by others the way you loved them. I heard a quote from an amazing song writer, Allen Toussaint, that basically said try to write a song every day. Some of them are going to be bad, but write them.

You got to treat it like a blue-collar job a little bit, you know?

Yeah, just keep doing it. If you write twenty songs, two of them might be really good.

Let's switch gears a little bit. Do you approach the instrument differently when you're a front man in Dumpstaphunk versus when you're a side man playing with the Rolling Stones or with Bonnie Raitt or with anybody else. How does your approach change?

It's not that much different to me. I don't approach it very differently when I'm playing as a band leader or whether it's an accompaniment. I always approach it by thinking what's appropriate for the music that I'm playing and what's going to make the music sound good. Obviously, when you accompany and you're playing with a Bonnie Raitt, Bonnie may want something specific, or she has an idea that's specific but she knows there's going to be some Ivan in it.

You can be playing and know that it's unique, but also I want to listen to what the other guys are doing at all times. I'm going to listen where the drums are; I'm going to listen to the bass players and the guitar player and whoever else is playing so I can see that I'm in there and I'm helping. I'm complementing what's going on and I'm not just playing to hear myself play. I'm hearing to make sure it's a good piece of the puzzle. I'm helping it to be a complete thing.

The listening aspect is so important because that's going to help make your decisions about what you're going to do rhythmically, what you're going to do harmonically.

Yes.

I like the idea of there's always going to be some Ivan in there, but the idea of it is you're trying to serve the song with whatever you're playing.

Yes, I'm trying to serve the song. Obviously if I'm playing with someone and I'm more of an accompaniment than a focal point of the music, there's a subtle difference, but it always involves listening. Listening to everything else is key. Your job is to accompany and to help and enhance what they already have going on and their style. You're going to conform somewhat to what they're doing and then you just put yourself in that.

When I'm playing with Dumpsta or an Ivan Neville solo thing, I'm making up what I want to. I'm making up something to bring to the table, but it still has to enhance and be a part of what the greater good is. It's all listening and being a part of the sound.

Tell me some of your thoughts about how you keep a band together on the road and musically what's most important to you to feel like the band is really clicking?

It's hard to keep a band on a road. Sometimes you have to take breaks and do side projects, other music that will keep you fresh and keep your interests piquing. If you've been out on the road playing with the same guys all the time, sometimes it gets a little bit too close for comfort. You know each other very well so you're like brothers or siblings and you can get on each other's nerves a lot at times.

But when you start playing together, there's that thing that happens. You know. You play with a lot of other artists and configurations as do I, so you know there's a certain thing with your boys when you all are clicking and it's just instantly great and happy. It's a happy place. We are like, "Oh my God this is so good." You're like, "Damn."

You can feel it when you are in that moment; you can feel the joy around the room. It's with musicians and you also feel it disseminating into the audience, too.

Every fucking body in the building or wherever you're playing knows there are moments when this may be some of the coolest, funkiest, baddest shit we have played anywhere, right now, what we're doing because we're connecting. And the chemistry . . . it's like you can wink your eye and another guy can feel it. You could fart and somebody on the other side of the stage answers. Things like that. You feel that connection. It's like you're weaving a basket together. Your pieces of a puzzle stick together. You feel that tightness and that unspoken commonalty . . . I can't think of the word . . . the unspoken *camaraderie* that you have. The connection.

I think that's the essence of what makes music so powerful. People want to feel that experience of "we're all in something together." We're all experiencing this one really fun thing or deep thing together. That's the essence of what really draws people to music.

Yes. You know it's funny how sometimes there are nights when a place is packed to the gills and everything's just seemingly cool and you might have some moments but it may not get to where you think it *should* have gotten that night. There are other times when it's a ho-hum kind of night and for some reason the music is all you've got at that point. There are some musical moments that are fucking magical. It may be a lesser crowd that night but the people that are there and the guys that are playing come together and create this moment you are all a part of . . . it's the magic of being involved in music.

Some nights it just flows and some nights it feels like you're pushing a boulder up the hill.

That's another thing, when you let it just flow or it's gone. Sometimes you have those songs that are confined to a certain arrangement but then they might have moments where this section kind of flows. It may go wherever we decide it goes depending on what we're playing.

Yeah, don't be afraid to do something different in the moment.

Yes. That's the magic of that stuff and what makes being in a band bearable at times when it's starting to feel almost redundant. Because you're doing so much with the same group, blah, blah, blah. But those nights when you know you're doing what nobody else can do when you're together, you're like, "Damn, *this* is why we do this. This is why we play in a band together."

No doubt.

I heard what you were playing and I'm playing some shit and you said, oh wow. When you played, I just played that and then this guy just played that and it made what I played sound so much fucking better. And vice versa. In fact, this "conversation" we're having, without saying a single word, you know?

That's exactly it. Would you like to talk about sobriety a little bit?

Absolutely. I really want to say something about sobriety.

There's an aspect of getting high and drinking and stuff that comforts you a little bit. Coming up as a youngster, I was nervous and sometimes had stage fright because when you're playing, you're exposing yourself, you're naked in front of these people. You're opening up your heart and your soul, so having a drink or smoking a joint or whatever, comforted me in some way.

Then there were times in the creative process that I would do drugs and I thought that it was enhancing my creativity. I came up with some amazing music during those times, but what I found out was I had to stop drinking and doing drugs because it stopped working for me. It stopped working for me, personally. I don't have anything against people who do that kind of stuff, but for me it stopped working. It was no longer fun and I started thinking the getting high and the drinking became more important than the music.

I was fortunate that I stopped, but I had a fear of how I'd play if I wasn't high and if I wasn't drinking. How would I feel? I found out that the fucking *music* made me higher than any high that I ever imagined. Like damn. I used to have this adrenaline after a gig and what do you do with that energy? I would get fucked up, right, but that never made me feel better than that initial adrenaline. I wondered why when I came down I really didn't feel that. I was trying to enhance something that already had a high that I couldn't imagine reaching anyway.

When I left the other stuff alone and just started dealing with the music and the high that I felt from being a part of playing music, being part of people feeding off of the music, giving something back, that exchange, that whole process—*that* became the high that I never really knew existed. I'm like, damn, this is fucking high, but now I don't have a hangover. I can go to sleep and all of that.

And you remember everything that happened, right?

I remember all of it now. I didn't have to do any of that shit. It's fucking amazing.

I still have slight nerves, but I like it. I got to tell you, when I'm doing a solo for someone else or playing some piece a little outside my element, if I'm not prepared like I should be, I'm more nervous. I'm like, damn, I should have practiced this shit a little bit more. Because I'm going to go play something that's not like the shit I know. It's not like playing with

Dumpstaphunk or playing some of that stuff that I can play in my fucking sleep.

Not only is natural nervousness a beautiful thing, but it's an extra little nervousness when it's tied to preparation. Preparation is key. You've got to over shed some shit. It's something you got to do that's a little bit outside your element and you need to practice this stuff. Fucking prepare your ass off. Even if you think you know it, go practice it some more.

Then when you know it really good, practice it some more.

It's crazy how different it feels from sitting at an instrument at home by yourself, to when you're onstage. It is a completely different feeling.

You playing some piano intro for somebody that you're, like, *oh my God,* then you are in front of thousands of people and you got to play this. So it's a little bit different. There's no such thing as overpracticing. You can't overrehearse in the band.

That's great advice.

What is the best advice you've gotten in the music business?

As long as you're doing this job, you got to make sure you're having fun doing it, playing music. You could have a serious job that involves some other kind of mechanics or what not, but you play music. You got a job that could be fun, so you got to let it be fun. As long as it's fun you can enjoy doing it and you'll probably get the best out of it.

That's very true.

When it becomes not fun, you need to figure out if it's something you're not doing right.

Well and the other thing is if you're a live musician, playing for audiences, they're most likely there to see you because they want to relax, have fun, and listen—so you better be 100 percent into it onstage because they're paying their money for you to share something with them.

Yeah. And you know I just thought of something else that's good advice. If you have a contract that somebody's trying to get you to sign—whether it be some recording thing or management thing—and using words that you don't understand, find someone that you trust, ideally a lawyer, and make sure you understand things you sign.

Absolutely, yeah. To even go a step further with that, I think in this day and age it's important that you at least understand the business side of things a little bit. You got to be involved in that to protect yourself and also to make sure that you're getting paid fairly.

Absolutely. Yes.

Any bad advice that somebody gave you?

I'm sure someone's told me some lame shit. Probably the worst advice is coke makes you fucking smart. Shit like that!

I was thinking the same thing. "Hey man, if you guys really want to be good, you should get into some coke," you know?

Yeah. "With blow, you get more creative." Somebody told me that shit back then. I can go sit at the piano and make up a chord change right now and record it on my voice memo. I'm completely fucking sober. I don't need drugs to make me transcendent.

SECTION EIGHT:

FINDING YOUR SOUND

Many of the most famous pop rock artists the past fifty years are people with personality and uniqueness. David Bowie, Prince, Freddie Mercury of Queen, Isaac Hayes, Frank Zappa and Bjork all come to mind as musicians with immense musical talent and fiercely independent and interesting personalities. They also all each have a signature sound that continued to develop over time. Even somewhat more mainstream rock artists like U2 and Led Zeppelin expanded their sound as their careers blossomed.

If you've gotten this far you probably already have an idea how you want your music to sound. Now follow your muse and just create. Try to think of working on music like a nine-to-five job. Not everything you produce is going to be your best material, but every time you sit down and work on music you're giving yourself experience. Trust the process of simply spending time with your music and you'll be more likely to have success.

When you're getting started, take some risks in the songwriting to find your voice or further develop it. Sometimes ideas work very quickly and it's obvious what's best. Other times you'll need to let an idea or song marinate and give it a chance to breathe. Try not to rewrite the same song over and over again. But also don't change your sound so drastically that you alienate whatever audience you've created. Many bands decide that they're going to change their sound after just a couple of years and it confuses fans.

Your odds of succeeding will increase if you stick with a similar if naturally evolving sound over the years. It's okay to make *some* turns and embrace natural development. Just don't do a one-eighty; be yourself. Real people with scars and flaws are more interesting than a façade or fake persona, in the more plastic sense. That said, many of today's successful artists create an alternate stage personality. Sometimes it works but be prepared to be able to separate yourself from that.

GETTING HONEST CRITIQUES

Where should you start in asking if your music is any good? Have friends over to your rehearsals and play your music for them. Tell them you want honesty! Record your rehearsals. Try to play the best version of a song you can and send it to someone whose musical opinion you trust.

PERSISTENCE VS. ANNOYANCE

There's kind of a fine line between being persistent and being annoying. Many people working in the music business just don't have their act together, so in those cases persistence might be needed. It's important to be able to read a situation. Every single person you interact with in the business is going to have a different method of getting things done. Keep that in mind as you interact with people, and don't be afraid to ask questions. But realize that if your persistence is received as an annoyance, you will do your art a disservice. Lack of social awareness could cause you to lose an opportunity.

CATALOG VS. HITS

Another important question is, are you writing to make a catalog or are you writing to make hits? If you're writing to create a catalog of music, the world is your oyster. That is to say it is much easier to be yourself and do what the heart pleases as you're writing. Do you have one sound that suits you or your band best? If not, which styles might complement one another on an album or in the live setting? Artists from the Beatles to Wilco to Dr. Dre have produced multiple arrangements of the same song. Trying different tempos and keys can be a good approach as you're trying to find a song's identity.

If you're trying to write hits, you're going to want to consider collaborating with a hit-making producer while trying to get a major label deal. Right now most hit songs are fairly formulaic, so you'll want to learn the idiosyncrasies of the content of hit songs. Making top 40 hits is a much more challenging path to forge these days. And the odds of you making it are much lower than if you're trying to write music for a career catalog. The list of recent people who have had a sustained career making hits is incredibly short. If you're banking on a career writing hits, consider this: You'll need to keep producing them. That's a formidable undertaking for even the most incredibly gifted.

FANS OF SONGS, NOT FANS OF ARTISTS

If you do intend to create a hit, know that hits don't always generate fans. There is a big difference between someone who likes a hit song on the radio and someone who'll put money down to buy a concert ticket for an artist's entire show. This is a crucial point to understand as you choose your direction in music, especially as live music has become a more primary source of revenue for most artists out there.

EXPANDING YOUR CRAFT

Three windows into increased musical comprehension are: reading, writing, and rote. Learn how to read music and you'll be a better writer as well. Finally, rote means being able to listen to someone play and then be able to play it back "by ear." These three skills can unlock the musical universe for you. With reading, you can play other people's complicated pieces of music. With writing, you can compose your own or transcribe others' solos or songs. And by developing your listening skills, you will learn how to hear and play music just as you hear and speak your native language. The transformation may take years, but if you put in the time, you will be able to "talk" music fluently.

LISTENING

The great bassist Kai Eckhardt has a series on bass playing that includes a section to improve your interval training. Interval recognition means hearing different notes played back to back or together as a chord and being able to immediately identify what the interval is and how to play it. Learning your intervals is at the root of being able to create music inventively and efficiently. Outside of working on exercises on your own, another way to learn is to study with other musicians or collaborate with them whenever possible. Playing music and actively listening to the other musicians will likely improve your listening most quickly.

LEARNING BY DOING IT

As long as we're alive, we should always be students of music, constantly open to both learning and new inspiration. When you're trying to learn how to play music with other people, it's important just to do it. Seek out other musicians, especially people that you feel are stronger musicians than you, as often as you can.

ARRANGING MUSIC

Arranging is different from songwriting, as it's more about recognizing how pieces fit together. Being a good arranger can be kind of like being a building architect. There are lots of ways to construct things, but only some parts go together and make sense when considered as a whole. Knowing at least some

172

music theory will increase your odds of being a successful arranger. Being familiar with as many instruments as possible will also be important, along with how to achieve certain sounds from each instrument. This is especially true in the studio setting.

RIGHT NOTE: Ignorance is not bliss when it comes to versatility as a musician. The more instruments you know how to play, the more variety you're likely to be able to create with your music. Try to master at least one instrument, but don't be afraid to branch out to others. Many musicians also find value from learning drumming rudiments, as you can apply more-complex rhythmic ideas to composition.

INDEPENDENCE OF YOUR LIMBS

Let's talk about reading music versus playing by memory or playing by rote, which is hearing something and being able to play it back. One concept worth exploring through both reading and rote is independence of your hands rhythmically. Two-way independence, meaning the ability to play more than one distinct part with your hands independent of each other, opens up even more possibilities for creation. If you're a drummer, you might need four-way independence. Otherwise, you'll be working on two-way independence plus possibly learning how to sing while playing two different things at once. This is one of the most challenging aspects of music. But again if you can play two things independently with your hands and sing at the same time you're going to find that your advanced techniques can be valuable in lots of settings.

INDEPENDENCE PRACTICE

When your hands are playing different rhythms, it's best to start by working on parts individually with your hands and then trying to put them together. It's almost as if you have trained your hands with muscle memory so that you do not have to think about one of the parts. It will just continue on autopilot, and then you can focus on what the other hand is doing. The more independence you have, the more complicated the ideas you're going to be able to execute.

RIGHT NOTE: It's a good idea to play along to songs you like or are trying to learn. It's also useful to occasionally practice with a metronome to work on your timing. Work on songs, work on improvisation, work on technique. The most important thing is just that you do something.

WHAT IF YOU PLAY A NOTE THAT SOUNDS WEIRD?

Usually, all you have to do is move in a half step one way or the other to make a weird-sounding note resolve. If you can do that, your weird note now just sounds like a passing tone. You might find yourself playing something live and you hit a note that sounds like a wrong note. Repeat it. The repetition signals intent and is heard as correct—just something a little more unusual or creative and outside the box.

PLAYING WITH OTHERS

It's always good to practice by yourself, especially as you're just getting to know your instrument. However, it's even better to play with other musicians. So *why* is it important to play with other musicians and how do you learn from collaborating? Victor Wooten gives a great example in his book *The Music Lesson*, of babies talking to adults and not knowing the meanings of everything. But does that stop them from talking to adults? No, they're still trying to communicate. What then happens is that the adults relate and talk back to the babies. The babies learn new words. Then they learn what they mean, but not necessarily all at once. The babies are learning to express themselves. This is exactly what happens in music.

SKILLS VS. SONGWRITING

Let's consider the balance of working on technical performance versus songwriting. Number one, the more technical proficiency you have on your instrument, the more creative you can be as a songwriter. If you don't want to write the same song over and over, proficiency and musical knowledge will help you achieve musical diversity. That said, more technical skill doesn't always mean you're going to make better music. So it's important to try to mix up your time working on both your technical playing *and* your songwriting. They're each essential to your development as a musician.

THE MICHAEL JORDAN RULE

You're going to need some tricks and ideas to avoid stagnancy. As you get used to the daily grind of being a musician, some of the initial joy and curiosity may be harder to generate. Basketball legend Michael Jordan has some great advice to keep your focus and drive in terms of improving your game. Jordan would constantly address what his strengths and weaknesses were, and then turn his focus toward improving the worst parts of his game. Always focus on getting better and you'll never get bored.

This mindset translates to music perfectly: No matter what, you're always a student as long as you still can learn. You should be trying to pick up new things along the way, and it's only going to make you a more interesting musician. You can improve by taking lessons, practicing your craft, or even by listening to other artists. You'll also be picking up life lessons along the way, so in general, pay attention and be in the moment. You *will* learn!

175

Another way to expand your musical world is to make yourself available as a session musician. Session work is not as consistent as it used to be nor does it pay what it used to, but it still does exist and can augment your income if you're not gigging as much during a certain time. Interval training and listening comprehension definitely apply. Another great trait to have is to be a good improviser in the studio. That is, knowing how to be creative within a framework of what an artist is looking to achieve. It's having the ability to do something original but not entirely out of bounds with what's being created. The ability to sight-read music is also invaluable as a studio musician.

Another beneficial thing to have in the studio is the ability to play lots of styles of music. Depending on who you're working with or working for that sort of versatility will open many doors. Some studios have musicians on call depending what is being recorded for a certain day. The more you know, the better your chance will be that *you'll* be the person they call.

PATIENCE AND GETTING OUTSIDE THE BOX

Ideally, you have the ability to turn on creativity at any moment, but also can be patient when there are roadblocks. Sometimes you'll get stuck, and there needs to be a new injection of creative ideas to make something work. Can you be that person? And, of course, you don't want to be the one who is part of the roadblock. Having as much knowledge as possible is going to keep you from being that person in the studio.

Producer and musician Brian Eno created a set of cards that he called "oblique strategies," featuring words or phrases that he would draw at random to try to help musicians get out of the box. Get your own set of his cards; they're a very interesting way to open the mind.

A CONVERSATION WITH VICTOR WOOTEN

Five-time Grammy Award winner is only the first of many remarkable ways to introduce Victor Wooten. Considered by most in the industry to be one of the greatest bassists of all time, Victor has made a name for himself not only as a performer but also as a record producer. Victor begin learning how to play the bass at the age of three and since has perfected his craft. Having released ten solo albums, as well as several as the bassist for the well-known Béla Fleck & the Flecktones, Victor is no stranger to recording. He is also the founder of Vix Records. Equally impressive is his desire to transfer his knowledge and passion for music to others. You can find him hosting music camps for all ages—all provided and produced by his not-for-profit organization, Victor Wooten's Center for Music and Nature. To quote Victor's mother: "The world needs more than just good musicians. We need good people." Victor Wooten is most certainly both.

JOEL: I'm curious, what's an important musical decision you made when you first started playing professionally?

VICTOR: I was lucky enough to be playing music almost from birth. You've met some of my brothers. I'm the youngest of five, and they were already playing. Regi was playing guitar. Roy was already playing drums. Rudy was playing sax. And Regi had already started teaching Joseph to play keyboards. So when I was born, they already knew this baby's going to play. I've never not done it. By the time I was five, we were out gigging.

So, you were a musician before you learned how to read or that sort of thing.

Oh, absolutely. The same way in English, or any language, you learn to talk before you can read it. That's the natural progression, is to do it first and then learn about it later.

Tell me, what do you remember from growing up and playing with your brothers at such a young age?

I remember a lot. I had a little toy Mickey Mouse guitar, and my brothers would set up to play, and I would just sit down and strum along with them the same way a baby is allowed to join the conversation, even though they only know baby talk.

I learned music before I learned the instrument. I was learning how to feel it. I knew what it meant if the high hat on drum set opened at the end of four bars and all these little things. The same way a baby knows the difference between a question and a statement by the pitch of their parents' voices. You may not even understand every word, and you definitely can't speak it, but you're learning a language first. I was doing the same thing but the language was just music.

So, when I was three or four, my brother Regi started teaching me where to place my fingers to produce desired notes. I was learning notes and how to play songs I already knew. Like a kid learns to speak, they choose the words they want to say first. And the words they want to say are words they already know. They already know the word "milk," or "Mama," "Dada," or more. They know what they mean before they can say them. A lot of the times in music, we're teaching kids things they don't even know what they mean. This is a C-major scale. Okay, I can play it, but what is it?

Right. It's kind of the opposite. Interesting.

So, I was learning music first. And when Regi started teaching me how to play the instrument, that came easier because I already knew music. By the time I was five or six, we, the five of us brothers, were the opening band on Curtis Mayfield's Super Fly Tour up the West Coast. We were living in Sacramento at the time, so we'd go to San Francisco, and Stockton, and all those areas. I get a lot of credit because I was very young, but if you think about it, my brother teaching me deserves the credit because he was only eight years older than me.

Wow. Is Regi just one of those people who is a natural at many instruments?

Yes. I know that he still teaches that way today. And where he got it from, I don't know.

If you give a bass or guitar to someone who's not a musician, someone who's never played bass or guitar before, they're going to hold it and start strumming it with their thumb. They're not going to try to use two fingers, like an experienced bass guitarist. They're not going to ask for a pick. They're just going to hold it from underneath the instrument and strum it with their thumb.

Me, as a one or two-year-old playing, of course, that's what I did with my toy Mickey Mouse guitar. But when Regi actually started teaching me the instrument, he didn't say, "Okay, you're doing it wrong. You've got to hold it this way and play it with your fingers." His mentality, whether he said it out loud or not, is, "Okay, you're using your thumb. I'm going to show you how to really use your thumb." And that's how he started me playing—using my thumb like a guitar pick, up and down. And that's what I'm known for now, but Regi started me like that right away. He saw that was my natural ability, and he made it better.

Yeah, because everybody is going to have their own, and should have their own, way of creating tone and the whole physical aspect of it. And it's going to be more interesting. Music is going to be more interesting, if everyone is doing that, as opposed to following a strict method of this is how it's supposed to be.

Absolutely. The same way we all have our own speaking voice. Right? And no one, including ourselves, has ever tried to change it. Because the tone of our voice was not the most important thing. Our parents just let us speak. And so even to this day, we all have our own voice, and we've never had to try to find a different one.

Regi was the same way. And on the bass he allowed—no, not only allowed, he *encouraged* and helped me develop my own sound, to where I never had to find it. We're always told to search for our own sound. You never had to search for your own voice when you were learning to talk.

Yeah, it's just there.

Music's the same way if we're allowed to express ourselves with our own voice from the beginning. And fortunately, I had that from my brothers.

I'm curious if you have something that you feel was a really important decision you made on the business side early on that impacted your career. And by early on I mean, this might be when you were in your late teens.

Well, my business sense kind of kicked in much later when I started touring on my own. But early on, everything was my parents. Again, I was lucky enough to be doing gigs at five, six years old. But I knew nothing about business. Nothing at all. My parents handled everything. I just played my part. Even throughout high school, I just played my part with the family band.

When I finally started making money on my own, in '81, because of a bad record deal, the five of us brothers weren't playing together. I had to get another musical job, and I worked at an amusement park called Busch Gardens. I played in the country and bluegrass band. Without thinking about it really, I was saving money. And really the only reason I was saving money was because I was still living at home under my parents' roof and I wasn't paying rent. I didn't have to go out and do all the things you have to do when you're living on your own, like laundry. It really wasn't until I had been with Béla Fleck & the Flecktones for quite a few years. And then I released my own first record and started to tour.

And that was A Show of Hands?

Yeah. So I did a tour, and I was using the Flecktones's management, booking agents, and all that stuff. And I did a duo tour with just a drummer. We drove from Nashville, Tennessee up to Northampton, Massachusetts for our first gig, opening for Medeski, Martin & Wood. And we got there and played an amazing but short set. And then the guy who was running sound for me and doing tour managing, he came over after the gig and said, "Hey, Vic. Here's the twenty-five dollars. Do you want to hold it, or do you want me to hold it?" And, I'd been through it with the Flecktones. Making some pretty good money. And he came up with $25, and I was thinking, *Okay, maybe that's a buyout for food.* But I found out that we had only made $25 that night.

Oh my gosh.

And I immediately got mad. It was late at night, but I called the manager on the phone. "You booked a gig for twenty-five dollars?" But after a while it hit me. Wait a minute. If I didn't know that, that's *my* fault. So, I learned right away, kind of the hard way, that I need to know what's going on. If there's a contract, I need to know what's in it.

Absolutely.

I need to know what money's being made, what money's being spent. And it wasn't really until then that I started paying attention to business. And this was in '96. I'd been playing music for a long time. I'd been touring with the Flecktones and letting other people handle everything. But after the first gig on that tour, I forced myself to get smart.

Wow. I think we've had one of those nights too, when we got paid twenty-five bucks, and I think we told the promoter to keep it.

Yeah, well, we took it.

Do you have a recommendation for how a young musician should split their time between playing music with others and writing songs?

I would say spend more time playing with others than anything else. Again, this is just my opinion, but I look at music like a language. Even if you're going to be a storyteller, you won't have a story to tell until you get out of that room, live a life, and mingle with people—talk and converse and listen. Music's the same way. If you spent most of your time in a room writing music, what do you have to write about, unless you've been out and gotten your heart broken, and had your house broken into and your car stolen. You need stories.

Yeah.

You need stories to tell. I say, just to make up a number, at least 80 percent of the time should be spent out there playing with people. Then you take what you've done, and you go in the room and practice it, or write about it. But, you have to have experiences.

I completely agree with that.

Music is about stories. If we have no stories to tell, I don't know what we're writing about, or playing about.

Yeah. That's a great point, and something that I don't think gets talked about or emphasized enough, that it's important to live your life. You can't just be a musician 95 percent of the day, working on music. If you have no other aspects of your life, there isn't going to be a balance.

Absolutely. You've got to have something to talk about. Again, just like in language. I want to learn Spanish. I could sit in a room all day, all year. I'm still going to come out of that room speaking with an accent. Anyone who's native to that language will know I'm not native.

Yeah.

But, if I get out there and I converse with other people speaking Spanish, I eat the food and live the culture, all of a sudden the accent will start to diminish on its own without practice. I say approach music the same way. The more you play with people, the faster you will grow.

No doubt.

That's how a baby learns to talk. They don't stay in a room by themselves. They learn it by conversing with people.

Yep, and listening. I think that's another thing in the more improvisational side of things that we do. There's more emphasis on listening. It's so important to be able to hear what your fellow musicians are playing, and to be able to then react to it, or make it a conversational thing onstage.

The more you do it and listen, the less you have to practice. I'm not saying don't practice, but an example is: If I go to Australia and spend two months, I'm going to come home with an Australian accent. That will not have come through practicing. It will not even have come through paying attention to: "Oh, how do they say that?" It will have become natural through immersion, through listening. Listening is that magic formula, that magic thing that allows you to pick up something quickly. That's my main method for learning music. If I have to learn music quickly, I'm just going to listen to it all day. Even when I'm sleeping. Like I said, a child doesn't learn a Michael Jackson lyric by practice, they just listen to it. By the third time, they're singing the whole song.

This is so true. When I'm flying sometimes, I really love renaissance vocal music, all the polyphonic stuff from the fifteenth and sixteenth century. I'll sometimes put that on when I'm on a plane and just trying to relax. I love when listening to music infiltrates the dreams. It's a cool thing. Do you think it's very important to know some music theory and/or history as you're learning how to be a musician yourself?

I think it's very important, but not at the beginning. The same way when a baby's learning to talk, you don't want to teach him nouns, verbs, and pronouns. You want him to talk first. I think in our typical musical curriculum, we teach theory too early. That's my opinion. I say, let's play a few years first. Let's enjoy playing the same way a baby talks for years before you even correct them. Even if a baby says "blankey" instead of blanket,

185

and they're six years old, you don't correct them. The parents start saying "blankey" too, because you know what they mean.

Right.

As long as they're communicating, that's most important. Again, a lot of times we start teaching theory way too soon. But, is it important to know it? I believe it is, the same way in English it's important to know how to read and write, and to know verbs, adjectives, and pronouns. It's very, very important. It doesn't mean you're a better communicator because you know it. But, you have the opportunity of being that. For me, my musical method is following the method that we learned to speak. When do we learn the rules of English, meaning the theory of English speaking and writing?

Not until years after you've started speaking it.

Absolutely!

It's down the road.

Right. In music, we want it to start the first year. I believe that's why most people quit.

Interesting. It gets too analytical. That makes sense. When improvising, is there a way to describe how to listen and create at the same time?

Sure. What I say first is, treat it like a conversation. Treat it like talking to someone. Make your responses based on what the other person said, not based on what you've practiced.

When I get a person who says they can't improvise, I may play a one chord groove, or something like that. I'll then have the person find three notes they like over this groove, not three notes I like. Now, we're not going to move away from those three notes. Just these three notes, which means you don't even have to think of these three notes anymore.

All we're going to do is express ourselves with them. That means we're going to use rhythms, space, dynamics, listening, things like that, the same way a baby knows only a few words at the beginning, but they still know how to talk. Just let them express themselves. There's no right way to do it. There's no wrong way to do it. Let's just do it. Having to do it right, is what screws most people up.

Yeah, a lot of times in music, the word "right" is a subjective thing.

In everything—religion, politics, everything. "Right" has screwed too many people up, having to be good or having to be right.

I feel the same way about the word "normal." What is normal?

Exactly. Here's the thing, everyone does it. When you sing in the shower, or when you sing driving to work, you're not doing it to be right. You're doing it because it feels right. It's bringing that kid or adult, whoever it is, back to the era when they were playing air guitar or air drums, or whatever. During those moments, it wasn't about the instrument. It wasn't about the right note. It was just doing it for the feel.

Sometimes I'll even have the person play that instrument and I'll turn their volume down. Just get them to play, or even sing the solo.

I just did a workshop at the Jazz Educators Network, including a lot of techniques to help people improvise. A lot of these techniques I demonstrated break traditional rules. One of them was, I invited a guitarist up onstage, and I had the guitarist sing while he was holding his guitar. Sing the solo over this blues progression; sing the solo you wish you could play.

Usually the hardest thing for people is to sing in front of others.

Right, yeah.

I had him singing this solo. Then, as he's singing, I said, "Without thinking about it, allow your fingers to start following your voice. Then if your pitch goes high, just let your hands go high. Don't worry about whether the note's right. Don't even think about it. Just allow your hands to start following your voice."

As he was doing that, and I'm making sure he keeps his attention on singing, I then slowly turn his volume up on his guitar. Even though the pitches may not match, the tone does.

Wow.

The feel does. The feel is magic, and wow. It's there. At first, when I turn the guitarist's volume up, he may hear that the pitch does not match his voice. If I hear his attention go back to the guitar, I will turn him down immediately and say, "No, keep your focus on singing. Don't worry about the pitch. Just keep singing. We'll learn the pitches later. This is all about capturing the feel."

When they can do it, whether the pitches match or not, everything else is right. The only thing that's not matching is the pitch. The feel, the dynamics, everything else is there. Immediately they sound like they know what they're doing.

It's so interesting because I think this speaks to a larger thing. That feel and tone, and phrasing, all of the stuff that has humanness about it, that's what's compelling for a listener to hear, not playing something perfectly.

Absolutely. That is what makes people feel. We have a pentatonic scale, but you feel it more if you put that flatted fifth and turn it into a blues scale. All of a sudden you feel that more. In every key, there's seven right notes. But, you feel those seven right notes more when you put in some of the five wrong ones.

Yeah.

A singer who just sings the right note is good. But the singer who eases up to the right note, from the wrong note, you feel that more. To me, it's the wrongness of it that makes someone feel it. That's what expression is, or even jazz, is about—the rightest ways of being wrong. The best singers do that. The best singers know how to massage a note. Bob Dylan, the way he sings, he wouldn't win *America's Got Talent*, or *The Voice*, with that tone. But he's doing it in a way that we feel it and we love it.

Some of my favorite singers sing out of tune a little bit. That's where the feeling is. If it's too right, it's too clean, it's like walking into a house that's too clean. You don't even want to move.

If you think about what vibrato actually is, it's pulling the notes slightly out of tune.

Yeah, exactly.

Then you feel that note even more.

Do you have anything that you feel was the best piece of advice given to you as a musician coming up, or something that you want to share?

I don't know the best piece, but I can remember one that pops into my head. There's a guy named Wayne Jackson, who's a trumpet player in a horn section called The Memphis Horns. They're the guys that played on "I'm a Soul Man" and so many other records. I was new to Nashville and got a chance to play on a record that they were working on. Wayne Jackson was very kind to me, and gave me a piece of advice, which was also a criticism. But, it was so kind. He said to me, "Victor, you have to remember, you have two ears. One of them is for you, but the other one is for the rest of the band."

That was his way of letting me know, I was not listening well enough.

Wow.

I've never forgotten it, and I hope I never do, because that was so powerful.

That's really great. That ties into what we were just talking about too, with the listening aspect. Last question. What is the worst advice you've ever received in your music career?

There's another teacher out there who said that you can't groove on the bass until you know the notes to play. His advice is to learn all your notes and your scales first, and then learn to groove later. To me, that's just as backward as it comes. It's like telling a baby, "Learn your alphabet, learn your verbs. Then you'll be able to talk." I say, just learn to feel music first and learn the rules later.

Anyway, that one is just backward to me. I can't call it wrong, because I'm sure it works for somebody. My approach is, let's just play. Let's feel it. Again, that's the way you learn to talk. A baby is not born speaking English, but they are born communicating. We're born with feeling. We will die with feeling.

When you play from the standpoint of feel, you can reach everybody. In other words, if a mathematician writes this formula on the board such as $e=mc^2$, with all these numbers and letters; if you don't get it . . . you're probably not going to look at that board and say, "Oh wow, that's beautiful." You have to understand the formula to fully appreciate it.

Yeah, no doubt.

But, if I just take all of this theory and paint a beautiful picture, you don't have to understand any of it to see the beauty. That's what music does. You don't have to understand it to hear it, appreciate it, or play it. You can just listen to it and go, "Wow, that's gorgeous. I feel that."

SECTION NINE:

BUILDING AN AUDIENCE

How will you know when it's time to step on the gas and start playing more shows while adding new markets? Once your act has gained some traction, you've gotten good reviews, and/or you've put music out there people are listening to, it's time. You never know when the momentum is going to continue to build (or slow down), so if you feel it building up, take advantage of it.

TOP FIVE THINGS THAT WILL TANK YOUR CAREER

Finding success and longevity requires quite a bit of thought, planning, and self-discipline. Then, a huge number of additional choices and variables come into play, many of which are not constant. There are, however, a few constants when it comes to long-term success and they are related to what you should NOT be doing:

1) A bad attitude. There are very few legitimate reasons to have a bad attitude and to always be complaining. You're a musician. You're lucky to be creating music. There are millions of people who live more difficult lives.

2) Taking every single gig you're offered. You'll burn out very quickly if you say yes to every gig. Saying no once in a while might also increase your payday down the road. What you offer is in many ways its own economy, with its own scale of supply and demand.

3) Being inconsistent with your commitment. Your career will take time. Invest in yourself every day. The best advice is to swap out the actions and activities in your life and routine that clearly have the lowest value or return and instead replace them with ones that move you closer to your goals. This isn't always

related to your music, and instead might be the things that create a healthy balance within your personal, professional, and physical life.

4) Not having any music or merchandise for sale. You're going to need to create revenue to live. This also means you'll need ways to promote your product or no one will know about it. But if you have nothing for sale, you have zero chance of selling anything. This doesn't mean you need to print ten thousand of the same T-shirts (actually please don't do that). Instead, test different things out. Create a few items in limited quantities and see what your fans respond to.

5) Getting wasted before you perform. The wild, drunk musician on the edge of sanity vibe gets old quickly for audiences and bandmates alike. You can't be at your best if you're wasted onstage. Give your paying audience what they deserve: your best!

IMAGE AND PERCEPTION

The first question you want to ask is: "What is the look or vibe you want identified with you?" Your image should influence *every* direction of your art, from onstage performance to the way you are marketed. Are you down to earth and performing as yourself? Are you cool and understated? Or are you wild and energetic?

ARTISTIC DIRECTION

Whatever it is you choose, you want any artwork and the branding to reflect the desired perception. It's important to create a logo that's both memorable and represents the spirit of your music or your band. If you can create something that's also easily recognizable, it will only help you down the road.

Your brand and image will also be important when it comes time to create merchandise. Most people only see your album artwork as little squares on their phones, so show poster and advertising artwork along with T-shirts will become crucial elements of your brand's image. Take your time with design to ensure all imagery and branding are consistent.

YOU'VE GOT THE LOOK

"Good drummer, great look," —Nigel Tufnel, Spinal Tap

Is your music best served with you as a persona or are you simply being yourself? This is an important thing to figure out from the get go, as it will inform the vibe around your music. Your look and persona shows your fans who you are and should mesh with the music unless you're being intentionally ironic. In other words, it would be strange to play Frank Sinatra style crooner music if you had a long beard and wore overalls onstage. But maybe that's the twist that makes it all work? Just keep in mind that there's a fine line between stupid and clever.

RIGHT NOTE: Never wear shorts or flip-flops onstage unless you're Jimmy Buffett, Bob Weir, on Warped tour, playing on a beach, or you're performing island music. It just looks more pro to be playing in *anything* other than shorts. If Wilco's Jeff Tweedy can play Bonnaroo in 95 degree heat with a jean jacket on, you can ditch the shorts for a set.

TOP FIVE THINGS THAT WILL MAKE PEOPLE DISINTERESTED OR DISLIKE YOU

1) Acting disinterested while you're performing onstage. You're disrespecting everyone in the room—from those onstage with you to those who paid money to see you.

2) Constantly being late. Making others wait for you is the ultimate show of disrespect. Always try to be a couple of minutes early and don't overbook yourself before a time-sensitive commitment.

3) Arriving at a gig or a rehearsal underprepared. What's the point of even showing up if you don't know what you're doing? You'll be wasting your time as well as others'.

4) Not paying other musicians or your crew what you promised them. If you have to go out of pocket to pay what you promised others, that's the right thing to do. You will ruin your reputation by stiffing people.

5) Turning up your amp too loud. We understand some artists need volume to achieve tone, but it should never come at the expense of the show sound. Your bandmates, crew, and audience will all suffer as a result of your excessive volume onstage.

GAINING TRACTION IN THE TWENTY-FIRST CENTURY

How do you get the word out about your music in the twenty-first century? Without a doubt, the best way is still word of mouth, or maybe more like word of Internet. There's no one you trust better than your friends when it comes to music.

While the modern world has a lot of modern ways that we can communicate, at the same time there are quite a few things that we can learn from pioneers of the industry. This knowledge plus some additional insight about how groups of people have been known to associate and then continue to be involved with one another brings us to the concept of "the tribe." While the concept of tribes is as old as these communities themselves, the idea of the modern tribe was brought to the world of sales and marketing with the best-selling book *Tribes* by Seth Godin in 2008.

While the notion of "tribe" has remained constant, the ways they come together, as well as why, are highly similar to ways some historic and well-known music acts have built their own audiences. To simplify, through the creation of a sense of community, encouraged discussion of the main subject matter, or in your case, your music, you can then create additional layers of interest regarding what you are doing. The result is a group of followers and fans that value this enhanced sense of community on many levels as much as the main draw itself, your music.

An early and very relevant example is that of the Grateful Dead, whose community of fans diligently followed them from show to show. The high level of engagement created a desire to not be one that missed out on the stories, memories, and occurrences that took place from night to night.

Overall, if you can, do things that get those interested in what you do to interact with one another, then you, too, can begin building your tribe. This is done in the modern world through a variety of online activities, some of which are likely to involve critiquing what might seem like every note you play, often with candor that might be hard to embrace. If you can't handle the criticism, opinions, or input, then don't read it. It might be better for some of you to do exactly that, meaning avoid it. One thing you certainly should *not* do is enter these discussions with a sense of anger. Remember, these folks are taking their own time to discuss what you are doing, so just let them do it. The chance of pleasing everyone is precisely ZERO. In the end, the more they are involved which one another, the bigger your community becomes, so embrace it.

Casting the Right-Size Net with Marketing and Publicity

In 2014, U2 released *Songs of Innocence*. The band and Apple thought it would be a brilliant idea to give away the album and simply have it pop up in five hundred million iTunes users' music library. After all, everyone would certainly love receiving a free album, and as a result they would make new fans! Unfortunately, A LOT of people got angry instead because the unsolicited new music took up limited space on their devices. The unforeseen consequences of the automatic download stirred a huge backlash against the band. The lesson to be learned is when you're looking for new fans, it's important to target those who are most likely to be interested. Those unlikely to be interested, for whatever reason, are a drain on your promotional budgets, time, and effort and regardless of your offering will continue not being interested.

USING SOCIAL MEDIA EFFECTIVELY

Social media is modern word of mouth. If your music is good, ask your friends and acquaintances to help spread the word online. This power of suggestion by those you know and find credible far outweighs anything you can purchase. Instagram, Snapchat, Twitter, Facebook Live, and Periscope are all great ways to showcase short video snippets of your music. Whether it's behind the scenes footage or actual performances, use these mediums to help spread the word. In addition to having official accounts spreading your music, personal accounts on these same platforms will help you interact with fans and potentially make new ones. When engaging those interested through these social media platforms it's important to offer something different, not just some same stuff easily found on your website, albums, or recent publications. Try some live Q&A sessions on these platforms. Give those that are paying attention the ability to access you on some level. It's amazing what some mild involvement with your fans through these channels can do for your growth.

CASTING A WIDE NET WITHOUT BREAKING THE BANK

If things are going well for you, then more and more people begin noticing what you are up to. Eventually, you are likely to come across opportunities that at first might seem like they will provide immediate revenue. However, using a long-term outlook, these situations may in fact have a lot more potential value when it comes to exposure as compared to the short-term income provided. In some cases you might exponentially increase the exposure factor by removing the revenue component altogether. The following is an example of how Umphrey's McGee did this when the opportunity presented itself.

CASTING A NET INTO NEW WATERS: AROUND THE HORN

A few year ago, Umphrey's McGee rerecorded and performed the theme music for a TV show on ESPN called *Around the Horn*. As a result, this version of the show's theme plays daily, and they also include a little bit of another song, "Bad Friday," as bumper music (aka, snippets used to buffer transitions between segments). This opportunity presented itself when the producer of the show, who is a fan of the band, asked for help trying to find someone to redo their theme. So we answered back, "Why not us?" And the rest is history. There are more than one million daily viewers of *Around the Horn*, so our music is regularly reaching new listeners, even if it's just a few seconds of music with an added credit line. Having music on a major television program adds credibility to your name and brand, regardless of whether you're getting paid for it or not.

CASTING A NET WITH MIXED RESULTS: CHICAGO

Not everything you try will work out the way you intended. Back in 2011, Umphrey's McGee was presented with the opportunity to create a theme song for the Chicago Board of Tourism. We were able to collaborate with Buddy Guy and the horn section from Chicago in the process, *but* were given specific lyrics to use. We did our best to come up with something that the city liked. By the time we reached the finished product, it was certainly more of an ad than an actual song. However, the public had a largely negative reaction to it and some people were confused into thinking it was an actual song Umphrey's McGee was releasing. The furor didn't last long, but serves as a good example of something that seemed like a great opportunity yet didn't turn out quite as expected.

INJECTING PERSONALITY INTO SOCIAL MEDIA AND TECHNOLOGY

When trying to connect with the outside world using technology and social media, it's important to note that the most sustainable connections happen when we treat things more personally and try to connect person to person. Ask questions and engage people on social media. There will be moments of agreement and disagreement, but interacting and responding is the most important action. Take a look at Joel's Twitter feed (@goldlikejoel) and you will see him connecting with people via conversations about everything from music to sports to travel. If what you are regularly posting doesn't invoke someone's desire to respond, then it likely isn't interesting or effective.

Unless your music is political or religious, it is probably best to avoid the topics altogether. Both are subjects that many are very passionate about. Since most have differing opinions, the chance that yours align well are slim to none. These topics and your comments are much more likely to invoke a negative set of emotions. You have more to lose than to gain.

ENDURING FAILURE AND HANDLING NEGATIVE FEEDBACK

There will be people—trolls and merely the over-opinionated—who don't like what you do and feel the need to let you know. Sometimes they'll be right and sometimes they'll be way off base. There's a difference between constructive criticism and trolling, but the point to remember is that once your music is out there, your intent no longer matters. People interpret music how *they* want to and that's okay. Accept that the public's perception of your music might not align with your own. Often what we believe is our strongest work is perceived to be average and what we as artists might see as average is viewed as excellent. You never know what people will like so don't get too invested in others' opinions of your work. Remember, those involved are taking their own time to discuss what you are doing, regardless of their opinion of it. They are involving themselves with what you do.

It's okay to take notice of what your audience likes, but don't let it inform you too much or your vision might become lost. Remember that without art there are no critics.

PERSONAL CONNECTIONS

When interacting with fans, be kind and say yes to quick photos as much as you can. Photos and selfies are the new autographs, and people love to have that visual memento of a personal connection to an artist they like. Some fans still want autographs, so carry a Sharpie with you just in case.

One thing you can do to make interactions more natural and less one-sided is to ask your fans about their lives. They'll likely be pleasantly surprised by your interest, and it'll make the interaction more rewarding for both of you. If you're feeling social, have a drink or two with show attendees and fans.

CREATING VIP EXPERIENCES

Once you've established yourself you can start to offer VIP experiences. These can be anything from meet and greets to a couple of songs performed for a smaller group during sound check to doing a step and repeat photo with people. The number one rule when offering VIP stuff is under promise and over deliver. You don't want to put too much out there and it's always great to have people who've paid a little extra receive something on top of what they expected. VIP experiences can help create personal connections while adding revenue to your shows.

ADDITIONAL WAYS TO CONNECT

One of the most important ways to connect with fans is simply giving away as much music as possible. Releasing music on individual platforms is a very good idea if you have a song that has a particular style that you think would appeal to a different demographic than your typical demographic. Once you're releasing music, put things out on different platforms and allow different publications or sites to have exclusive rights to a song's debut. Also, any opportunity to create video content to accompany your audio will only give you a better shot at more people hearing your music, which should be the ultimate goal.

TOP FIVE THINGS IMPOSSIBLE TO FAKE (FOR LONG)

1) **Talent**. If you're a below-average musician who is aided by Auto-Tune and other technology, it won't last. Just ask Milli Vanilli.

2) **Experience**. You will learn most from doing what you do over and over again. And there are no shortcuts. You just have to keep doing it. That's how you're going to learn.

3) **Hype**. The hype train is usually a short-lived burst of interest. Be able to deliver on the hype or people will eventually see through it.

4) **Honesty**. Don't be a liar. It's going to bring you and everyone else down around you. Building trust in all your relationships—internal and external—will earn you respect.

5) **Profitability**. If you're consistently losing money you may want to consider looking at reasons why and make a change. A short-term loss is one thing, but to exude an image of success, you need to actually be successful.

TOP FIVE WAYS TO REMAIN LIKEABLE

1) Take the music seriously but don't take *yourself* too seriously. Be real and show that you're human. Demonstrate that you care but also be willing to make a self-deprecating joke about yourself.

2) Put on the best show you can regardless of the crowd size. You never know who might be in the audience.

3) Be efficient with your load in and load out. House crews and other artists will appreciate your show of respect and the fans will enjoy less downtime between artists. Being organized is always a plus.

4) Give to local charities with your show. Giving back to a local community is an excellent way to make a difference while you're on tour, while also spurring more interest in your music.

5) Take chances. Don't play it safe with your music or your shows. Keep people on the edge of their seats.

A CONVERSATION WITH ALICIA KARLIN

It's likely that everyone you know has been to a concert, festival, special event, or venue of some kind. What's less likely is that they know how the process of getting those involved in such events happens. That is where booking agents, talent buyers, and talent procurement professionals often enter the picture. Alicia Karlin, the vice president of Talent for Madison House Presents, knows all about artist management, festival and event production, artist relations, and VIP services.

Madison House Presents, a division of AEG Presents with whom Alicia has worked with for more than a decade, has a long history of producing live events, festivals, and special events. Some of the more notable amongst a long, long list are the Electric Forest Festival, the Mumford & Sons's Gentlemen of the Road Tour and the Fare Thee Well performances that brought the remaining members of the Grateful Dead back together for their 50th anniversary. All of that said, let's hear more of what Alicia has to say about the industry.

JOEL: You worked on events when you were in college. Did you know at that point that that's what you wanted to do in the music business?

ALICIA: I was at University of Florida and started dipping my toe into events and music business stuff. I immediately decided that that's what I wanted to do, and started working outside of school on events, like at the radio station in Gainesville, and getting internships at different music business companies.

What were some early lessons you learned as a promoter?

I quickly learned as a promoter that money is very easy come, easy go. And a lot of people are here today, gone tomorrow. I think being smart and responsible, building a good reputation as a normal, responsible person was important.

Do you think it's important early on to take as many opportunities as possible?

Yeah, I do for sure. I was able to build my network a lot quicker that way. I was booking shows at University of Florida with national agencies and nationally touring bands and making relationships with agents from the time that I was nineteen.

After you graduated from college, what was the first step that you took?

I interned at Artist Group International in New York, working for Dennis Arfa, who reps Billy Joel. Their agency also reps Metallica, Rod Stewart, and a bunch of different bands. I enjoyed it and thought that I was going to work there full-time. I got a job offer to do so, too, but some friends that I had gone to college with had moved out to Boulder, Colorado and were working with Madison House Publicity. They said the quality of life in Boulder was amazing and suggested I come check it out. I did and soon started interning at Madison House Publicity and Madison House Booking and Management simultaneously. Within a month or so, it turned into a full-time job, and then the stars kind of aligned when AEG Live opened a Denver office. Don Strasburg, who had recently left Live Nation to come over to AEG, asked who he could hire as an assistant. He interviewed and hired me that same day. After the interview he said, "Okay, go upstairs and get your computer and come downstairs. Now you work here."

That was how it all started, being in the right place at the right time. I was able to help open up the AEG Denver office, which is now one of the biggest promoter offices in the country.

Is there any decision that stands out as one that really set you on your current path?

I always thought that I would be in New York. Always. I'm from South Florida, an East Coast Jewish girl. I didn't know anything about Colorado. Then I just decided to move there, after coming out here once. That definitely changed the direction of my career path.

When you're working on events, what are you looking for in up-and-coming artists before you book them at an event?

Number one, you look for some sort of traction, whether it's a single, radio, streaming, or live touring, depending on the genre, or where the event is. For Electric Forest, I look at people who are making a splash or up and coming in Michigan and Chicago, and able to sell tickets across the Midwest. Also, I listen to trusted agents and managers who tell me, "Hey, I just started working with this person." I know that they have limited time and limited space on their own rosters, so if they're willing to invest in these artists, they're probably worth checking out.

If you're giving advice to an artist, what do you think they should be focusing on so they can earn money and get noticed by promoters or management?

It depends on what type of artist they are. If they're a producer or DJ, you can make a lot of money on streaming and not ever have to tour. If you are a band, you need to focus on your live show when you're first starting. Focus on building a fan base wherever you are and growing that. Support bigger artists when they come through your markets. This gets the local promoters to know who you are and saying that you're a reliable band with a good draw, a good opening act. These are all great first steps to being noticed in a bigger way.

Electric Forest has been a huge destination event in the United States for fans of EDM, rock, and jam-centric music. What are the most important elements of Electric Forest that have led to its continued success?

Well, I would love to say that it's just the music, because that's what I oversee. But it's not. It's the total experience. It's the art. It's the immersive nature of the event. The fan community there is really different from any other festival in the country. We've taken ten years to hammer home the message that there is going to be diverse music at that show. You can see a four-hour set or a forty-five-minute set. There's no set rule for any stage or set length or the way that the schedule works, and I think that's one of the most important elements in the music programming. I really try to pay attention to every single act on the bill—when they're playing, who they're playing against, what time they're playing, and take six months to build that and move it around, to make sure that it's perfect. It's never perfect, but we try.

What advice do you have for women in the industry—both as an artist or someone on the production or promotion side?

I think being around other women in the industry, and learning from them and talking to them, being part of networking groups or social groups, is a really great way to understand the similarities and differences, the struggles, and the things that are great. That's been helpful for me.

Is there any area in particular you see women achieving more success than in the past?

I definitely see more female general managers of venues, production managers, and tour managers since I started. I think that speaks to the openness of the business in general, and women feeling empowered to start careers in venues and production.

Do you have anything that stands out as the best career advice you've ever received?

I have not ever subscribed to the "just keep your head down and do your job" mentality. I've always been a big mouth, and kind of pushed my way into wherever it was I was trying to go. For me, that's been part of my success—not just being okay with whatever comes next or pushing down one door at a time. I have personally tried to jump over obstacles and through doors in order to fast-track certain things.

I think that's very true. There's value when it comes to being assertive and speaking your mind. There are all kinds of things that can happen if you're not afraid to take a chance.

Lastly, do you have anything that stands out as the worst career advice you've ever received?

Yeah. "Don't rock the boat." Or "This is how things are done here."

SECTION TEN:

MARKETING AND MERCH

Merchandise serves the dual purpose of creating a revenue stream and providing free advertising. You should have a merch table at every show where people can also sign up for your mailing list. Point out the location while you're onstage and consider dropping by the merch table when your set is done to meet fans and help move some merch. Even if the venue has a local person selling your stuff, you'll be more likely to sell things if you or someone working with you can interact with potential buyers. While your ticketing revenue and percentages can vary wildly, most venues will give the artist 85 to 90 percent of merch sales, so you can see how it's advantageous to sell merchandise at shows.

TECHNOLOGY AND STREAMING

The days of downloading music are quickly coming to an end. In fact, by the time you're reading this, Apple might no longer be offering downloads from their iTunes store. This is a perfect example of how quickly technology can change things and how you have to pay attention to where the future is leading. So where *is* it leading? Streaming!

STREAMING PLATFORMS AND IDEAS

Once considered to be the mortal enemy of the recording industry, streaming music, or what was once file sharing, is now the most favored delivery method of the industry. Once you have some recordings, get them on streaming platforms like Spotify, Amazon, YouTube, Apple Music, and Tidal. The goal is to get as many spins as possible—not just for potential payouts, but because that's how something starts going viral. Streaming platforms are now lead indicators for what might become a hit on the radio. That's right, streaming is now ahead of radio. Focus more on getting the spins than getting the sales.

Syd Schwartz, formerly of Sony Music, states that playlists and songs are moving beyond genre descriptions to moods or time of day. Think "morning coffee," "afternoon workout," or "breakup songs." This is how playlists now get traction, and they're constantly updating. Ask yourself, what's the context that a song of yours is most likely to fit? Target specific themes and words to help find an audience and get your music on playlists.

UMPHREY'S MCGEE'S SUPER BOWL: UMBOWL

Back in 2010, when many of the social media platforms popular today were beginning to take hold, we decided that we would create an event featuring as much fan interaction as we could imagine. We called it UMBowl and announced it on Super Bowl Sunday as the Super Bowl of Umphrey's events. There would be four quarters and each would feature a unique way the fans helped select the music we played, with some voting in advance and some voting in the moment at the show.

One of the most interesting of the quarters featured live texting from fans guiding the band's improvisation. Input and suggestions could be as specific as "metal disco groove" or as oblique as "sand passing through the hourglass." The best part: There were really no wrong answers for us musically. The ideas only required us to use our collective imaginations. The second most interesting quarter featured past improvisations that we then reworked into songs. In this case, the fans voted in advance for their favorite past improvisations from a selection of thirty to thirty-five we presented. After voting concluded, we then tried to see what we could piece together from the winning improvisations to create a song and/or recreate the best parts of the improv. It was one of the craziest things we've ever attempted. We felt that creating new material out of popular segments of music would be a hit with fans, and it very much was.

UMBowl was a unique opportunity for the band to interact with fans in one of the most personal ways imaginable, involving them in the creative process. As a result, roughly fifteen songs we regularly play were created using the techniques described above, or through fan-sourced songwriting.

TOP FIVE DECISIONS THAT WILL HELP YOUR BRAND

1) Work with people who are as passionate as you are about your art. Inspiration is one of the best things to have, so make sure you're creating with people that inspire you and, hopefully, are even better musicians than you.

2) Create music that you believe in with true intentions. If it's from the heart, it will likely reach someone else. If it's superficial, it probably won't resonate long term.

3) Interact with your fans on social media. Give them new insights into music and your craft. Share your successes, failures, and moments of levity.

4) Learn from your mistakes. It's okay to make a mistake once, but don't learn the hard way twice.

5) Be thankful to anyone who helps you, be it a radio DJ or stagehand. Being a thankful and grateful person to someone who is out there working on your behalf will bring goodwill.

A CONVERSATION WITH SYD SCHWARTZ

After an impressive thirty-year career heading up the digital marketing for many of the world's most well-known bands, such as the Rolling Stones and Beastie Boys, Syd is now a vice president for Legacy Recordings, a Sony Music Entertainment company. As the founder of his own marketing and strategy firm, Linchpin Digital, Syd is also involved in the Mockingbird Foundation, which is dedicated to supporting and funding youth music education.

JOEL: Say you've recorded some music now. How do you get people to hear what you're doing?

SYD: The good news is that distribution is no longer a barrier. There are no shortages of ways to get your music out there. What is important to remember is that, from a digital perspective, unless you are up there in the hundreds of millions of streams and enormous amounts of downloads—and my guess is by the time this book is published, the notion of downloads may actually be the old way of doing things, which is mind-boggling—you shouldn't look at any of those ways as your primary way of earning revenue. They may generate *some* revenue and income, which is nice, but all (including YouTube) are largely ways to help you and your audience find one another. Getting it out in as many platforms as possible is really important yet equally important is thinking very carefully about metadata so you can both be found AND be properly compensated.

One of the interesting things about being a musician in the current age is that you have to have a much broader skillset than the musicians of, say, the fifties, sixties, seventies, and largely eighties, where knowing how to play your instrument and write and arrange and maybe produce a little was about as much as you needed to do, in addition to maybe knowing how to dress so that MTV might actually play your video.

Now you need to know a little bit more about how people are likely to find your music so you need to think a lot about not making words in your songs particularly difficult to be found via a Google search.

There's a quote in *This Is Spinal Tap* where they talk about there being a fine line between clever and stupid. That has become truer than ever. And context has largely replaced genre. What I mean by that is you used to go into a record store or a Wal-Mart or Tesco and go, "Oh there's the rock section and there's the country section," etc. For the most part, what we are seeing now is that people aren't really looking for music that way anymore. People are thinking about music in terms of "morning jog" or "afternoon workout" or "relaxation." They're thinking about the context in which they're living their lives and what music is going to fit into that context. So instead of musicians thinking, "We're kind of an Afro reggae polka metal thing," imagine as much, "*Where* is this song/album/collection of music likely to resonate?" I don't want to say that playlists have replaced the album but I think that they kind of sit alongside it as a mechanism for containing a collection of tracks.

So how do you get noticed if you have, say, a "morning coffee" song? How do you get noticed by somebody who's putting up playlists that lots of people are listening to with this particular idea?

It's a great question. I mean the first thing is that you may be very convinced that a song is the perfect "morning coffee" song. And you may not be right.

The good news is because of data, and all the ways in which you can slice and dice it, now you can actually test that theory. Spotify in particular can measure two very important things. One is called skip rate. How often are people skipping your song within a playlist. And if you have a high skip rate, that's probably not great news. That means you're in the wrong place within the playlist or you're in the wrong playlist. There's also something called attach rate and it's a really important metric. Attach rate is when someone is so into the song that they click on that little plus sign (if they're on Spotify), which adds it to their collection. Statistics show that person is four times more likely to play that song again if it's in their own collection. And this is very much a game of bulk and volume and numbers, so attach rates are important. If your song has a high attach rate but also a high skip rate, it means people like your song but they don't like the context in which it's in. Even if you think it's a great "morning coffee" song, maybe it's in their "breakup song" or it's a better "jogging" or "driving" song.

If you're trying to figure out what is the song good for, do you talk to your friends?

Talking to friends is great provided the friends are good enough friends that they're not just going to tell you everything you want to hear. Music is very subjective; it's very personal, but the truth of the matter is absolutely you want to ask as many people as possible to get an objective perspective.

All right, let's shift gears and talk about something that is really specific to you. How do you get started as an artist? And is it even important to get signed by a label at this point?

I would say that that the second question is the one you probably need to answer first. When people talk about getting signed—and certainly you have to go back a number of years to relate—I lay the blame for the desire to get signed squarely on the shoulders of Jon Bon Jovi. He had that song where he rides "the steel horse" and he stares pensively out the window of his private jet rapping his knuckles on the window at the rain coming down and he leads a tough life after his manager has wrapped him snugly in a fluffy bathrobe . . . apparently it gets chilly after you've rocked them all. Everyone who saw that video was like, "I want that. I want to rock them all! Have people take care of me and fly private jets!" etc. And the reality is that's probably not going to happen if you get signed to a label. Signing to a label is a strategic decision because you decided you need a team of experienced executives who are going to help further your career. You have to decide whether a label is what you want to do versus taking a do-it-yourself approach, such as Umphrey's McGee has done by surrounding themselves with people who have built their own experience and a circle of trusted friends and colleagues who can help them get from place to place in a manner of their own choosing, doing it at their own speed, and on their own terms. That has upsides and downsides.

It definitely means that access to the movie and TV music supervisors of the world and certain other things are not as open to them as they would be if you're with Warner Music or Universal or others who can with one phone call get the Super Bowl people on the phone or whomever it happens to be.

But also understand that those slots are one in ten thousand. One hundred thousand. One in a million. That's gambling. And you lose a lot of freedom. It's what some people might refer to as indentured servitude, going to sign for a label.

Now would you say in general, and of course this isn't true for everything, if you're trying to produce something that is more top 40 music, the label might be more important? Whereas if you're trying to do something that is a little more niche-oriented, as far as the genre, that may not be as important.

Yes. As we're speaking here in mid-October 2017, pop music is largely hip-hop. EDM is pop music. And it's a very crowded marketplace. You need the support of streaming services. Of radio. The artists that are having success there, if you look at their stream counts you're talking in the tens and hundreds of millions in singles. Three hundred and fifty million streams may sound like a whole lot but because oftentimes they may have eleven cowriters and five producers, that's not a lot of money at .0084 cents per stream or whatever the formula might be once you do the math.

You divide that amongst a whole bunch of people and if that's the *only* big hit in a seven or eight-year career arc you don't get to retire on that. You have to think about whether you're a career artist or you have a hit single and then go on to become an accountant. If you're really thinking about being a career artist where you develop a base of a couple of thousand or a few thousand fans and you want to tour x number of nights a year, maybe put out some new music at your own pace, and maybe do some teaching, write some music for film or television or video games, and do a variety of things. In an economy now where people are coming out of college or high school and thinking about *I'm going to work at this store for a while. Or I'm going to do some work in the evening. Or I'm going to teach for a while.* It's no longer the notion of this kind of nine-to-five job and you work at a company for twenty-five years or whatever it is.

I'd like to hear what the biggest upside and the biggest downside is to getting signed to a label and then the biggest upside and the downside to doing it independently.

As I mentioned, the upside to signing to a label is you are getting a large team generally of experienced people who are connected. You are going to be funded and people can help. It smooths out some of the rough edges. One of the things that I think labels do pretty successfully is media training. Part of what you need to do in building your image is to get in front of a camera and speak in public. Labels will help train you in those things. The downside of that is that the label is going to tell you to do things you may not be happy doing. For instance, they may go to you and say you need to shave forty seconds off of the single that you thought was absolutely perfect in order to get it on the radio. Or you have an opportunity to be on *The Tonight Show Starring Jimmy Fallon* but you have to cut a song down to two and a half minutes instead of five minutes. You may view some of those things as artistic compromises. Art and marketing are sometimes enemies and there can be difficult conversations. And the other thing is that sometimes the label will stop paying attention at a time you feel they should be paying attention.

As for going independent, the biggest pro is that you can do things on your own terms and build and surround yourself with a team of people that you know and trust and believe in. You know everyone shares the value system and your belief in what you want to accomplish as an artist. The downside to that is they may be struggling as hard as you from a financial standpoint. Or they may not have the juice to get to Jon Pareles at the *New York Times* to get the review that you're looking for and it may be an equally frustrating battle to cut through the clutter.

I think the one of the hardest things is figuring out what you should do first. What advice would you give to someone just starting out?

Don't sign anything. Never. Seriously don't sign unless it's a contract with the venue for a gig. Even if you're going to sign a contract with the venue for a gig, if you've got a friend who's in law school, make sure he's there at your side so that you're not signing something that ends up coming back to bite you in the ass.

I always recommending that the artist be the one who initiates the contract. Have a kind of statutory contract to use so that it's not something that you're getting roped into with a lot of fine print.

If you don't know what you're doing in a negotiation, you're going to get beat. That's good advice for life in general. If you don't know what you're doing, stop the conversation and find someone who knows what they're doing. This is why you need a team, whether it's a label or a team that you built yourself. The other advice I would give is get paid. There are any number of people in the music industry who will tell you that you should do something for free because it's good promotion or it's good for *awareness*. I have news for you. If you try to pay your rent or your mortgage with awareness, or you go to a store and at the register ask, "Can I pay with awareness?"—you're not going to get a very good reaction. Always get paid. Establish upfront that the work you do has value and make sure that's the baseline you start from.

What are some other opportunities to create revenue streams early on in your career?

As cheesy as this is going to sound, I have heard more income stream success stories from up and coming artists who find local businesses who are making television commercials for a local cable access who are looking for something other than crappy incidental music to use as backgrounds. They are looking for people to compose something for them and they don't have a lot of money. No one can afford to license "Satisfaction" by the Rolling Stones. But you know what they *can* do? They can pay you a couple of hundred dollars to record a cover of "Satisfaction" because they don't have to pay master licensing use for something like that or an original instrumental thing. If you're interested in doing such things and you have a band members who are into video games, try jamming along to someone playing a racing game or a fighting game or something to see how that comes out. You never know. Upload those things to YouTube and you never know when someone's going to stumble across something and go, *"That's* exactly what I'm looking for!"

But how do you get into the video game licensing or something that sounds like a little bit more national platform?

There are a number of online platforms similar to Angie's List, where artists that do this type of work basically say, "We are a metal band and if you need music for a video game, here's what we can do and how we do it," etc. These include Synchtank and Jingle Punks.

What are ways that you can build an audience? Is there a secret to how to do this most efficiently or successfully?

I don't know that there are secrets as much as there are a couple of obvious things that I think sometimes get overlooked. You definitely want to make sure to capture people at the moment they decided that they're interested. For example, many artists don't get this right with their e-mail list. An e-mail list sounds like ancient technology. Who reads e-mail anymore? It's all about social media and texting and Snapchatting, etc. Wrong—because 93 percent of people who have computers check their e-mail at least three times a day. Somehow or another this one bit of technology has not evaporated out of our lives.

But it's vastly under-utilized. I guarantee you right now if you were to go to find your favorite artist and sign up for their e-mail list, you'd type your e-mail address, click a button, and on the screen it says, "Thanks. You'll hear from us soon." Well, okay. And even if you *do* get an automated reply, it says, "Thanks for subscribing. Click here to unsubscribe." That's not a welcome e-mail; that's an unwelcome e-mail. If you're going to set up an e-mail list, welcome people at that point in time when they're most interested. They just gave you their e-mail address. Offer them something right away and then tell them you've got a Twitter, Facebook page, and Instagram account. And by the way here's 20 percent off at the merch thing. Here's a link to it by the way if you want a T-shirt. And if you invite three friends to the e-mail list we'll give you whatever but really make them feel *appreciated* for the fact that they're interested. Like really show them that you're interested. It's not that hard. There are free tools out there to do this. You don't have to sit there and do your job. Put a little thought into it. Stay in touch with your fans. Don't ever have to have that horrible conversation that starts with "so how are we going to reconnect with/reactivate the fan base?"

What's a good way to have this same sort of connection and experience at a live show? How do you get them to sign up for your e-mail list or something. What should you promote from stage?

It's a similar thing. "Text us at X and we'll hit you back with the set list you heard tonight." There are so many ways that one can do that. Tweet out the set list as it's happening. Things like that make it easy for people to connect with you. If they bought tickets, thank them for coming to the show. Drop me an e-mail. Offer a free ticket for a friend if they bring one the next time. There are any number of ways of making people feel appreciated.

This seems like a good segue to whittle that into social media. How much focus should the actual artists be putting into social media? And what is a good balance of keeping things more artistic versus trying to promote what's going on?

Easy question, complicated answer. First of all, it's very personal. Social media is a very personal thing. People have a different relationship with it. Some people are more private about it. Some people are more public about it. I think the challenge is that expectation management becomes a full-time job.

If you start off really aggressive out of the gate—you know replying to every tweet, thanking, etc.—and all of a sudden you get busy and don't have time to continue that, you can unfairly be seen as bad guy. I would say, if there's a particular social platform that you enjoy, that's great. And think about initially starting it as more of a broad "conversation." If you're into photography, use Instagram and broadcast out. This way people have a lens into another facet of your world and you can do it at your own pace and it's not necessarily a dialogue.

Continuing about social media, how do you expand your social media web? Other than hashtags, what are ways to have other people notice what's going on with you?

Don't rush into doing it before spending some time studying how others are doing it. Some people are just really preternaturally great at certain aspects of social media. Start following them and seeing how you can get into the conversation. And once that starts happening you develop a bit of a feel for it. Certainly, hashtags are important, but we all know the people who use like nine thousand of them in every single post. That level of desperation is probably not a great look.

Also, I feel it's smart to keep somewhat specific to what people are interested in talking to you about. In other words, if you're doing musical things, try to post videos in various content that's about music. It's fun to engage people who enjoy your music about *other* music and even possibly introduce them to some other new stuff. That's a really fun way to open the dialogue a little bit. All of a sudden, your fans are very excited because they feel like, *Oh wow, this person is a fan too. We can relate on that level.*

Ask fans for recommendations. You know you're getting on the tour bus. What should we add to the Netflix queue? That can be a terrific conversation starter. And give thanks for the recommendation. Do so and you just made some fan's year.

Are there things you should stay away from on social media? Politics? Religion?

Yeah, both of those. And be extra mindful of humor. It always sounds funny in your head but coming out of your mouth or in

280 characters, it is not nearly as funny. There are really funny people on Twitter. Unless enough people have told you you're as funny as those people, you're not that funny. And when those jokes fall flat it can be costly. Also, I hope by the time this book is published we're in an era that maybe people have learned how to disagree with each other online respectfully. It seems like right now every topic is sensitive and if you kind of stick to the music thing it's probably okay.

The other thing your mom probably said at some point is if you don't have anything nice to say, don't say it. It's really great advice. But here's the best advice I have ever been given.

When I called my grandmother to tell her that I was getting engaged, she had just celebrated her fifty-fifth wedding anniversary. I asked her, "What's the secret, Grandma?" I'll tell you, this is the first and only time in her life I ever heard her swear. She said, "It's really pretty simple. When you're wrong, admit it. And when you're right, shut the fuck up."

And I will tell you that in marriage, business, friendships, and just generally in life, no one likes to hear "I told you so." And everyone likes it when you're man or woman enough to say, "I was wrong about that and I'm sorry." If you can remember those things, and act on them, you'll be fine. So thanks, Grandma!

SECTION ELEVEN:

MANAGEMENT

There are ten thousand sayings that could be but won't be inserted here—most of which reference the importance of having a strong foundation. When you start out you'll likely not have management, which leaves you handling most managerial tasks yourself. That's okay. It's actually better for you to appreciate firsthand this part of your business. In the beginning, you should be focused on creating music and prove that you can draw crowds big enough to garner interest in your work before you become overly concerned with your representation. Do your best to stay organized and keep things simple as you're getting the ball rolling.

RIGHT NOTE: If you're multitasking at the start of your career, don't reveal that you are the actual artist when reaching out to talent buyers and clubs to get gigs. You'll be able to get more leverage if the talent buyer doesn't know you're in the band. After your first gig at a given club the talent buyer will likely figure it out, but it always looks better if it appears that someone other than a band member or artist is representing the band.

The Ins and Outs of Securing Management

How do you want yourself represented within the industry? This is an important consideration when trying to determine or choose management. Your manager will likely be your point of contact for everyone in the music industry. Knowing this, it's important that this person has people skills. A manager should also have experience with money, business, and business management, as this person will likely be highly involved in both short-term and long-term money management. Your manager should also be someone with the ability to mediate relations between band members or other artists when needed. Finally, your manager will need to have a good idea of balance for short-term and long-term vision, in addition to helping you develop that vision.

Let's take a look at some of the factors that will help you find the right person to represent YOU and your art. Most artists start with this question: Do I want a manager who only works on my music or should I find someone who has experience and works for other artists as well? There are good reasons why both choices might be right for you. As you meet other artists, it's often a good idea to start talking to them and their managers to help you decide which route to pursue. Your manager will likely require 15 to 20 percent of your revenue, so it's very important that you choose someone you feel will be the right fit. Remember, what seems like a small amount of money now, might very well be a whole lot later. It's okay to want a return on this investment and expense.

MANAGERS WITH A ROSTER OF ARTISTS

A manager who is already working with other artists likely has some things going for him or her. They should have established connections with talent buyers, other artists, and possibly agents. The possible downside resides in time drain. Your manager's time will undoubtedly be spent according to who makes the most money. If you're not doing well, you may not get much attention. This comes down to the classic scenario of being the small fish in the big pond.

MANAGERS FOCUSED ON ONE ARTIST

A manager who is only focused on you and your art has some advantages. The number one advantage is that your success is paramount to theirs, so there's a mutual trust and commitment that will run deep. Chances are also likely that someone just managing you and no one else really believes in the music that you're making. It's a lot easier to sell an artist when the person selling is a staunch advocate. Inexperience might be an issue, but if your manager is personable, he or she could seek out other managers for advice or when questions arise.

WHAT IF YOUR MANAGEMENT ISN'T WORKING OUT?

Establish from the beginning what will happen if things don't work out. A big mistake with creative agreements is only planning for what can and will happen when things go well. If things don't, hopefully you can agree to an amicable split, as it's never good to burn bridges. Always try to make adjustments or changes before you terminate someone, unless they've been dishonest with money or some other aspect of your business. Dishonesty runs rampant in some parts of the business so having a manager with good character and a moral compass is a wise idea. Communication will solve most problems, but if they can't be solved, move on and try to learn from the mistake of making a hire that didn't work out.

UMPHREY'S MCGEE AND MANAGEMENT BY JOEL CUMMINS

We started with one manager, Vince Iwinski, who was a friend of the band and expressed interest in representing us. Vince loved our music and believed in everyone involved, so it was a very natural fit. He didn't have much experience but immediately dove in and learned as much as he could. He started while holding down a forty-hour a week job, yet eventually left that once it became financially realistic for him to focus on the band full-time. Vince worked very hard to learn about the business and to meet as many people in the business as possible. He is a great example of an artist finding someone on the outside of the business who believed in the music enough to become a successful manager.

By 2010, Vince was stretched thin as our business expanded and we realized that we were missing some opportunities because there was too much work to get done. We turned to an internal solution and brought on Kevin Browning, our former front-of-house engineer, to comanage with Vince. Vince now handles the day-to-day and touring needs while Kevin tackles content management, technology, and social media. Kevin's also the point man for our own record label, which we started back in 2014. Adding Kevin to the management team changed our business in a myriad of positive ways, as it created some new revenue streams, relieved pressure where it was becoming overwhelming, and allowed us to focus more on putting out consistent musical content in addition to the many tour dates.

BOOKING AGENT

A booking agent is someone dedicated to getting you gigs, making sure contracts are signed, and helping to execute a long-term vision. Most artists first hire a manager who then helps them find the right agent. If you're playing mostly local gigs, you might not need an agent yet, as the agent's expertise should be national and sometimes international touring. Some agents operate independently, while others have very high-profile agencies, such as William Morris, Paradigm, or Creative Artists Agency (CAA). Some have differing opinions on booking agents. Keep in mind that they are more or less performance-based salespeople that work for you. Meaning, if they don't get you work, then they don't get paid either. It is in their best interest to get you work, and this is a good thing.

WHY THE AGENCY MATTERS

When booking agents are part of a larger agency they not only have access to much more information, they also likely have a stable of artists with whom they work. This is important for a few reasons, but most importantly, you will have direct access to other similar artists. This can potentially lead to a number of productive and interesting things, including collaborations and co-bills or tours with these other artists. Depending on your genre, some agencies are more inclined to a certain style of artist. In the end, the one that does the best job for you is or was the best choice. However, it might be a lot easier to establish a relationship with an agency that is already working with other acts that are considered to be in your genre.

WHAT WILL A GOOD AGENT DO?

A good agent will help you:
- Develop a plan for touring both short-term and long-term
- Get you the best deals possible with the right promoters in an given market and be looking out for you at every turn
- Know the signals of good and bad deals through their previous experience
- Find opportunities to put you in front of new fans
- Put together sensible tour routes so you're playing in the right cities on the correct nights
- Get involved in settlement if there is a discrepancy

WHAT WILL A BAD AGENT DO?

A bad agent:
- Does not pay attention to the details, or worse, neglects your band
- Does not look out for your best interests nor create a sensible long-term plan for you
- Is unreliable or unavailable

In order to avoid the bad-agent scenario, set expectations and goals right from the beginning so that your agent can try to properly execute your vision. This is back to our previous discussion about creating agreements and contracts that account for the good *and* the bad. This is all just part of running a solid business.

EXPENSE AND PERSONNEL MANAGEMENT

If you're only touring for a couple of months and then going off the road for an extended period, it doesn't make sense to put people on salary. However, if you're making your living by playing live shows, it *does* make sense to find and keep the best people. Put them on salary and offer healthcare because this is going to be your team and, in a sense, "family."

When putting together a crew for the long term you want people who are hardworking and go above and beyond what they're what they're supposed to be doing. You don't just hire your buddy who wants to come out and party on the road with you. That only makes things more fun for the very short term. These are the people you're going to surround yourself with for many years, so these decisions are important. Working with the same people means they don't have to be retrained constantly and allows them to grow with you. This leads to a lot more consistency with your shows and much more fun if everybody gets along.

Next is the question of do you choose those with expertise or ones with less proven skills but undeniable passion? The answer is specific to your band, finding a balance of both kinds of people can work best. A lot of times having someone with experience running front of house roles, like running your lights and the more technical things, is important. But some of the other positions can be filled by people who are willing to learn what is required. Their passion aims to get it done right.

Your crew is an investment. Do they want to do this for five years? Ten years? Or are they just looking for something for six months? It's important to find out what other people's intentions are to help you narrow down your search and succeed.

Before we move on, there are a few things that will universally lead to those around you either losing interest or, more importantly, a passion for you or what you are doing. This translates not only to those that come to see your shows, but also those that help you put on the shows.

With all this talk of shows, gigs, agents, and tours, it's probably a good idea to give you an accurate portrayal of what the remaining part of tour life is like. From the outside looking in, it might seem great, and yes some of it is, but there are a lot of things you may not have even considered. Let's get into what those things are and some tips for making the best of them.

CONVERSATIONS WITH KEVIN BROWNING AND VINCE IWINSKI

How do you become the manager of a rock 'n' roll band? Answer: You figure it out! This is at least true when it comes to story of how Kevin Browning and Vince Iwinski became comanagers of Umphrey's McGee. Both now have twenty years of management experience, all with Umphrey's McGee. In fact, Vince is even credited with helping the band get their first show in Chicago, at the Elbo Room, which was the fifty-fifth show in the band's time line. Kevin, once the band's soundman, as well as a list of other things, has now joined Vince as the band's comanager. Along the way, both learned quite a bit about what to do, and what not to do.

JOEL: What should a young artist focus on?

KEVIN: There is no substitution for putting in the hours. No shortcuts. No easy ways around. You just got to do the work.

I would certainly focus on being great and getting the word out. If you're not great, there are a hundred other choices in today's environment for somebody else to go listen to. You've got to focus on getting the word out because if no one's ever heard of you, it doesn't matter how great you are. You will be the greatest unheard artist of all time, of which there are many. Be patient. Getting good is not a fluke. It takes a ton of effort and persistence.

What are the most important things on the business side that bands should focus on early in their careers?

I suggest that young artists and veteran artists alike play to their strengths. I think you should sit down and make a list of what you are good at and what you suck at, because everybody will have features in both columns, and it doesn't serve you or your band well to try and pretend that you're a bunch of things that you're not. Figure out what differentiates you from the pack. What are you better at than the next artist, or what are you willing to work harder at than the next guy? Those things will help guide your decision-making process early on.

I highly suggest the divide and conquer strategy within the organization. Who does what well? From touring logistics, to math and numbers, to social media, fan interaction, who is going to excel most in your group? The things you're good at, you should do. The things you're not good at, you should find somebody else inside the organization.

Don't ever be afraid to ask questions, regardless of how dumb you may think they make you look. That's how I taught myself to engineer, to mix, to record, to produce, and to do a lot of the things that I'm doing today. Over the years, I learned from asking people how they did it. I paid particular attention to those who I thought were doing it especially well, who I admired, or even if I didn't admire musically, I appreciated the way in which they were approaching those tasks.

While practice is essential early on, good content is certainly a paramount. Figure out what content means for you. Again, what is it that you can do better than the next guy? What kind of content can you provide that is captivating and entertaining? Is it putting out live recordings? Is it putting out video snippets of backstage rehearsal or hilarious commentary on all gas station snacks from coast to coast? Ultimately, if you entertain people, they will hang around, even if it's not about your music per se. Music touches on everything, and so can you, so make the content captivating and you will grow an audience.

That said, while good content is paramount, getting attention is even harder. You can have incredible content, but if you don't have an effective way of distributing and getting people's attention, people unfortunately don't hear it. So, not only do you have to think about what is going to separate you from others while creating good content, but you've got to think about what's going to separate you in the way that you go about getting that content out there. Find something that can differentiate you from others on both of those regards.

As important as anything else are the relationships that you build and maintain over time. More often than not, a good relationship is what makes the difference between a door opening or not. As mentioned earlier in the book, you never know who's on their way up and who's on their way down, and ultimately, it shouldn't matter in terms of how you treat people. Foster and grow relationships in all parts of the business, in all parts of the trade, in all parts of the gigs, and as your Rolodex grows, the opportunities available to you will grow with them.

I'd like to hear about your pivot from engineer to your current role as comanager and record-label guy. Other than wanting to get off the road, why did you make that career pivot?

There were a number of factors that went into the decision. Some people are more aptly suited to life on the road than others. And family was a big factor, without a doubt. My wife and I were pregnant with our first child, and by my wife and I, I mean exclusively my wife. But, I absolutely loved the eleven years that I was on the road and wouldn't trade it for anything. Traveling the world opened my eyes and has been incredibly valuable from a business perspective.

Another big factor was that I started to burn the candle at both ends. We'd be on the road and I'd be mixing and recording full-time, and then as soon as we got home, I would be working, effectively, a nine-to-five in the office trying to pursue various creative and business ideas. Being on the road full-time was a roadblock to pursuing those ideas with the kind of attention that they deserved.

Whenever you're hiring someone new, try to hire someone smarter than yourself. We accomplished that by hiring Chris Mitchell to take over my role as live front of house engineer so that I could refocus on a whole laundry list of things, which included everything from starting and managing our own record label, building out a lot of the unique events and shows that we put on, crafting and fine-tuning the fan experiences, and some of the interactive elements, both in person and digitally.

Generally, I spend my time broadening the reach of all things Umphrey's. Managing the record label and overseeing a bunch of the distribution, marketing, packaging, artwork, and all the elements that go into it, is another full-time gig, particularly when you're working on any new project. So, that was another reason that I ultimately decided to get off the road.

At that point the most value that I could add was to figure out how to make the band as a whole sound better, to learn how to engineer. Then I had to learn how to get better at recording, so that we could both listen to the material and make improvements, and then to give away and eventually sell and promote the music as a whole. From there we started getting more serious about studio projects, so I pivoted to learn how to studio engineer.

I realized once we finished a project, that the packaging, the distribution, and the marketing was a place that we really needed assistance. So, I did that. Finally, I started to spend a good amount of time pursuing business development ideas. I changed positions to keep adding the most value to Umphrey's McGee as a whole. That and my inability to sit still and my never-ending curiosity for how all this stuff works forced my need to keep doing new things.

What are the most important qualities of a good manager?

The most important qualities are really the obvious stuff, such as the need for trust. At the end of the day, if you don't trust your manager, there's a problem. You have to know that they have your interest at heart and that they are not beating around the bush with you. They're not obfuscating; they're not hiding. They're not trying to cheat or steal. It's basic, but it is paramount.

Artists need to always feel like they're getting the truth from their manager, whether that be hard to hear or not. I will say that a good manager does need to have a way to frame or massage things in ways that help different personalities internalize the same message, but there's a significant difference between caressing the nomenclature versus being even moderately misleading.

You want a manager that has great ideas. If not great ideas, at least so many ideas that *some* of them are great. You are going to have a thousand questions and you're going to want feedback. A manager should be a great resource for that and they should have enough ideas to help, if nothing else, spur on the artist's own creativity.

You want people that can get shit done and people who know people tend to get shit done. If they don't have all the relationships necessarily to begin with (which we absolutely didn't), you at least have to have people who are personable and have the ability to establish quality relationships as you go.

The last thing I'll add here is, especially if you are in a band with multiple members, a manager should be helpful to generally just keep the train on the tracks and keep the team together. In Umphrey's second record, *Songs for Older Women*, I believe my title was "sound corrector/voice of reason," which spoke primarily to my ability to arbitrate or to generally just be a therapist when needed.

Much like any field, relationships can be tricky and complicated. A good manager ought to be good enough with people that they can help you smooth through some of the difficulties that you are inevitably going to face.

What's the best music business-related advice you've ever received?

The best piece of music business and even life-related advice that still sticks with me was actually a piece of advice that was intended to be about engineering, but I found it to be an apt metaphor for life in general. In 2005, Umphrey's was playing shows with The String Cheese Incident and Peter George was the system tech on the tour. I was asking him some questions about engineering and he said to me, "Kevin, don't ever forget that the knob goes both ways."

Now he was meaning it in the context of sometimes you think you need a little less of a certain frequency, but don't forget that sometimes you actually need a little bit more of it. Don't paint yourself into a corner of thinking that you always know what to do. The idea that the knob goes both ways is incredibly appropriate for trying to find your way out of jams or solve problems way beyond the engineering realm. Sometimes you convince yourself that it could never work a certain way and so you don't even consider the possibilities. The knob going both ways is a frequent reminder to me that you never know how things are going to shake out and you should never be afraid to try all sides.

———

JOEL: *Why did you start managing Umphrey's McGee?*

VINCE: I started managing Umphrey's McGee because I loved the music and I had a lot of passion for the what was happening with the band. I believed in it from the very beginning. I wanted to help out so much and wanted to be involved.

What does a manager need to know if they're getting into the business?

Many people want to be involved in the music business, but they don't know how to do it. I was at the right place at the right time with some incredibly talented musicians who were just getting started and I had my own set of sales and marketing skills to contribute. Those two areas of focus gave me lots of insight that I think helped the band.

What should a manager do for their artist right from the get-go?

One of the things that artists can really benefit from is having somebody who believes in and has passion for the art they're creating as much as the artist themselves. I feel like I had a lot of belief in what Umphrey's McGee was doing so it gave me the opportunity to preach the word of Umphrey's far and wide and try to get people to listen.

Assembling a strong team from the early stages is also really important. You have to find people who are willing to take the risk and share the passion for the art that you're creating.

Do you have a label or distribution or are you going to do that yourself? Do you hire a publicist? Who's handling your social networks? Who's handling your graphics? Who's handling your merchandise? Do you have enough personnel to go on tour?

Lots of mistakes can be made early on that can cause headaches down the road. Pay attention to the legal side of the business—especially when you start playing shows and signing contracts. Have someone look those things over for you before you sign your name to something, so you understand what you're signing. The music business can be cutthroat in certain ways, so you need to have somebody taking a look at that stuff to make sure it's okay.

It's also important to your financial situation right from the beginning. Nobody wants to have problems with the IRS. In addition to having your finances in order, having a financial plan in place and knowing what you can actually afford to do is incredibly important. You want to go out and play shows, but if you're going to need money that you don't have, then you have to take a look at what you can and can't do. It might involve playing more shows locally to build up funds so that you can play new markets. You might need to hold off on some of your plans to go outside of your strongest market in order to have enough money to do it.

One thing that I've heard from many people is that it's important to have three plans: a short-term, a mid-term, and a long-term plan. What are your thoughts there?

I couldn't agree more. If you're starting a career and you think this is what you want to do for the long term, it's *incredibly* important to make sure that you know what you're going to do this week, as well as what you hope to do in three to five years, and everything in between. You have to plot it out. If you just hope for the best and go out on a limb, there's a good chance that you'll come back with your tail between your legs.

Improvising on the business side is not as fun as improvising on the musical side.

Exactly. You can definitely get burned.

What do you think are the most important qualities of a good manager?

One of the strongest attributes of a good manager is that you have to be a bridge builder, not a bridge burner. You have to have strong relationships with everybody that you contact in this business. If you're nice, easy to work with, respectful, AND you don't have an ego, you'll get a lot further than if you've got somebody that tastes a little success and gets a chip on their shoulder. I've always aspired to be a team player, willing to set aside any sort of ego and just work hard and build strong relationships. That goes a long way in a business that can be plagued with a lot of egos and strong personalities. When you're nice, you get a lot accomplished and people want to help you.

What are the challenges of preserving your artist's artistic integrity while also trying to run a smart business?

Whether we're playing a huge show to ten thousand people or playing to one thousand people in a smaller venue on a Tuesday or a Wednesday, the willingness of the artist to play their best in both of those scenarios helps preserve the art and the product as a whole. As a manager, I think that you need to help keep expectations realistic that not every show is going be a sold-out stadium. I want to make sure that the band is as comfortable and happy on the road in both of those two scenarios, as different as they may be.

What is the best music industry advice you've ever received?

The best advice was from a fellow manager telling me to never be afraid to ask for help. If you don't ever ask, you'll never get what you need. It goes back to never letting ego get in the way of your success.

What is the worst music business advice you've ever gotten?

The worst advice that I ever received was when somebody once told me that we were never going to succeed because we were too niche of a band and we should just keep our expectations low. They obviously didn't believe in the product that we were putting out in the early stages. Don't ever let anybody tell you that what you're doing will never be good enough. If your faith in your product is shaken at the early stages, then you're going have a hard time achieving the goals that you set out.

Have you reached back out to that person recently, twenty years later?

I don't think that person is even in the music business anymore.

SECTION TWELVE:

THINGS YOU NEED TO KNOW,
OR AT LEAST SHOULD HEAR ONCE

There are a few things that those with experience would likely tell you that they wished someone had told them prior to figuring it out the hard way. Part of the reason this book even exists is to try to help those without experience avoid the pain, heartache, anguish, frustration, or financial loss associated with many of the things we are about to discuss. In fact, if something in this section helps you with any of the following subject matter, then you made a very positive return on the investment associated with buying this book.

SEEK DOUBLE AND TRIPLE BILLS

It's going to be much harder for you to garner an audience just doing shows by yourself. This is especially true if you're only getting started. As previously mentioned, finding like-minded artists can help you rapidly expand your fan base. Plus, getting added as an additional performer on existing shows is easier than trying to book gigs as an unknown. In the beginning, getting your music in front of and heard by as many people as possible benefits your growth more than anything else. Think of it this way: You are trying to get to the top of the mountain. What is easier? Climbing it yourself, or letting those already up there pull you up?

That said, don't expect that a given artist's fans are just going to show up for your set. Try to promote awareness of your music amongst that artist's fan base and create some excitement if you're the first act on a bill. You will likely play to some empty seats. Sometimes you need to create fans one at a time and that's okay too.

FESTIVALS AND CAMPING SHOWS

Creating a fan base is easier when an audience is already in the mood for music. The festival scene—both city fests and camping festivals—is alive and well, with more live performance options than ever. Some are called "soft-ticket events," meaning it's a very low cover charge for the value a patron receives. "Hard-ticket events" mean the tickets are more expensive and likely just feature a couple of bands.

Most cities, big, medium, or small, have a variety of neighborhood festivals where you can build your audience. Since these events typically extend over long hours, they need a big stable of performers. In fact, so much, that the booking agents might add you quickly and easily if you have the proper presentation.

Camping festivals tend to be more genre specific, but they are another excellent way of playing for new people, as you have a captive audience of live music-loving patrons ready to have a good time. Sometimes artists will even do "pop-up" shows in the parking lots or campgrounds of camping festivals. It's occasionally easier to go where the people are as opposed to hoping they will come to you

Most festival promoters will only book bands with history in surrounding markets, so it's advisable to have at least a few gigs under your belt before trying to land a coveted festival slot. Some camping festivals have voting slots where you can submit your band to be added to a festival. This is especially useful for bands that aren't that well-known yet but might still be able to drive some festival attendance. It's a win-win for both you and the promoter, so if you have the ability to drive sales, point that out!

WRONG NOTE: DON'T EVER PAY TO PLAY! It's bad business plain and simple. This does nothing other than set an unfair precedent for future acts. It also empowers the promoters of the world to a level that isn't healthy for the industry. If paying to play is your best option, perhaps it's time to go back to the drawing board.

WHEN AND WHERE SHOULD YOU GO?

During the process of lining up a few gigs, give some thought and consideration as to how you can start building an audience in multiple markets. With that consideration, it is important to know that major cities, college towns, or secondary markets may require different strategies.

For major markets, start by playing them every month or every other month. If your audience builds quickly, you'll want to add more space between gigs—typically three to six months once you've established momentum and are moving up venues.

For college markets, make sure you check the university's academic calendar to prevent the mistake of planning your show during finals or spring break, or even worse, during the summer when the town might be mostly dark. In regards to scheduling and booking shows in college towns, check with student organizations and other groups at the school itself tasked with booking talent for school-related functions.

In the end, markets react to acts in different ways, but a smart, well-thought-out approach is the best one. Just try to put yourself in situations where you have the highest chance of success if possible.

THE POWER OF BEING COUNTERINTUITIVE

In general, go where your competition isn't. Think of this as having a cowardly approach! Yes, you read that correctly. What does that even mean? It means, why fight the giant and subject yourself to the most competition possible? Instead, gravitate to spots where the competition has inadvertently left you alone to compete with no one. *Everybody* wants to play Florida or California in January or February. As a result, you're going to have more competition if you follow suit. But if you go to places like Minnesota, Michigan, Massachusetts, Maine,

Vermont, and even New York in January or February, you'll find that you have a lot less competition.

More often than not, by being counterintuitive you'll avoid going up against bigger shows in your genre and might not even have another show in town to compete with at all. Yes, winter conditions provide other challenges that might make your days harder, but people who live in cold markets still want to go out and do things too.

RIGHT NOTE: If you're in a big city, aim for a few different venues because different people go to different places. If you only play the same club over and over again, it limits the likelihood of gaining new fans. While playing different venues in major cities is ideal for fan growth, you'll need to keep in mind which promoters book which rooms. You also don't want to unintentionally piss off a loyal promoter because you didn't give them a concert. Luckily, most promoters in major cities have a variety of venues where they can host you.

PLAYING OUTDOORS

In the summer, try to play at outdoor venues, as more people will wish to attend outdoor shows than indoor shows. That said, make sure you check a market's average weather at that time frame or you could unwittingly increase your chances of playing in the rain—or worse, snow.

BUILDING SOMETHING WITH LONGEVITY

It's likely going to take a hundred to two hundred shows and a couple of years to build your fan base. But the long-term goal should be to play seventy-five to a hundred shows a year touring around the country. That's a huge commitment to start with, but one that needs to be verbalized so everyone involved understands. In 2003, after touring the country for two years,

Umphrey's McGee played a career-high 162 concerts. While that number is unsustainable, it was so large because the band was introducing new markets while also trying to make ends meet. Are you going to try to tour internationally? These are all excellent questions to talk about, even if some are further down the road.

CONCENTRIC CIRCLES

Umphrey's McGee was based in South Bend, Indiana when it first began touring. As such, it made sense to arrange the tour cities in concentric circles, working our way out from South Bend. We played places like Indianapolis, Grand Rapids, and Chicago. The touring then expanded to college towns like Madison, Wisconsin; Champaign, Illinois; Bloomington, Indiana; Kalamazoo, Michigan; and Ann Arbor, Michigan. In general, following concentric circles make for more affordable and smart touring. No one wants to play a show after being in a car for eight hours.

MARKET EXCEPTIONS

Depending on the style of music you're playing, it's important to identify markets that you feel make sense for your genre. For rock 'n' roll and EDM, New York is the top US market. Las Vegas, Miami, and Los Angeles are also top EDM markets. If you're a singer/songwriter or a country artist, maybe this means Nashville for you. Consider adding the most important markets like New York City, Los Angeles, Nashville, or Chicago earlier on. These markets are big. It's that simple. They have more people that in turn can fill bigger venues. This results in the possibility of more word of mouth. Really, more everything. These cities are also the cultural hearts of various music scenes and have more people working in the music world than other markets around the country. In the Umphrey's McGee world, they've had visits from important musicians like Buddy Guy in Chicago, Garth Brooks in Nashville, Al Dimeola in New York, and Matt Groening, the creator of *The Simpsons*, in Los Angeles. This is not to mention the hundreds of other important music business executives, managers, and agents. When collaboration is the name of game, getting to know important players personally early on makes a difference.

This doesn't mean that you shouldn't play markets of all sizes, because you absolutely should. Just structure these stops on the way to and from the bigger markets. This healthy mix will lead to well-rounded exposure that can really help you in the long run.

TALENT BUYERS AND VENUE OWNERS

It always helps to build a personal relationship when you're working with venue owners and talent buyers. Make the effort to keep things familiar and friendly. There are going to be times when you need to fight for something—and that's okay—but do it respectfully and never burn bridges. Other times you may need to do the talent buyer a favor to help them out with something. Always try to be gracious if asked. If the talent buyer likes you and/or your music, the likelihood of you getting the gig that you want is going to go up.

It's also important to work with the talent buyers on a more long-term growth plan in their markets. Ask questions about how to build your audience, as they'll know their market best. Ultimately, every time you play a concert somewhere, it should have a big picture strategy attached to it, setting up the next play in that market. Remember, while in the beginning it might seems like an endless sea of venues, markets, and options, but in the end that isn't the case. If you get the longevity you seek it will come through growing, respecting, and appreciating these connections and opportunities.

TONIGHT'S SHOW IS SOLD OUT

You sold out a show! Congratulations, it's a really great feeling, right? But before you rest on your laurels, could you book a second night there? In order to do so you'll need to have enough material to play two concerts back to back. But one of the important things that gets you from bars to clubs to ballrooms to theaters is creating demand. You do that by leaving people outside who want to get in.

What does that mean? While it sounds counterintuitive it is a good measure of true growth and can pay off with additional shows. This is a long play too. When it comes to selling tickets you are competing with everything else in people's lives. There are a limitless number of things that might prevent your "day of show" buyer from walking up to the box office window. Knowing that the possibility of doing so might not exist gives people a sense of urgency to commit well before the day of.

Along with this sense of urgency to buy tickets, there are also logistical advantages to playing a two-night stand: Travel expenses go down, there's only one load in and load out and you'll have more free time on the second day since you're not traveling.

STEPPING UP

Once you've sold out a night, or multiple nights, at a smaller venue, it's time to move up to a bigger venue in the future. Finding the right day(s) and time of year for your next play will be crucial in mitigating risk as you try to increase attendance. The worst thing that can happen is you play the bigger venue so poorly that you have to return to the smaller venue again. Don't ever send your career in the wrong direction. It's exciting to think about playing a bigger venue, but jumping the gun can be a huge career mistake.

One of the things to consider with a larger venue is that while it might add exposure, it's also likely to add expenses. Your five-dollar ticket at the bar is not going to get you the same amount of revenue as a five-dollar ticket at the club. Generally speaking, start your pricing on the lower end of things, as the first priority should be to get people through the door. Charging too much at the beginning of your career will only hurt your long-term chances. The right price point might be different for every market and may even vary from place to place. Typically, the bigger cities will be able to absorb a slightly higher ticket price while college markets need to be less expensive.

THE FREELOADERS

How will you handle the guest list? This is a huge decision that will matter more and more as you ascend. If you have family members who you want to comp tickets to that's fine, but you really should be taking care of music industry people on the guest list as opposed to your friends.

If your friends can afford to pay for tickets, they should be buying tickets. Do you show up at their place of work and want—or worse, *expect*—free stuff? Hopefully not. Most will understand this; those that don't might not be the people you want around anyway.

Another good general rule is to say no to "plus ones" on the guest list. It's okay to sometimes say yes, yet it's equally okay to say no about this stuff. Remember, this is your JOB, and your friends' and families' party. They're coming to have fun. You're here to make money. Every "plus one" keeps you further from that goal.

Now that we established what NOT to accumulate, let's spend a minute talking about something that accumulation of IS a good idea.

CO-BILLS AND SUPPORT

The more shows you play, the more likely you will meet other artists. Occasionally you'll want to join forces to help expand each other's audiences and fill up rooms. Again, look for like-minded musicians, as it makes no sense if you play very mellow music to do a co-bill with a heavy band. Other artists you work with don't have to sound *exactly* the same but should be something that will appeal to the audiences of both bands.

If you go out and personally introduce the other artist, your fans are more likely to respond positively. Figuring out a way to collaborate *during* the show is even better. Plus, most collaborations will make your show more interesting.

RIGHT NOTE: This is music, not sports. Friendly competition is good, but it's a lot easier to work together than to try to undermine or sabotage other bands' sets. You never know when you'll be sharing the stage with another artist again, so try to keep things friendly.

KILLING TIME PRODUCTIVELY

Up to this point, we have talked about adding or shedding certain things in and around your act. Some of that you can control. Unfortunately, time is a pretty uncontrollable factor, but what you do with it is very much up to you. If you've made it to the point where you have a backstage room, consider creating a small, makeshift practice space. One of the major limitations of the sound check is that it presents a finite amount of time to get things done. Sometimes things will go wrong with sound check and you have to adapt in the moment. Try to roll with it and not get frustrated. Bring some small cube amps or even just your guitars backstage and you can sing through and work on material. That will take the pressure off having to get everything done at sound check.

Always use your down time productively.

We have really come a long way since those early moments of planning and recording your first demo. While this section was about creating momentum, keeping it going, investing in yourself and your music, as well as a few cautionary points for not tanking your own progress, what come next is just as important. As your career grows, so will your responsibilities, needs, and then demands upon you and your time. That's right, it's time to discuss creating a completely different type of support act for your band.

GEOGRAPHY AND LOW-HANGING FRUIT

Practical touring means first looking at where you live and then identifying which markets will be easiest to target. If most of the markets you think will be good for your music are far from where you live, you may want to consider moving or the travel issue could seriously hinder your progress. Convenience matters and being in a geographically advantageous location will save you both time and money.

Cities like Chicago or Nashville make sense as good places to call home, as their central locations make many markets easily accessible. If you live on the Eastern Seaboard you also have a lot of options that will be easy to access, as cities are closest together there. The West Coast of the US is the toughest place to live as far as touring goes. Cities are further from one another and you're extremely far from important East Coast markets.

RIGHT NOTE: When you're starting to tour you might also want to consider living in a smaller city that is cheaper than major markets since you'll be spending a good chunk of your time on the road. Choosing an affordable place to live as you're getting started might also be beneficial if it helps the musicians focus on music. If you don't have to get another job, especially one unrelated to music, it will only help your career. Perhaps you'll want to start in a smaller city and eventually plan to move to a larger city with a bigger scene.

AVOIDING COMPETITION FROM MAJOR SPORTING EVENTS

Depending on your genre, sports may or may not be important to your fan base. Regardless, it's likely worthwhile to consider major sporting events when planning a tour. For instance, don't play in the southeast where SEC football markets are happening in the fall. College football is going to be a massive competition for you on a Saturday. That said, Friday nights or Thursday nights before college games can work. Once the NFL schedule starts in the fall, try to avoid playing on Sundays going up against the NFL. For major league baseball, you'll want to avoid things like the World Series and playoffs, though baseball is tougher to plan around since you might not know which teams are playing when you're planning. Another big one to keep in mind is March Madness, aka the college basketball playoffs. March is a great time to tour the West coast, as your shows will start after all the games are over due to the time difference. There are also many market specific sporting events that will need to be considered, so always ask the promoter what's going on in town before you confirm a show.

RIGHT NOTE: One person should ideally make a daily schedule—both a physical and an online version that everyone can access. Having a daily schedule (or day sheets) will help you stay organized and efficient on the road. It's also a good place to keep all relevant info, like travel time, venue contact numbers, hotel reservation info, and the exact timing of every part of the day. In general, plan as much as you can in advance so you can focus on music the day of the show.

CONSIDERING SCALE WHEN PLANNING A TOUR

Try to play similarly sized venues each weekend so you can use the same gear each night. It will be impractical if you play a much larger place followed by a tiny club where you need half the gear. So if you're going to play a few bigger venues think about doing those together on the same run or weekend. Conversely, consider playing smaller sized venues together. Things might not always work out in the most ideal way, but if you can control these variables you should.

RIGHT NOTE: Always keep some extra cash handy in the event there is an issue with your vehicle or trailer while touring. Purchasing a AAA package is always a smart move so that you have assistance with your vehicle should something go terribly wrong.

AFTER YOUR FIRST SUCCESSFUL GIGS

When you've drawn a great crowd or sold out a show you might think, *We need to get back to that market as soon as possible!* But most of the time the opposite is true. You'll want to give that market more space to help ensure the demand expands. You may have to find a delicate balance between markets where you can make money and continue to develop new markets.

SHORT-TERM VS. LONG-TERM GROWTH

Once you've played ten or fifteen different markets you'll likely find a few that earn more than others. Don't play for the short-term money; play for the long-term growth in your best markets and make sure that you space your shows accordingly. It's always better to leave a healthy attendance number up on the board and not rush back to play somewhere once it has done well.

Spacing of markets can be a very challenging thing to do correctly early in your career and will likely continue to be a major question throughout your career. Thankfully, your manager and agent should be able to help you decide. When you start, as a general rule it's okay to revisit most places in one to two months.

LONG-TERM TOURING THOUGHTS

After a year of returning to a market every six to eight weeks, you'll want to consider spreading out plays to once every three to six months and hopefully playing multiple nights at the smaller venue or moving up to a larger venue. If you find sustained success, you'll want to involve your manager and agent to help plan each market. The most important thing is to keep the positive buzz going and to continue to create demand for tickets to your concerts.

ARTISTIC VARIETY

Another reason to wait until you try to put together a national tour is that you'll want to play a different show when you return to a market. Does it have to be completely different? Of course not, but you definitely want to have at least some new material to play every time you revisit a market. Playing the exact same show in New York six months after your first play there won't help you get fans to return the next time. The goal should be to make the listener think, *I can't miss a show anytime this artist comes to town because you never know what they're going to do!*

RIGHT NOTE: Try to use just one vehicle, share hotel rooms, or even stay with friends to save money. If you're young and adaptable, maybe consider finding a spot from a couch-surfing website. Love nature? Camp while you're touring in the summer! The most important lesson is simply to not spend money on unnecessary things while on the road.

WHY YOU SHOULD SUPPORT RELATED SECONDARY MARKETS

Athens, Georgia, the college town home of the University of Georgia, feeds the Atlanta market. Providence, Rhode Island and Worcester, Massachusetts support Boston. It's important to eventually add these secondary markets to your routes because they will help grow adjacent major markets. That way you will have more options for cities to play as your career develops and you won't be stuck repeating specific markets and venues too frequently.

PERSISTENCE AND INVESTMENT IN MARKETS

Eventually you're going to have to take chances with new places. Go somewhere once and you've already made an initial investment. It's in your best interest to return a few times and see how things progress. Going to a new market and immediately abandoning it because your show didn't go as well as you hoped is a poor strategy. It took Umphrey's McGee around ten shows in Milwaukee, Wisconsin, to draw more than two hundred people. Now, twenty years later, Umphrey's is selling out multiple nights at the 2,500 capacity Riverside Theater. Persistence is important.

TOURING RIDER

Once you're touring you'll want to ask for a rider at each show, which mandates a few food and beverage items be provided by the venue. While the venue will procure these items, they're likely coming out of the night's expenses, so be smart. A typical small rider might include a case of water, beer, a bottle of hard alcohol, and a few food items to snack on.

It's a good idea to create two different riders and alternate them, so you have a bit of variety from day to day. If you're traveling from city to city, it's important to ask that your rider be present when you arrive in the afternoon, as it relates to having a few snacks there waiting. You'll probably want the alcoholic drinks closer to showtime, but the food you ask for doesn't help if it shows up right after you've eaten dinner.

THE OTHER TWENTY HOURS OF THE DAY ON THE ROAD

One of the biggest challenges of touring is figuring out what to do with the other twenty hours of your day when you're not playing music onstage. The most important place to start is getting to know your bandmates off the stage. This is just as important as getting to know them onstage and you'll likely spend more time with them offstage than onstage if you're touring.

Team-building matters. There will be laughs and there will be tears, but doing things together will only strengthen your unit. Find silver linings in challenging moments. When you have to carry your gear up and down two flights of stairs, you've just done your exercise for the day.

Doing non-musical things as a group or with someone in the group while on the road can bring inspiration and stimulation that will add value to your touring life. Choose things that are exciting, fun, and maybe even educational. If you're not making music on days off, plan dinners, golf, bowl, ski, hike, play paintball, visit theme parks, go to the movies, or attend other shows. It's good to give yourself and your bandmates a break from music after a grueling five or six days in a row of shows.

The other option, of course, is finding a studio or a practice space and further working on music on days off. That's a great thing as long as you're not burning yourselves out. If you're playing six concerts in a row, you might want that seventh day off from music to do something else. After a few days touring you'll have a better feel for the balance needed as a musician on the road.

AND MILES TO GO BEFORE I SLEEP

When you start touring, you'll likely be traveling for a good chunk of your day. Listen to music together, play cards, or try to come up with anything that'll make the drive time more fun. After a couple of shared trips, you'll hopefully have somebody who wants to drive and another to stay alert and ride shotgun while other people can kind of rotate in and out of taking naps. Always safety first! If you are not a good driver, it's okay to tell your bandmates that from the get go. But you should figure out another way to contribute if you're not going to take your time behind the wheel.

OTHER GOOD USES OF TIME WHILE TRAVELING

Taking a nap in the van is a good way to catch up on sleep. If you can't sleep, traveling is also the perfect time to listen to other artists. Get to know as much music as possible and share music with each other! There's more music for you to access than ever before in history, so take advantage of that. Consider it homework.

RIGHT NOTE: Recording your shows and listening back to them constructively as a group is going to help your performances. Remember, it's just as important to compliment the good stuff as it is to critique things that fall short.

MOBILE PRACTICING

Balance on the road will mean something slightly different for everyone. Surprisingly, one of the most challenging things is finding the time and space to write or practice. So how can you continue to improve as a musician while on the road? One of the things you can do is try to allow for time to play your instruments when not onstage. If you're a guitarist, singer, horn player, bassist, or a DJ, you don't even need more than your instrument and maybe a set of headphones. If you're a drummer, you might want to get a practice pad. For keyboardists there are excellent small keyboards ideal for traveling. If you have a little extra time or a day off and an opportunity arises to do something fresh and different with your music, just do it. Be spontaneous on the road. You're in the music business, and creativity should be encouraged.

A CONVERSATION WITH CHUCK LEAVELL

Best known as the touring keyboardist and musical director of the Rolling Stones since 1982 (they even call him the "Sixth Rolling Stone"), Leavell is a self-taught musician. Playing in a handful of bands through his teen years, he was then recruited by The Allman Brothers Band in 1972, and was a key contributor to their chart-topping album *Brothers and Sisters*. After their breakup, Leavell started his own blues/rock/jazz band, Sea Level, releasing five albums and touring tirelessly for many years. Author of five books and seven solo albums, Leavell won the Lifetime Achievement Award with The Allman Brothers at the 54th Grammy Awards.

JOEL: You've mentioned attending a Ray Charles concert as an epiphany for you musically. What did you do immediately after attending that concert that started your musical road?

CHUCK: Well, I was quite young at the time. Thirteen, I think. It was my sister, Judy, that had a date to go see Ray, and my parents also were going out, so they suggested that Judy take me along, which she graciously did. Our family had that great record, *Modern Sounds in Country and Western Music*, which we all really liked. So, I was familiar with him. But man, I wasn't prepared for the sheer power of his performance. Not just him, but the whole band. Fathead Newman on sax, Billy Preston on Hammond organ, the Rayletts. And Ray was just so cool, with a kind of understated command. His voice and his playing were just superb, and I left that concert saying to myself, *If I could ever be in a band that is anywhere near that good, that would be my dream.*

What decisions as a young man, musical or music business-wise, stand out to you as things that later impacted your career path?

Well, my dad told me at a young age to be aware of the business side of any profession. That helped me immensely when I was old enough to read contracts and such. He also told me, "Son, you make your own luck." That was great advice. To me, that meant in part how to "be in the right place at the right time with the right attitude." And, of course, there is that thing called "practice." For most of us, that means hours spent on learning our instruments, learning the general principals of music. I love the saying of the five *P*s: "Proper preparation prevents poor performance."

You've been a band leader, a musical director, and a side man. What are some of the differences in how you approach each role, if any? If you've had to consider different gigs at the same time, what factors in to how you decide which gig to do?

To the first part of the question, I think it has a lot to do with "going with the flow." If I'm working with an artist and musicians in a situation where there might be some uncertainty going on, stepping up with ideas and more of a leadership role can help the situation. But, on the other hand, if I'm on a session or in a rehearsal with an artist or producer that has definite ideas, then I want to try and please them. Not that I won't speak out if I have an opinion on something, but I want to do my best to deliver what they are asking for. As far as being a band leader, my best advice is to come in very prepared but also to listen to any comments from my fellow musicians. The bottom line is to do your best to enhance the creative process and work toward the best possible outcome.

As to the question of deciding priorities in a situation where you have to decide between gigs . . . that can be really tough. You just have to weigh all the options carefully. Give it all the consideration you can on all sides. For me, the top priority is what is best for my career. It's more about what the best decision is for the long term. And, of course, your gut needs to be listened to.

You're one of the great rock 'n' roll soloists on keyboards. What makes a great solo? What do you do to differentiate between solos? Is there anything you shouldn't do while soloing?

I believe soloing is a learned art. It's like telling a story. You don't want to give away the plot straight away. You want to do a bit of teasing, cajoling, pique the interest of the listener some before you carry it to fruition. Build the house from the foundation up, and when you get the roof on, *then* you can try to blow it off. Also, be aware of the support you have or need from your fellow musicians. The bed that they lay is important to allow you to go where you want to go. And if you hear something from a fellow musician that inspires you, try to do something to compliment that. It can result in good musical conversations in soloing. Don't be afraid to push yourself, but not so much that you get too far out of your comfort zone. I think it helps to sometimes sit with your instrument, clear your mind, and just improvise. And do it in as many keys as you can. That kind of exercise can help when you are asked to do a solo in any particular situation.

You've toured with many legendary artists over the years. How do you stay balanced and happy on the road?

Every situation is different depending on the individual, but for me, exercise is essential. I like doing weight training and a bit of cardio for about forty-five minutes to an hour usually four to five days a week. I also enjoy looking into activities available in any particular city. Could be anything from parks to museums to shopping areas. Being a tree farmer, I have friends across the planet that I can visit with who own forest land or who are engaged in the outdoors in some way. My wife, Rose Lane, and I always travel together these days, and have for many years now since our two daughters are grown. It's great to have her with me.

In more recent years you've played with many popular country artists in addition to being the musical director for the Rolling Stones. What's different when you're contributing to that style of music?

I think, to a degree, Southern Rock has morphed into some styles of country music. So I think it is natural for me to engage in country. But the bottom line is that I'm happy to play on as many diverse kinds of music as I can. You can always learn something from playing different genres, and it can be fun to blend things together.

What are some things that make for a good collaboration? And what's something that can ruin a collaboration?

I guess I would say that the chemistry has to be good between collaborators. I think you have to enjoy the process, so if there is a situation where there is a rub of some type, either personally or professionally, then it may not go as well as you'd like. But one essential thing is to be a good listener to your fellow collaborator. Try hard to understand his or her point of view and work together. On the other side of the coin, be honest about your feelings to whoever you are working with, so that everyone has a good and honest understanding of what the goal is.

You've invested a lot of energy into environmental concerns and sustainability. Why did you choose these types of world issues to get behind? Should we as musicians use our platforms to promote other things we believe in?

First, I don't think it is a good idea to "preach" from the stage. When I'm up there playing, it is to entertain and not to try to sway someone to my particular point of view. But yes, I do have a passion for the outdoors, the environment, nature and forestry. Rose Lane and I are Tree Farmers, meaning that we grow mainly southern yellow pine on our land. Some are eventually carefully harvested over a very long period of time— like sixty years—for various products. The first things we do, around age twelve to fifteen, are mainly for paper and packaging products, and further down the line for lumber and other building products. But let's be clear, I believe we not only need working forests, we need forests that we protect for recreation, hiking, and pure aesthetic reasons. For me, just like we want balance in our lives, we want balance in nature. And it's not just about the trees; it's about ecosystems, wildlife, the environment. Don't forget that trees sequester carbon to help clean the air and that they filter the water that goes into our streams and rivers. They provide home and shelter to all manner of wildlife. I am the cofounder of a website called the Mother Nature Network (www.mnn.com). We have become the most visited independent environmental website in the world, getting between five and six million hits a month. The goal is to be the most accurate Internet source for environmental news, education, and information and I believe we have achieved that.

What's the best advice you've ever received about music or the music business?

Well, what I said earlier that my dad told me: You make your own luck. You make luck by practicing and getting proficient on your instrument, by learning the principles and theory of music. And by learning how to "be in the right place at the right time with the right attitude." And by learning the laws and principals of the music business, understanding contracts clearly, and nowadays knowing how to use social media and other promotional tools. Finding your own unique way of performing.

What's the worst advice you've received?

"Oh, don't worry, we'll take care of that."

What should a young musician be focusing their time if they want to create music as a career?

I think we've covered most of that in the above but I would add: Have fun with it!

SECTION THIRTEEN:

BEING A GOOD BANDMATE

W e've stressed the value of finding suitable, or like-minded bandmates. But what about how to be a great bandmate yourself? Everyone in your band is going to be different. It's incredibly important that you accept them for who they are and know it's human nature to change some over time. In general, open-mindedness will make it easier for everyone to find their identities in the band. Communication and listening to each other are also crucial for the continued success of your music. All this helps you have fun making music together.

Keeping It Light

If you're playing music for a living, you're bringing happiness to other people. You're not making life or death decisions. It's important to remember that people are coming to experience your music as a way to escape whatever it is that's happening in their world. It's your *job* to entertain them. So take your music seriously but don't take yourself too seriously. We're musicians, not heart surgeons.

Communication Is Many Two-Way Streets

Communicating effectively with others can be tough. Why? Because we are all different. That's obvious, right? However, there are a few things that aren't "different" from one to the next. The first being that we all want to be heard, especially by those who we spend a lot of time with, care about, respect, or want to be respected by. So listen to those you are working and creating with. Next, we all have good and bad moments, and if you spend enough time with anyone then you are guaranteed to catch some of both. This goes the other way too; others are likely to see your best and worst qualities. Let's talk about how to deal with that.

There will be things you disagree with amongst your bandmates or collaborators. Those disagreements might be musical or logistical. Learning how to talk about them and a willingness to compromise are essential. Picking your battles is important. Is your gripe really worth it? If so, how you present your issue is of crucial importance.

Whether you're at your practice space, on tour, or in the studio, being able to assess when and how to present your "issues" is imperative. Some prefer one-on-one conversations. Others don't mind discussing issues in front of everyone. Regardless of the setting, make sure you communicate with one another. All that said, know that right before you the hit the stage, or worse, while you're *on*stage, is certainly not the right time to raise concerns!

CONSTRUCTIVE CRITICISM AND CONSTRUCTIVE COMPLIMENTS

No one truly enjoys criticism. However, your choice to become a performer means that you are going to get plenty. If you want to make a career out of music then you've got to be able to take and give constructive criticism. But an often overlooked part of working together is telling others that they did well. Finding a healthy mix of both goes a long way.

ACTIVE LISTENING

You learn a lot more listening than you do speaking. Active listening is a really important part of maintaining a productive, long-term relationship with your bandmates. You've got to intently listen to them, take in their thoughts, and try to put yourself in the other person's shoes. Almost every disagreement seems smaller after someone is able to verbalize their thoughts, so always take the time to talk through issues.

It's essential never to let a small problem become a big problem. Find the right time and approach and talk about it. Active listening is a great place to start. If you actively listen to one another you may even be able to have a peaceful disagreement. When it comes to relationships in general, one of the most common complaints from the disgruntled is that the other person isn't listening. Don't let that be the case with you and your bandmates and the payoff will be a solid foundation.

Keep Pushing (But Celebrate Progress, Too)

It's all right to be self-critical when it serves as motivation toward improving your music or show, but it's also beneficial to acknowledge when as a group you have done something well. You don't want to look back on your career and ten years into it realize that you haven't enjoyed any of it because you've been so harsh on yourself. Keep pushing but also stop and smell the roses once in a while.

OFFSTAGE RESPONSIBILITIES

There are lots of things that need to happen to get from your practice space to the gig. Figure out a general plan for who will handle the crucial elements of the gig, from planning to driving to packing gear at the end of the night. Not doing so can leave certain members repeatedly performing certain tasks and some possibly doing none. This can lead to petty disagreement that erode positive progress made in other areas. Remember, if you continue producing positive results then soon enough you will have more help.

A Simple Example Taken from the Road

The members of Umphrey's McGee think of responsibilities on the road much like a family might when it comes to chores.

The following is taken straight from Joel's history and experience on the road with the band.

UMPHREY'S 1.0 BY JOEL CUMMINS

The Keyboardist

In bands before Umphrey's McGee, I made around ten different contacts at bars and clubs in South Bend, Indiana, though none of them were true live music clubs. (Not a single one even had house PA systems!) When Umphrey's started, and I got to know the other guys in the band, it seemed like a good fit for me to continue those venue relationships. I took on being the point of contact for talent buyers, handling concert bookings and promotion. Our bassist, Ryan, and I would typically walk around college campuses and hand out fliers day of show as well. This sort of personal interaction definitely got a few unlikely people on board to attend the shows. Whether it's handing out fliers or figuring ways to connect with potential attendees in a personal fashion, it's an important aspect of expanding your audience. Also, once our manager, Vince, was on board, I tried to serve as the conduit between band and management, making sure there were always open lines of communication.

The Bassist

Ryan, our bass player, would typically be the guy who packed the trailer at the end of the night because he was good at that Tetris kind of thing and a hard, physical worker. As the bassist with just his instrument and amp, he was always the one who was done packing up first, so it made practical sense for us to have Ryan pack the trailer for maximum efficiency.

The Percussionist

282

Andy our percussionist loves to drive and happens to be a very consistent, solid driver. He also doesn't like to drink very often at shows, and that's a very important thing to have at the end of the night: a sober driver. We would, of course, rotate between the three to four of us that we felt were the safest drivers and would typically discuss who would drive before the gig and then after the gig for the next day. You didn't want to slam a bunch of coffee in the morning planning to drive and then find out someone else was already behind the wheel.

The Singer/Guitarist

Brendan was a very poor driver, which we all acknowledged, so we let him drive much less. His important role was often to sit shotgun and keep the driver company—especially during the super late-night shifts, which are the hardest ones for the driver to stay awake. In the early years, Brendan also did a good job making sure we had something fun to do after the show if we were staying in town. He and our lighting tech, Adam, were the social coordinators.

The Guitarist/Singer/Drummer/Keyboardist/Studio Guru

Finally, Jake found his best contribution to make on the road was as the traveling DJ. When we started touring it was actual CDs and tapes that we played in our van. Jake's collection of music is pretty astounding, so not only did we get a veritable education on all sorts of music but he was always playing us new things that he wrote and recorded in his studio. We had a lot of great exchanges of music and ideas thanks to Jake. Of course, we all played different music for one another from time to time, and I think that added to the fun.

Drummer

Mike, our original drummer, was just an all-around funny guy. He would drive occasionally but was famous for going for a half hour one day then pulling over and saying he's done. That said, he probably got most of the biggest laughs out of all of us while we were driving around, and that was something that you can't quantify. Good laughs to break up the time and bring you together make lasting memories. Mike was also a huge proponent of band card games, so we did that for mostly small change with a few of us in the back of the van on longer drives. Playing cards and gambling with one another was a surprisingly good team-building exercise, though once in a while someone lost fifty dollars on a drive. When we were off the road, Mike had a collection of drumming videos that we would watch together as we tried to learn more complicated patterns and open our minds to all kinds of rhythmic possibilities.

MAINTAINING HEALTHY HABITS ON THE ROAD

Eating healthily on the road can be a huge challenge. It's especially tempting to eat crappy comfort food after you've been rattling around in a van all day traveling to the gig. It can also be difficult to eat anything healthy after the show when most places that are open late involve pizza and fried foods. If you're younger, you might be able to get away with not eating as well, but the healthier you are, the better you'll feel from day to day and be able to tour longer.

Staying healthy on the road also means getting enough sleep so you can give the audience and your bandmates the best performance possible. Being well-rested often has a lot to do with having a good attitude throughout your show days. If you are under-rested you're likely going to be grumpy and probably not going to be as sharp as you should be. Some days we're all more tired than others, so try to take a nap if you need it. Or if you know you just can't wake up, go get a coffee or some form of caffeine instead of alcohol. That's going to be more beneficial to your performance in the long run. When you're younger you may be able to bounce back quicker, but you can't keep shortchanging yourself on rest or it *will* eventually catch up with you and you'll get sick.

1) If you only have one room for everyone, use the lobby restroom to poop.
2) If more than two people are using the bathroom to shower and shave, clean up the sink!
3) If there are people showering after you and you got the last towel, call the front desk and ask for more before you shower.
4) Don't take a twenty-minute shower while others are waiting for you.
5) If sharing a room and you need to talk on the phone early or late, walk outside the room.

BE ACTIVE ON THE ROAD

Once you're at your gig and have everything ready to go, take a walk. Check out the town or at least move around a bit to get the blood flowing. Stretching, running, hiking, or biking can all be done on the road, and you'll feel more alive onstage if you are active before your gig. In general, try to create healthy daily habits that are sustainable and you'll find that your touring life is going to be a lot easier and more interesting.

HOW MUCH FUN SHOULD YOU HAVE ON THE ROAD?

After the gig is over, should you go for the sunrise party or go to bed? It's all about the context. You want your touring life to be fun but you also don't want to let the fun turn into a party that exhausts you. Start working backward from what you need to do the following day. If you swing too much one way or the other, it's going to ruin the experience regardless. Measure your stamina and be smart about where and when you join the party. There are certainly right and wrong times. If you want to hang, try to cut loose after the shows *not* before or during them. And it's also smart to have the fun night when you don't have to play a gig the next day or drive ten hours.

RIGHT NOTE: If you *do* decide to stay out all night before a gig the next day, respect your bandmates and your audience by being on time, focused, and working a little harder than usual to have a good attitude. Partying and then complaining about how terrible you feel the next day is a really bad look. Don't be that person.

TOP FIVE WAYS TO BE A JERK WHILE TRAVELING

1) Being late.
2) Show up to leave and say you need to eat or go to the bathroom right away.
3) Falling asleep while riding shotgun.
4) Having such bad personal hygiene that you make the van smell bad.
5) Distracting the driver and putting everyone's safety in jeopardy.

WHEN IT'S NOT WORKING OUT

I've been in the same band now for twenty years. I was probably in four or five bands before that and did three or four different side projects that were very serious. And the only one that's continued to work out for me is Umphrey's. There are a lot of things that can become frustrating factors or even a clear signal that it's time to move on. If you are spending time wondering why you're not getting along with one another, or when it's not fun anymore, then that's probably not the right fit. And I think it's also important to be able to acknowledge that and to not drag something out longer than it needs to be because if it's not the right fit, then you're just wasting time that you could spend finding somebody else to collaborate with. It should be fun onstage and hopefully it'll be fun offstage. It's going to be a lot more exciting and enjoyable journey if you can figure out ways to make things enjoyable.

TOP REASONS BANDS BREAK UP

There are a number of reasons why your band may have split. Here are few of the most common.

MONEY

The top reason for stress and fighting in a marriage is money. It can certainly be the same within your band. This can stem from two different sides. Either there isn't enough money or payoff to warrant the effort or commitment. Or the way the band's money is being split, spent, or saved is contentious. Regardless of whether there isn't enough money, or disagreement about where existing cash is going, do what you can to figure it out. Otherwise, the result is likely to be you talking about the band you *used* to be in.

PERSONALITY DIFFERENCES

Things change and so do we. A separate book would be needed to really get into all the reasons of how and why. To keep it brief, success, lack thereof, or simply aging are all potential reasons why you may no longer see eye to eye. Some of this can be tempered or mitigated with good old-fashioned adult behavior, some not so much. Once bigger personality differences begin to surface, not addressing the things that accentuate them can turn into bigger issues fast.

As previous discussed, learning how to communicate is an essential part of ensuring your act's longevity. That being said, you should listen twice as much as you talk. Too often communication can be one-sided. Over time the feeling that someone you work with, or are friends with, isn't truly listening to what you say will likely result in major friction. The idea that you will get along with everyone all the time isn't a realistic expectation. There will be disagreements. What *is* realistic though is the expectation that all parties can, will, and should be heard. If you want to keep your project together for the long term, do exact that.

CREATIVE DIFFERENCES

Where to even start with this part might once again require an additional book. The simple fact is, making music that everyone is and continues to be passionate about is HARD. Period. Not finding common ground to meet on is likely to result in bigger disagreements or infighting that can lead to a breakup. Remember, you all decided to do this together, so do what you can to meet the creative needs of everyone involved.

EGO

There are a lot of mildly clever musician jokes that could be inserted here. Yes, they are largely about lead singers and guitarists, but they aren't the only ones commonly infected with the ego bug. It can really happen to anyone. This often occurs when someone feels they are pulling off the majority of the work onstage. No one likes an ego maniac. As musicians— especially successful ones—it is sometimes easy to let our heads get too big. When someone tells you that yours has swollen up a bit, take a few minutes and think about that. Maybe they are right, maybe not. But NOT being an egomaniac is what's best for your band and your own future. An oversized ego is one of the least desirable qualities that you can find, as you are all in this together.

FAMILY

In the end, this is really what can, will, and should come first. Remember, the one constant we can count on is change. The likelihood that this factor influences changes in your music career is high, especially as you age. For those who have kids, you likely aren't going to embrace tour life in the same way you did prior. Then on top of it, your life partner might not end up being as supportive as you hoped when you leave them at home to do all the heavy lifting raising your kids while you are out playing shows.

CAREERS AND AGING

If you aren't a full-time musician, that means that you and your bandmates likely have other jobs. As your music career grows, you might find that members of your band or yourself have other careers that grew as well. If your music career isn't generating the same level of money, then it's likely that a decision will need to be made. Mix in a few other variables from this section and it quickly becomes a breakup.

IMPROPER SPLIT OF WORKLOAD

Who really likes doing all the worst jobs? No one. Earlier we recommended amicably splitting up the work and responsibility associated with your performance. If you chose to ignore this advice, then it is highly possible that it led to some animosity or loss of respect for those you are working with. It's understandable. No one likes the person that always dumps the worst tasks on others, or worse yet, disappears when it's time to do any work at all. If you can afford it, consider getting help with set up and tear down sooner than later. That is a common friction point, and if you can avoid it being yours then you are best off finding some help because it sounds like you need it.

SUBSTANCE ABUSE

Unfortunately, in the music industry this is a common problem. Whether it comes with activity associated with shows, or just in general, being around someone that is constantly wasted or high gets old. Worse yet, if it's all of you, then it might become even harder to deal with. Both on a personal and professional level, high levels of drug and alcohol abuse are going to leave you in situations that are often less than ideal. Enough said.

TIRED OF IT

What was once fun, may no longer be. This is not uncommon, and certainly isn't isolated to music. Realistically, things sometimes become stale. What was once invigorating might now feel like a burden. For those of you that have been at it for a long time, you will go through minor periods where your level of excitement might sway a bit. However, if the peaks turn into valleys and you *stay there*, then your passion may have faded. That's not good and will likely lead to you not having fun, which leads to just not wanting to do any of it. Regrettably, there's not much you can do about this one if it happens.

LACK OF RESPONSIBILITY

Let's get right to the point on this one. No one likes flaky people. In fact, it doesn't take long at all to not want to be around these kind of people. Don't be a flaky person. Please.

Everything we just discussed can singularly or collectively be enough to cause a split or end to your project. Talk to anybody that has been at it for a long time and the odds that one of these things became the reason for a project's end is overwhelmingly high.

CHANGING LANES OR THE FULL PIVOT?

Before we get too crazy and talk about a full-on change of plans, have you considered a slight modification of your existing plans? There are a number of things that can trigger this need, some wanted, most not.

The number of well-known acts that have had to, or chosen to change lanes, meaning a slight change in direction, is high. On the heels of a hugely successful album, *Pyromania*, British rock band Def Leppard suffered a horrible setback when drummer Rick Allen lost an arm in a car accident in 1984. What appeared to be a career-ending tragedy became a huge challenge to the band and Rick, who wanted to continue playing. The band spent years crafting a specialized hybrid electronic/acoustic kit for Rick and by 1987, they were playing shows again. By 1988, their new album *Hysteria* surpassed the success of *Pyromania* and the band found bigger success than ever.

Grammy-winning electronic music artist Skrillex began his career as a vocalist and guitarist for post-hardcore band From First to Last. When he started having vocal problems, he was forced to have surgery. When the surgery did not solve his problems, he pivoted to creating electronic music and has subsequently become one of the most recognized DJs and producers in the music business.

Here are a few common reasons to consider a change, or maybe be forced into one.

BAND BROKE UP

Did your band break up for whatever reason? If so, then your decision to continue a music career necessitates a change in direction. This means that you need to figure out what comes next for you. Maybe you find a new band, re-invent the current one by adding new members, or do something completely different.

WHAT YOU WERE DOING WASN'T WORKING

Perhaps what you thought was going to work, didn't. A countless number of possibilities as to *why* may exist. If you are trying to make a living through music, then you might need to figure this out. It certainly isn't an uncommon issue, but the solutions to this problem aren't quite as common. Why? Because making a living as a musician is hard. There are a lot of performers, or people that want to be performers, out there. Then coupled with the myriad of choices that exist to compete with you as a performer, the overall window, or perhaps keyhole, that you have to pass through to be successful is narrow.

Sometimes those that stick with something longer than the rest are the ones that end up winning. At the same time, at some point you might also need to be realistic about what is going on with your career. If you are happy and enjoying what you are doing, then everything may in fact be fine. On the other hand, if after whatever amount of time you feel is appropriate, you aren't getting what you want, then it quite possibly might be time to examine what other options exist. In the end, this is up to you.

CHANGE IS TOUGH—NO WAY AROUND THAT

Making changes in life, whether big or small, is one of the hardest things to do well. In fact, many people refuse to do it even when very much necessary. Regardless of what circumstances brought you to this point, real decisions need to be made about how and when you are going to address needed change. How you handle impending change and the potential adversity that comes with it is paramount to where you end up.

A CONVERSATION WITH NIKKI GLASPIE

Among some the best drummers of today, Nikki Glaspie has made waves in music. Raised playing the drums in the church choir, Glaspie made her way to study at Berklee College of Music. It was there she started drumming at Wally's, Boston's most famous jazz club, and it wasn't long until this talented percussionist was playing in some big-name bands, including **Maceo Parker**, Dumpstaphunk, The Neville Brothers, as well as many other New Orleans-based bands. In 2006, she auditioned for Beyoncé, and after landing that gig she toured worldwide for more than five years. Knowing she had more work to do, she and a few other members founded The Nth Power, a band on a mission to spread light and prove that soul music can be greater than ever before. They operate on the belief that synergistically they can make more impact than any one individual could.

JOEL: I'm curious about some of your early inspiration. You started playing in the church to gospel music. How does that connect with the drummer that you are now?

NIKKI: Playing in church definitely had an influence on me, because very early on I made a connection with music and the spirit. That's just something that I've carried with me my entire life—the importance of music and how powerful it is to the soul.

Music goes beyond language and connects people, both the people creating the music and the audience. There aren't very many things where all these other differences can be dropped and left behind. Music connects us all, you know?

Yeah, I know. My grandmother, she was a musician, I mean still is. She plays keys, but she played every instrument in the band. She played drums. She played saxophone. She played whatever they needed to be done, she just did it. There's this story of her playing the bells. The bells player was sick and they had to march the next day. The band director said, "Ethel, I need you to play bells." She took them home and learned it overnight. Then came back and marched the next day.

That's so incredible. What a good inspiration to have as a kid, right?

Yeah, absolutely. I definitely get my musical influence from grandmother. She's the matriarch of the family and a super-awesome musician. She's also a pastor.

Very cool. Were you singing a bunch back then too?

No. I was not singing at all.

Interesting, because you have a great voice. You're an awesome singer now.

Oh thanks. Singing came a lot later for me. Because I never really wanted to sing. My family had a great number of singers. I was like, "I don't even want to sing. I want to play drums."

What are some early decisions you made that impacted the rest of your life? Is there anything that really stands out that you're like, "Wow, I'm glad I made that choice." or, "Wow, I'm glad I didn't do that?"

Oh yeah, absolutely. I can definitely name three important ones just right off the bat. When I graduated from high school, I was slowly planning on becoming a cardiovascular pathophysiologist. I was going to be a heart surgeon. For some reason, I figured out I wasn't going to get out of school until I was thirty-six and the average life expectancy of a doctor is fifty-two. That doesn't give me a lot of time to operate, you know what I mean.

That gives me like about sixteen years of my profession.

That's some great critical thinking there.

Yeah, so I really wanted to help people. I thought, *I can help people by playing music.* It was like a switch went off in my head. It was as if something clicked. Oh, this is completely possible. I could touch way more people playing music than going to school for twenty years and becoming a heart surgeon.

That is such a cool concept. I love it.

Yeah, so that's basically what happened.

Well and as a musician you also don't have people's lives necessarily in your hands. It's a little less pressure, right?

Yeah, a little less pressure. But I just decided it was something that I could do. I honestly had no idea how I would do it, what capacity or how it would happen. I was like, you know what, I love music, and it is a huge part of my life. I never really thought that being a professional musician was even an option. I actually had no idea what I was going to do with it, but I thought, *I'm just going to study music and see where this goes.* I didn't have a plan or think, "I'm going to be a performer," or, "I'm going to be a music therapist."

None of that crossed my mind. It was just "I'm going to study music and figure it out."

I had kind of the same experience until I met the guys in Umphrey's McGee. I knew I loved music, but how am I going to fit into this big picture somewhere? It can be hard to grasp a specific vision when you're younger too.

Definitely, because there's just so many options. The thought of being a professional drummer is kind of daunting and impossible, honestly. If anybody had told me then that's what I'd be doing, I'd be, like, no way. I wouldn't have believed them.

So there's your first big life-changing musical decision. What's the second one?

The second one was when I quit the wedding band I was in. It was called Felix Brown. We were just your typical R & B/top 40 band. We played clubs around Boston and Fanueil Hall as a party band and weddings on the weekends.

The money was probably pretty consistent?

Yeah, the money was consistent. I was definitely making great money for a twenty-one-year-old. At that point, I had actually left school. I quit school because I couldn't afford it. Berklee was super expensive. I didn't have a full ride; I just had a couple of grants.

Got you.

I was already working. I didn't need a piece of paper to tell me that I can work. I could be a professional musician without anything else.

That's a great realization, you were already doing it.

Oh yeah, so I just did the things that professional musicians do. I started playing gigs, and I was like, "This is already happening." I'm making money, I'm doing this. I remember this particular wedding, it was at Abraham Lincoln's summer home. It was so decadent and just ridiculous. These people had so much money. I just remember being treated like a peasant. There was a kitchen that connected outside down a ramp. It was the loading dock, sorry to say. That's where they set us up to eat dinner. It was by the serving trays and everything. When they served us dinner, it was three slices of rare steak, two carrots, and two potatoes.

Oh wow. What a slap in the face, that's not cool.

I looked at it and I thought to myself, "I don't need this. This is the last wedding I'm ever doing."

Sometimes it takes those stark moments to really hit you. I've definitely had a few of them too.

Yeah, but that's the thing, there were so many of those moments before. Just feeling like second-rate hired help, a second-rate citizen. I thought to myself, this is not my life or who I am, or—

It was time to make a decision for your soul part of the musician.

Yeah, it was for my soul part, for my psyche, for my self-respect. Honestly, I had no idea. I just thought, "I'm quitting, that's it." Then, once I decided, that was the last gig, I also decided to move to New York. God told me, "Go to New York." That's what happened. I literally packed up my stuff. I remember it was December 19, 2005, I moved into my apartment in Brooklyn.

What was the third decision?

The third one was going to the Beyoncé audition.

That kind of set you on your own path.

The decision to move to New York was really the one that sent me on the path because it was just six months later that I auditioned for Beyoncé. The thing about the audition was I had a gig in Nantucket with the Sam Kininger Band, and it was a Monday and a Tuesday night. If I didn't go Monday, I couldn't play Tuesday.

Right.

I had fifty bucks in my pocket. I said to myself, "Well, what am I going to do?" I could go play this gig, and I can eat for the next two weeks, or I can go to this audition and try to live off of my friends. I went to the audition. At the time, I thought it was a gimmick. I thought, "Oh she'll have a female band for about two months, just to do a late-night TV tour": the Lettermans, the Lenos, etc. Then, it turned out to be five years.

Looking back on it now, what was it about your playing and your personality that stood out, that got you that gig?

I think that as far as my playing was concerned, I was solid. I was a solid drummer. That's what made me stand out. It was just how I hit the drums, and how I interpreted the songs. I went through the school of hard knocks.

When I was at Berklee, I went to this club called Wally's. It was like a cesspool, a breeding ground. It was sink or swim. You get onstage, and if you mess up, they stop the song and you're out. That's kind of where I got my chops, and where I got my musical sensibility from. I learned how to play songs.

It's important to learn from the greats.

Because a lot of people don't know how to play songs. People will play all over and not play the part. I always use "Billie Jean" as an example. The bass line is such an iconic one. If the bass player doesn't play that, it's no longer the song.

So you're talking about approaching the drums in the same way. These are parts; these are compositions.

Yeah, they're compositions. All of those things work together.

Leon "Ndugu" Chancler was the drummer on "Billie Jean," right?

Yeah. And what an incredible musician he was.

What a great example of a classic drum part, that it served the song. As a drummer, that's what you need to do, that's what you should be focusing on.

It's funny because I feel like me being a female definitely plays into that, into me wanting to, or desiring to fill the role. Do what's supposed to be done, and not any more or any less. That's my natural inclination as a female. If something's not being done, I want to do it.

Let's talk about your experience of being a woman in the music business—some of the challenges, and what advice you have particularly for women coming up in the business.

I would say, first off, don't look at yourself as a female musician. We're all just people. Even being in the Beyoncé band—it's an all-female band—we never once looked at each other, or ourselves, as female musicians, we looked at ourselves as musicians, which is why I think that we played music at a certain caliber, or part of the reason. People love to focus on the fact that we were females playing all the instruments. For us it's the farthest thing from our mind. We are focused on playing music and making it feel good. I don't think, "Oh my God, you're such a great keyboardist for a dude."

That's an excellent point, Nikki.

For a man, like oh my gosh. That could go any way. It's like, "Oh man, you're such a great ballet dancer for a dude. You're a great housekeeper for a dude," or anything. Whatever. There are idiots out there saying things like, "Oh you're good for this or that. You're different because you're a female." For me, that's just more fuel to the fire. That's what I did growing up. People constantly told me, "Oh, girls can't play drums." I'm like, "Oh really, they can't?"

Do people really need to say that or even think like that? We have something in music that can be a positive, life-affirming experience that breaks down barriers. Some people still choose to sully it with stupid stuff like that.

Yeah.

I want to talk a little about how you approach situational drumming. How is your approach different from when you're collaborating with somebody versus being the leader of the band? What kind of different things are you thinking about? As far as you both approach to music, and then the gig too, in general.

It's not really different. Obviously when I'm leading the band, I do what I want!

Well, you're the drummer, so you kind of get to do that anyway. You're driving the train regardless.

Yeah, exactly. That's the thing, even when I'm not the leader, I am. It's like I'm always the leader. The approach isn't really different. When an artist or someone that's leading the band tells me what they want, I give it to them. I provide that. When it's my thing, when I'm leading it, I do what I want but I also take ideas and suggestions. To me, music is a group effort.

I think being open-minded to others' ideas tends to be a more enjoyable experience.

Oh, absolutely. I've been in situations where it wasn't a group effort, and it was less enjoyable for sure.

I think that's good advice. If you're working with a band, to try be inclusive about the musical decisions.

I think that's how we are who we are. Every person's voice is heard. That applies to all parts. I might have an idea about a bass part, I might have an idea about a guitar part, and vice versa.

Being open-minded to at least trying other ideas is helpful. I know that's something in Umphrey's that we try to do. If we have a couple different suggestions for how something might happen, let's try it, and see how it feels.

Yeah. To me, that's the recipe of a good band.

Anything stand out that you feel is the best advice you've ever been given, and also the worst advice?

Horacio "El Negro" Hernandez, told me, "Practice now. Once you, like, start playing gigs, and start traveling and touring, you're not going to have time to practice."

Wow.

Especially as a drummer, it's really hard to get time to sit behind the kit. We have practice pads but it's not the same when you're trying to work out ideas. You have to sit behind a kit and really play to work ideas out and figure out what you want to do. His advice to me, was to get all your shit together now. Figure out all the possible combinations, do everything that you can, practice as hard as you can now, because once you get to that level, it's just not so easy.

That's such a great point. Once you're on the road, practicing as a touring musician, you're also trying to save your energy for a concert if you're playing that night. On a day off, after you've played five or six days in a row, you probably don't want to get back in the practice room right away.

Yeah, yeah for sure.

I think that's awesome advice.

Yeah, and as far as the worst advice, I can't think of anything that someone told me that was just terrible advice. I approach every situation as a learning situation. Let's say I see someone playing a gig, and they're completely butchering it, it's terrible. *That* is a learning situation. That's how you learn what not to do.

As far as bad advice, honestly, I just put it out of my head, because I knew it was bad. You know what I mean?

Yeah, no reason to hang on to that.

I was like, I know that's not real, so bye.

I think another big thing I can share, just from knowing you both as a person and a musician, is that there has to be a level of passion. Because if you're up there and you don't believe in what you're doing, no one else is going to believe in what you're doing.

That is the truth. Also, I tell kids: "High risk, high reward." I'm sure some of their parents would not like that, but it's true. If you really believe in something, if you really believe that it can be done, it can. That's the risk, walking in the belief.

Absolutely.

Once you do that, the rewards are plentiful.

SECTION FOURTEEN:

GEAR TALK

F iguring out what you need to buy and in what order can be a daunting challenge. You likely already own your instruments and amplifiers. So what's next? If you've already played some gigs and have money to reinvest, you're going to want to start to purchase gear. These are the tools of your trade, and doing this can and should be considered a long-term investment in yourself and your craft. Let's talk about where you should start.

WHAT TO INVEST IN

CABLES

You'll want a decent collection of instrument cables on hand. Always have a few extras in case something goes down when you don't have time to repair them. Nothing is worse than a faulty cable derailing a guitar solo. The cable itself seems like it's pretty straightforward, but that isn't always the case. In fact, terrible cables can lead to a terrible sound even when plugged into the finest of instruments.

Know the difference between speaker, instrument, and XLR cables. These are the three most common ones you're going to see, and they all serve unique purposes. The XLR cable connects to microphones. The instrument cable connects an instrument to either a DI box or a sound board. And the speaker cable connects either your speakers for your PA or your monitors to the sound console. They aren't interchangeable, so don't mix them up.

RIGHT NOTE: Cables typically have a natural coil. You'll notice when you buy them that they're kind of a circle looped around each other. If you continue to wrap them the same way, your cables will stay in a lot better shape and ultimately save you loads of time in set up and break down because you're not untangling cables. There are YouTube videos worth checking out to demonstrate the natural coil.

MICROPHONES

Anyone who has used house microphones at a bar knows that they don't always work properly or smell very pleasant. Most importantly, using the same mics night after night will help keep your music sounding consistent. Learn the basics of microphone directionality and microphone placement to help inform your decisions as you start to buy your own. The world of microphones can seem broad, expensive, and downright confusing. However, there are some microphones that have more or less become industry standards.

There are two professional microphones that everyone starts out with—the Shure SM58 for vocals and Shure SM57 for everything else. These are the most popular microphones in the world. In fact, Umphrey's McGee is still using two of these that were purchased twenty-five years ago! For nearly everyone, these mics will get you started. If you're looking to move beyond those, your first purchase should be a kick drum microphone such as an AKG d112, Shure Beta 52, Audix D6, or Sennheiser e902. Condenser microphones would be the next items you purchase. They are better for picking up room sounds and instruments you're not mic'ing directly. All the microphones mentioned here can be purchased for less than $200 each, some closer to $100.

PA / MONITORS

Owning a relatively small PA (public address) and monitors opens up the potential to play venues that might not have a suitable or even available PA, such as well-paying private parties. If you're really smooth, you can also rent out your PA to other artists when you're not using it. Regardless, until you're playing larger venues that all have a good house PA, it might prove extra useful to have depending on your needs.

If lighting matters for your shows, you may want to purchase your own equipment. Intelligent lights are now smaller, more powerful, and more affordable than ever. It can be an element that makes the music more impactful.

Also consider bringing a small element of staging that will help project the image you're looking for as an artist. It can be as simple as a logo, your name, or something completely abstract depending on the vibe.

RIGHT NOTE: If your group has a drummer, consider getting some sort of visual representation—whether it's a decal or artwork—on the drummer's kick drum. This is an efficient way to add a small visual element to your act without incurring a huge expense.

FRONT OF HOUSE AND MONITOR CONSOLES

The ultimate way to reduce the variables of your live show is to invest in a front of house console and/or monitor console. You can save your work on a night to night basis and virtually eliminate the lengthy process of a daily sound check for each channel. Owning your own sound consoles will simplify your days on the road and help maintain a consistent production.

WITH GEAR, LESS IS MORE ON THE ROAD

You will face limitations of time for nearly every gig and sound check, so efficiency is needed in your setup. Each piece of gear adds work moving and sound checking it for each show. Every time you add a piece of gear or channel to your rig, it exponentially increases the work and the time needed for that instrument, as every person onstage with you will also likely need to add it to their mix. Try to keep your rig as straightforward and simple as possible. As you start to play bigger venues you can add to your rig, but in general choose versatility and practicality at the beginning.

RIGHT NOTE: Make a visual representation of how the stage is set up for your act. This is known as a stage plot and you will want to share it with the local sound engineer in advance of your show, as it will make your set-up process more organized and straightforward for everyone involved (and lessen the chances for mistakes as you wire the stage on a nightly basis).

Hopefully that clarified some of the mystery that comes with equipment and how to handle the accumulation of it. One thing that you don't want to accumulate too much of is what we need to talk about next.

A CONVERSATION WITH ROBBIE WILLIAMS

As we previously stated, the majority of the music industry is like an iceberg with the largest part of it not visible. This is especially true for the crew of any band, big or small. However, for those performing to focus on exactly that, a great team is a must. That is why bringing Robbie Williams in for some advice is a good idea right now. An industry veteran with twenty years of experience, Robbie has spent the last fourteen years of his career as the stage manager for Umphrey's McGee.

MATT: What does a stage manager do?

ROBBIE: I try to see the big picture of what lights are coming in, what sound is going in, how much space we need, where we're going to put everything?

How do you keep track of all this stuff?

It goes in the truck the same way and comes out the same way, every day.

Is there a diagram? Do you literally have a sketch?

We numbered the cases. It's like a big game of Tetris.

I custom-designed most of the drum and percussion cases and the keyboard cases.

What's the worst you can do to your gear as a touring artist?

Not investing in a road case for all your gear. Everything has got a case. It protects it and your investment. It might seem like a lot of money on the front end. Like, "I just bought this one thousand dollar whatever and I now have to spend seven-fifty on a case?" That sucks, but you're still going to have that gear for, like, fifteen years.

What's the best thing you can do?

Have your equipment serviced.

You're talking like solder joints and stuff like that?

Yeah. Just like the older stuff, like the Hammond B3.

Do you have an extra one for parts on those?

We have a guy who is in Minneapolis who really takes care of our gear. Whenever we go through there, I set up way in advance and he can send me stuff or tell me how to fix things on the road. I have a good relationship with him.

A lot of people don't give credence to the fact that when you're moving electronics around in a truck all the time, it shakes things loose.

Yeah. It's constant. All of a sudden, you're like, "Wow. There are only three screws holding the bottom of this keyboard on. I'm glad I caught that before there were no screws left."

When you're not at the point of having a semi to bring everything, what are a couple of things that you won't go on tour without?

Batteries, spare cables, spare power adapters, gaffer tape, and zip ties.

When hiring someone, what are the qualities you want in a crew member?

Number one for me, and I think other people, is make sure you can live with the person.

Like personality-wise?

Yes. Because you're going to be spending a lot of time with them. You need someone who respects you and who you respect as well.

Dependability?

Dependability and accountability. We've always had a thing where it's like, "You're an adult. Nobody's here to tell you how to live your life. If you want to stay up drinking or whatever all night, so be it."

Just make sure and do your job?

Yep. But when it's on, you're on. We're nobody's mother.

What's a red flag if you're interviewing crew members that makes you immediately know that person is not going to be right?

The whole me, me, me thing. Nobody is here to see us.

So someone I can live with who is a team player, plus is able to do numerous jobs.

That's one of the things we talked about—finding a Swiss Army knife before you find a specialist. Someone that does a lot of different things, wears a lot of hats.

Yeah.

Who do you think is the most important crew member to hire?

Probably a sound guy, so you actually have consistency from show to show.

What's the worst thing you've ever left behind at a venue?

All the practice gear. Every bit of it.

Has that happened more than once?

No, just one time on my first tour. And I had a friend of a friend bring it back to us.

Wow.

Yeah. He loaded all the practice gear in his small car and returned it. To this day, he takes credit for me having my job.

SECTION FIFTEEN:

CREW

I t can be a challenge to determine when the right time is to hire new people without overextending yourself. One of the things Umphrey's McGee did as a band was to ask new hires to show us how they thought they could make the band more money and pay for their own salary. That type of personal ownership and investment keeps your people focused and motivated. We also made a promise to ourselves to only hire people that we felt were smarter than we were, and tried to look for people with skill sets that were not already our strongest.

Whether it's the music business or a completely different industry altogether, the most successful operations are the ones that seek, hire, and then retain the best people possible. You are only as good as the people that exist within your business. It comes down to three Ps: people, product, and process. Any deficiency within those categories can easily, and quickly, derail your path toward success.

ACQUIRING CREW

For a while you're going to be setting up and tearing down your own gear. Eventually that operation will become involved enough that it is beneficial—and financially feasible—to have other people coming out and helping you. In the beginning, who should you hire first? Strong consideration should be given to someone that can act as your "front of house engineer."

The front of house engineer is the guy who controls how you sound to everyone else. The reason why it's the most important person to hire is a lot of the resident engineers in bars and clubs probably don't care that much about how your band sounds. That's just kind of the reality out there. You'll come across good local sound engineers occasionally, but you don't want to count on that especially in larger settings. That's where you need your own sound engineer. Ideally the sound engineer can also assist in other tasks, whether it's tour management, helping to book shows, or whatever else you can shed off the band's duties as soon as possible. You also now have somebody to act as a go-between if the band needs anything during a show. That way no one's ordering bar drinks over the microphone.

Your second hire, if you're in pop rock and doing somewhat complex music, or if you're a DJ who wants to have more of a production, should be a multipurpose, Swiss Army-like person who might be able to raise the level of your production as a "lighting tech." Most venues have house lights, but some are way better than others. Plus technology is changing. More acts prefer having intelligent lights, which are programmable lights you do not find at most venues that still use old analog cans, which are just a light with a gel on top of it. These new multifunctional lighting units are reasonably cost effective to rent or even buy. It might be to your advantage to invest a little bit in a light rig that you can bring along with you on the road show to make sure there's production value consistency regardless of the quality—or lack—of the venue's house gear. Of course if you're more of a solo singer songwriter, you might not need your own lighting engineer. It all depends on the music and how much of a production the show warrants.

The third person to add to one's crew would be a "tour manager." Their role is to take care of every organizational detail and to be responsive 24/7, depending on the band's needs while on the road. This is an essential person to have as the touring dates get more intense to keep things in order and running smoothly. The tour manager is also the person that settles with the promoter at the end of the night and takes care of any previously agreed rider terms, which are what you require the promoter or the venue to provide, including food and beverages. The tour manager might also be your point person with merchandise, which could mean they sell merch or they set up merch with a local seller. Above all, the tour manager keeps everything together and on time, relieving responsibility of anybody in the band.

That said, of course, keep yourself on time. DON'T BE THE LATE GUY.

Your crew may continue to grow as you succeed. Perhaps you'll want to hire a "guitar tech," a "drum tech," or maybe a "merch guy" to bring with you on the road.

RIGHT NOTE: If you're on tour, someone will need to address where you'll sleep on a nightly basis. This means booking hotels, setting up Airbnb's, or contacting friends for sleeping arrangements. If you're willing to take a chance to save money, there are also many sites now that will book last minute discount lodging.

SECTION SIXTEEN:

TIP OF THE ICEBERG

In reality, the likelihood of you becoming the next arena or stadium act are slim. Sorry, it's the truth and always was. However, that doesn't mean you can't have an enjoyable, lucrative, and fulfilling career and life in music. Whether or not you have considered other options, know that many *do* exist. Not discussing these in some detail would be a huge oversight on our part.

THE TOP CAREER CHOICES IN THE MUSIC INDUSTRY

Valid career options in the music industry are vast and plentiful. Many in fact are quite lucrative too. Some are directly related to the general subjects of performance, recording, and promotion, while others are related to musical instruments, teaching, or perhaps media. Regardless, there is music everywhere, paired with often overlooked jobs and careers.

LIVE PERFORMANCE, MANAGEMENT, AND SUPPORT

Many that started as performers and touring musicians stay near what they know best. There are a whole lot of options for you here, albeit several include the sacrifices associated with touring and the road, without the glory of stage performance. If you are good with that then there are many avenues available. At this point, you also might be thinking that you don't have any related experience. First off, that isn't necessarily true. Plus nobody had experience doing anything until they did it. Meaning, as long as the interest, desire, and passion exist, learning something new won't be that difficult.

PROMOTER

Up to this point you may have logged quite a bit of experience doing this for yourself. So why not try doing it for others. The same relationships, connections, and knowledge that you

323

cultivated for yourself or the band should be equally helpful when it comes to doing it for others. Depending on what and who you are promoting, it is possible that you might need additional financial resources to pursue a career as a promoter. If that isn't something within your grasp, then perhaps the next option is a good one.

Booking Agent

At any given time, there is always a brand-new generation of up and coming acts trying to find gigs. Or perhaps the venues themselves seek help booking their next gig. Your experience and connections when it comes to booking your own shows might really pay off here. If you're starting at an agency, you may have to work your way up the chain of command. If you're doing it on your own, you can consider the dual role of manager/agent.

Management

Did you learn a lot about how bands, tours, and general operations work? If so, then you are probably qualified to manage. Sure, there are likely to be some things that you need to learn to pursue this direction, but once again, if the desire exists then learning is easy. On the flip side, finding clients could be a little challenging. This choice will likely require patience, persistence, and a strong desire to make shit happen!

If you choose to pursue this option, it is recommended that you pursue acts within genres that you enjoy and are passionate about. Why? Well that's an easy answer. If you believe in it, enjoy it, and more importantly *believe that those you rep have what it takes to make it*, then your job will be that much easier. If you can't put a checkmark next to those particular factors, then reconsider this choice, or at least which act to dedicate your services.

TOUR MANAGER

An absolute linchpin of a successful, productive, and profitable touring operation is its tour manager. But let's get one thing out there. This position is not for everyone. Without a doubt, it requires some specific attributes that you must have, or very quickly develop, if you expect to find any level of success. These include being super organized, having the ability to deal with all kinds of people, being able to have tough or difficult conversations, and graciously doing just about any thankless job or task along the way. The tour manager often has the longest hours on the road and must be ready to work at the artist's whim, even if they need something in the middle of the night. If that is a job description that you still feel good about, then this just might be the role for you.

LIGHTING AND SOUND

There are a number of positions that exist under this designation. It could include everything from running front of house sound to being the one that helps set everything up. Once again this isn't for all. When on an active tour, everything in this category is not only going to be a whole lot of work, all that work—and often related problems to solve—occur within a tight and stressful time frame before each performance.

In addition to being a lot of work, these types of jobs and careers are highly process oriented. Planned and executed properly, these things can occur with precision. But if done poorly, well, this can be a living hell, both for you and those that you are working for and with. These jobs are best suited for those that are driven and have the ability to solve problems on the fly and often under pressure.

In regards to the lighting aspect of this, as previously mentioned, there is a whole new world of smart technology out there. It's actually really exciting. As the overall affordability and ease of use is becoming a lot more accessible, additional jobs and careers have come along. For some, this is a really fun and rewarding segment of the business.

GUITAR TECH

Can you effortlessly tune a guitar? Can you restring, repair, or make adjustments just as fast? If the answer is yes and you love guitars, then this might be just for you. Pursuing guitar tech doesn't offer the most plentiful of options, but if you are in fact great with guitars you just might find yourself in a long-term gig with a performer that not only needs but *values* your ability to help them sound the best that they possibly can. Depending on the gig, some guitar techs are also required to know much of the artist's material in the event an emergency sub is needed. Being able to play the instrument well could help you land a shot to get into the performance side of the business.

DRUM TECH

Okay, same stuff applies here as did a guitar tech, but with drums. The setup, tuning, and general readiness of a drum kit isn't exactly simple. If you have experience and a love for drumming, then exploration of this career path might be worth it for you.

STAGE MANAGER

Does the idea of making everything not only fit, but also work on a different stage, in a different city daily excite you? If so, you just might be the next great stage manager in the industry. Just don't expect a lot of notoriety. Example, name one stage manager? Despite the lack of public recognition, this is another linchpin of the touring machine. This isn't an easy job. It requires the ability to not only plan ahead, but also to understand the technical details that might come with making different "stuff" work with other different "stuff" each and every day.

RECORDING, SOUND, AND TECHNOLOGY

While the recording industry as a whole has gone through a massive set of changes over the last two decades, the number of those recording is greater than ever. This expands past just music. Entirely different categories exist now that didn't fifteen to twenty years ago. An example would be the recording industry that is related to audio books and then podcasting. Did you know that 25 percent of Americans listen to at least one podcast? In fact, while we are on the subject, check out the podcasts that the authors of this book made for you.

In addition to new and interesting segments of recording, an entire industry related to music technology, gaming, and everything else that comes with it is very much something to consider. If you really want to stretch it out, you can even include video production, too. The same skills and experience used to produce audio are used to produce video. Enough said? Let's go ahead and talk about some of the established and rising possibilities here.

RECORDING STUDIO ENGINEER

A whole lot of people are completely overwhelmed with the act of recording. They would much rather just walk into an existing setup, do their thing, and, despite the associated expense, have something professional come back to them as a result.

If you recorded yourself or others and have been someone that has the patience and persistence to not only get the recording but the postproduction right, then being a sound engineer might be the right choice for you. Much like many of the other options, this one will require some technical know-how as well as a patient approach toward helping others create and produce what they are satisfied with. If that's you, this warrants consideration.

PRODUCER

This is much more of a niche, and with that, can be hard to get into. A producer can perform a variety of roles when it comes to the recording process, some of which include the ability to get others involved or finding the necessary resources for other things to occur. A producer's job can involve trying to motivate the musician or chiming in creatively about what's working and what's not. Most of all, the producer is the outside resource that helps bring the best out of the artist and filter out what isn't their strongest material. You likely know and understand what it might, will, and could take to do this. If you don't, it's probably best to start somewhere else for now.

SESSION MUSICIAN

Are you REALLY, REALLY good at any, or many, instruments? You'll need to be if you want to be a session musician. Why? The entire point of this job is to get it right, and quickly. Being a session musician requires the ability to operate with swift precision within many types and genres of music and, oh yeah, be as good or better than whomever you are working for.

SONG WRITER

Do music and lyrics flow freely from you? They will likely need to if you want to pursue a career as a songwriter. This can be a tough career to pursue. Not only will you have to get your music in front of those that have the desire and means to purchase your material, but you will also have to have material worth buying.

VIDEO GAMES AND TECHNOLOGY

Well, someone has to write and then perform all the music associated with video games and other technology that surrounds us. Why not let that be you? There are all kinds of options for you here, and all within an industry that is, and will likely continue to grow.

A&R, OR ARTS AND REPERTOIRE

Someone has to find the next big thing. Landing a job in A&R can be a dream come true. Meaning, yes, you're paid to do nothing other than go out daily/nightly and listen to live music, then potentially convince these acts why a discussion with your employer is in their best interest. The coveted A&R positions for major labels are few and far between, as profits continue to shrink from recorded music. Jobs like these will continue to become more and more scarce in the twenty-first century.

THE MUSICAL INSTRUMENT INDUSTRY

It is estimated that the overall market size of the musical instrument industry will meet or exceed eighteen billion dollars by 2020. That's right, you read that correctly—a *b* for billion. That makes this particular path one that has quite a few options. Anyone that has ever been to the NAMM, or North American Music Merchants convention, will attest to the overall size of this industry. With nearly a hundred thousand people attending this convention, that means there are a heck of lot of career opportunities available.

Companies such as Roland and Yamaha operate worldwide. Roland alone generates over four billion dollars a year in sales and is the world's largest manufacturer of electronic musical instruments. With that huge amount of volume come a few interesting facts too. The first is that Roland's founder, Ikutaro Kakehashe (lovingly known as Mr. K), is also the inventor of MIDI, for which rather than licensing he made available to all. Understanding how influential and powerful what he had created would become, the one-time watchmaker turned pioneer of electronic music felt this was something the world needed access to. So on behalf of everyone, thank you, Mr. K.

In addition to that fun fact, most don't realize that Roland is also the world's largest drum maker when it comes to sales volume. How you ask? Well, making amazing digital drums that can be played at only a fraction of the volume of traditional drum kits is a good start. But wait, there is more. Roland is also the parent company of BOSS. Yes, the maker of seven of ten of the world's most popular guitar pedals of all time, including the DS-1, which has sold more than a million units, and for many of us was the first foray into the world of electric guitar distortion.

Believe it or not, all that doesn't even make Roland the biggest musical instrument manufacturer out there. Yamaha holds that title, largely due to the wide variety of musical instruments produced by the company, which includes everything from the orchestral band instruments kids play growing up to drum sets, pianos, guitars, and well, you name it. Yamaha accounts for a massive slice of the industry. While many associate Yamaha with boat motors and motorcycles, they had made musical instruments long before that. Want proof? Look at the Yamaha logo. It is three tuning forks laid across each other.

Okay, you get it, the musical instrument industry is HUGE. Now what can you possibly do within it? The answer to that question is just about as broad as the industry itself. So let's get a little deeper into the possibilities.

It's fair to start here. After all, someone has to sell the billions of dollars of instruments produced annually. These kinds of jobs aren't technically associated with the manufacturers themselves but more so with the retail operations that sell the instruments. Now before you rush out to find a job within this segment of the industry, despite the high volume of sales, the music instrument retail business has been in a state of decline, or massive change for years. Huge amounts of competition coupled with easily shippable items and razor thin margins have made it difficult to operate retail operations. While companies such as Guitar Center or Sam Ash still operate national chains, many retailers have either gone out of business (as is the case with most of the piano industry) or been forced to alter their business model to include a variety of different services or offerings.

Despite the musical instrument retail industry embracing some evolutionary tendencies, there are still many above average paying jobs and career within it. If you have a knowledge of musical instruments and the ability to sell, then you too can be one of those making a great living from musical instrument retail. If you have a knowledge and love for *orchestral* instruments, then you have an even greater chance of finding success, as traditional band programs are still very much existent in schools across North America.

JOBS WITH MUSICAL INSTRUMENT MANUFACTURERS

For those not interested in a life of retail, there are quite a few possibilities that exist working for the makers of the instruments we are so fond of. While some of these possibilities may only be possible for those located within the geographical area of the manufacturers' operation hubs, not all require this. Companies such as Roland, Yamaha, as well as the other manufacturers, all employ a variety of "in the field" employees. This includes some straight sales jobs as manufacturers reps or district sales managers, much like Matt DeCoursey once was for Roland. Other career paths are related to instruction, demonstration, or performance related jobs. While some of these gigs are full-time, many are not. However the part-time effort associated with these piecemeal jobs usually pay well, albeit they definitely require travel.

In-House Careers with Music Instrument Manufacturers

If you do happen to live within range of a musical instrument manufacturer, then you might be in luck. Both Yamaha and Roland have US headquarters located in Southern California, at which a large number of employees work for either company. Companies like these have a wide variety of needs. Some are related to the support mechanism needed for those buying their instruments. Others are related to product testing and development. Add in the variety of jobs that are associated with sales, marketing, artist relations, or logistics and you end up with a whole lot of job possibilities.

These jobs can be kind of hard to land as most people that work for similar companies do whatever they need to do to keep these jobs. After all, doesn't it sound pretty cool to get paid to work with all the instruments that you would love to own, or perhaps be involved in the research and development of those to come? If you are able to get a job with a company like Yamaha or Roland, then congratulations. Both have a stellar reputation as employers, and as instrument makers too.

TEACHING, INSTRUCTION, EDUCATION, AND THERAPY

You probably didn't pick up a guitar, or sit down at a piano for the first time thinking that you would later become a teacher or instructor of the instrument. But doing so is a very popular path both for musicians embracing change, or for those with an entrepreneurial spirit to start their own small business related to teaching lessons, or perhaps operating a studio in which several instructors operate and teach lessons.

This path is a noble one. Consider yourself tasked with teaching fine arts and the skills needed and wanted in order to enjoy music for a lifetime to the next generation of musicians. Within this path there are a few different types of instruction or education that are possible.

INSTRUCTOR

The first and most straightforward path is that of an instructor, or someone that offers lessons either to groups or, more commonly, privately to students of all ages and skill levels. This is a valid option for those wanting or needing to earn a little extra money on the side, or if you choose can very much be a full-time job and career. In order to pursue this, you will need to have the fundamental skills and knowledge required to teach students how to play music. If you are prepared, then this might be a great choice, at least for now.

MUSIC EDUCATOR

This career path involves a lot more formal education, training and usually credentials. Consider this path to be more like that of a school teacher or similar position than that of a private instructor. While budgets for school-based music programs aren't exactly setting records for their size, such programs exist in pretty much every level of institution from elementary through college. Before you get too excited, many of these jobs are done by those willing to do them more for the love of the subject and those receiving the knowledge than they are for the associated paycheck. If you can accept that, this might be for you.

MUSIC THERAPY

The field of Music Therapy has been around for a while and can and should be considered a very valid and rewarding career path for those interested. Used in association with various types of treatment or learning, music therapists perform a needed and noble task when it comes to alternative therapy for the elderly or quite possibly those with special needs. Pursuit of this career path likely requires credentials or education. If you already have these credentials, in many cases and places this can provide a great living.

MEDIA AND JOURNALISM

The world of media and journalism, much like that of the music industry, has gone through a total metamorphosis. What was once in the hands of a chosen few is now quite the opposite. Meaning, anyone now has the ability to quickly, easily, and effectively publish content related to music and the industry itself. In a more traditional sense, there are hundreds of media outlets that employee thousands of writers and journalists who create and produce content for their online platforms. What are those jobs? Here a few that might interest you.

JOURNALIST

Pretty much anybody can publish articles related to music, their opinion of it, or perhaps a recap of the experience they had at a live show. There are also a whole lot of full and part-time positions writing for credible and established media outlets. You might have to first hustle up several non-paying articles in order to establish enough credibility to get ones that pay out. If you are able to do so, then you might find yourself in a position where you can create content from anywhere. The best part is your association with these credible and popular outlets is likely to help you gain access to people and places that most can't. Performers want the exposure, so what's an extra name on the guest list, or a VIP pass to come backstage after the show?

Now before you quit your day job, a lot of these gigs are barely considered paying. The reason being, there are about a hundred more of you waiting to take your place if you decide that you don't like that fact. But, if you don't mind and you have a passion for the subject matter, this can be a heck of a lot of fun, as well as something loaded with just as many unique memories.

PUBLICIST

Can you generate hype? If so, being a publicist might be a good fit for you. Before you start applying for jobs in this field, you should probably understand that many parts of this profession are in fact highly repetitive. You often, if not every time, have one message to deliver, but are expected to do so to hundreds if not thousands of recipients. Then on top of that, many of these recipients don't or won't even care about what you have to say. Being a publicist involves having and constantly garnering more media connections and accepting the fact that it's a number game. Meaning, you have to send your message out to a large number of people in order to get some form of participation from a few. If you are persistent, and not afraid to often hear "no," then you might have what it takes to work as a publicist.

MUSIC DIRECTOR

A wide variety of companies and institutions have positions for musical directors. One of the more common institutions in need of this position are churches. Music is a huge and serious part of many types of worship. With that, churches and those attending are willing to provide the means necessary for someone to coordinate, improve, or maintain the standards of the members.

Other careers available for musical directors could be at radio stations or other media outlets where these individuals are tasked with determining the overall content associated with airplay or other forms of distribution.

RADIO AND INTERNET

Do you have a passion for music and at the same time aren't afraid of a hot microphone? If the answer is yes, then you might be able to pursue a job as a DJ or Internet radio host. These positions come in a variety of shapes and forms, some paid, many not. If you want to pursue this avenue, it is very much possible that you will be doing so for the love of the subject matter. Much like some of the other opportunities discussed in this section, these positions are highly sought and thus the demand far outweighs the supply. Normally this is a good thing in regards to economics, however in this case not so much for those wanting to host shows online, or on the radio. Sure, some major outlets do offer some pretty solid compensation. However, there are what on some days seem like a huge supply of low or no pay options here.

THE STORY OF ROY SCOTT OF HEALTHY HIP-HOP

Way back in the beginning of this book we described Matt DeCoursey as an entrepreneur, an investor, and an author—all which is still true, especially the entrepreneur and investor part. That brings us to the story of a Kansas City area entrepreneur who Matt and his company, Full Scale, have recently partnered with.

Roy Scott was once known as "Macc James," a "gangster" rapper who has recording credits with the well-known Tech N9ne amongst others. Roy is a Kansas City native and grew up with a father who was also a musician. Roy spent a few years in the Kansas City rap scene. He did exactly okay. We aren't going to tell you that he was a star, but he was making a living. In fact, enough to support a wife and children.

This is where Roy's story takes a hard pivot. One day Roy picked up his son from preschool and while heading home heard his very adult lyrics being recited from the back seat. Roy was absolutely turned upside down hearing his own son spit his lyrics. *What have I done?* he thought. And even more important, *What am I doing?* He knew something had to change and that was certainly the last moments of Macc James, Gangster Rapper.

Now searching for a way to deliver something positive and meaningful to kids, Roy created Healthy Hip-Hop, also known as H3. What is that exactly? It's hip-hop music made for kids that has a healthy, positive, and upbeat message. The concept was quickly embraced, and Roy soon found himself pitching his idea on the über-popular entrepreneur TV show, *Shark Tank*, in September of 2015. Well, at least filming an episode.

Sounds exciting, right? It certainly was, as during the episode Roy and his performing partner received a "deal" from one of the sharks. *Wow, this really is going to big!* Roy thought and headed back to Kansas City to wait and prepare for the episode to air.

Waiting is exactly what Roy did—in fact, six months' worth before the call came. The problem was, it wasn't the call he was expecting. Instead, it was a call informing him that his episode would NOT air. No explanation, no reason; it just wasn't going to air.

Understandably, this rocked Roy's world. Left to wonder *why* this had happened, another month passed by when the phone rang. It was an anonymous person at the network who felt terrible about the situation and wanted to let Roy at least know what had happened, and that was that Disney, ABC, and *Shark Tank*'s parent company, had invoked a clause in everyone's contract that gave them the right to nix any business or partnership that had been made during filming. But why? Simple—they thought it could create competition.

Now, midway through 2016 and saddled with debt from product he was planning on selling after the show aired, Roy needed to figure something out. Fortunately, he had created a decent income from performing shows related to H3, yet Roy still wanted more.

In an effort to continue pursuing his dream, Roy applied for grants, funding, and other sources of capital to produce a content delivery network and mobile app that could be used by kids in schools as well as their parents. Much like the career of "Macc James," this went just okay, as Roy won several small grants allowing him to continue proving out his concept. This went on for the next year and a half.

Now, in February of 2018, our story brings us to Roy being a guest on the *Startup Hustle* podcast. Hosted by Matt DeCoursey and his business partner, Matt Watson, the show that now has listeners in a hundred sixty countries was then on Episode 6 and also trying to prove it could be viable. For roughly an hour Roy told his story of triumph and heartbreak and everyone went about their business after.

It wasn't until June of 2018, when another significant call was made. This time from Roy to Matt DeCoursey. The simple summary: "Matt can you help me figure out why I'm not getting as many investors as I think I should?" Having always liked Roy, as well as the concept Roy had, Matt agreed.

It didn't take Matt long to see a few things. The first was that the business Roy had created was trying to do too many things without first mastering one. The solution was easy: Just simplify your approach. The next thing that became apparent was that Roy and H3 were really on to something. As Matt did the financial projections and planning review, he realized that Roy had come up with a strategy that not only could be very profitable but would also deliver a highly valuable and positive message to schools and their children and do it at no charge to the schools!

It was just one week later that Matt's company made the first of what have become multiple investments into Healthy Hip-Hop. Set to fully launch Summer of 2019, the H3 network will deliver the fresh and positive message of Healthy Hip-Hop to schools across the country. Also included in the H3 offering is a mobile app that allows its users—meaning parents or children—to create their own Healthy Hip-Hop songs and share them with one another via its pre-approved friends network. While this story is still very much being written and no one knows how it will turn out, the point is that Roy stuck to it, found people that believed in him, and also those able to help him with the resources he needed to try.

WE DIDN'T FORGET ABOUT YOU

So much of this book, in fact nearly all of it, is dedicated to the pursuit of rock 'n' roll, or other types of modern music. But for those that are classically trained in orchestral-related categories, yes you do also have the ability to participate in many of the education fields we mentioned, but you also possibly possess the ability to land a job for which only those specifically qualified can get.

ORCHESTRAL MUSICIAN

Yes, that is correct. If you play strings, brass, reed, or other orchestral instruments, then you might be able to land a variety of gigs uniquely associated with these instruments. I mean how many oboe players are there in your local market? Yes, all the times you drove your parents nuts learning how to play that thing can or could pay off! Just kidding, but maybe not. If you played in band and orchestra growing up and stuck with it, there are likely several kinds of gigs available for you. Some as simple as ensemble performances, and others with a lot more depth such as full orchestra or symphony gigs.

Hopefully something in this section helped you find a solution to wanted, and hopefully not *unwanted*, change that might be coming for you. Keep in mind, the music industry as a whole is huge, and there certainly are a wide variety of jobs and gigs that can and very much should be considered successful careers in the music industry—including many more options than we could address. If you are looking for something, be diligent and thorough in your search. You never know what you might come across!

APPENDIX

HELPFUL MUSICAL WEBSITES

1) Find venues and other artists' tour itineraries — Pollstar.com
2) Oblique Strategies — http://www.rtqe.net/ObliqueStrategies/
3) Lefsetz Letter — http://lefsetz.com/wordpress/

ACKNOWLEDGMENTS

JOEL CUMMINS

Thank you to my wife, daughter, my parents and grandparents, who have all encouraged my desire to pursue and love music: Dasha Davis, Willa Quinn Davis Cummins, Susan and Jerry Cummins, Lowanda and Leslie Easterday, and Mable and Robert Cummins.

To my bandmates and book contributors: Brendan Bayliss, Jake Cinninger, Ryan Stasik, Kris Myers, Andy Farag, Mike Mirro, Vince Iwinski, Kevin Browning, Huey Lewis, Chuck Leavell, Susan Tedeschi, Victor Wooten, Taylor Hicks, Jeff Coffin, Nikki Glaspie, Chris Gelbuda, Pete Shapiro, Alicia Karlin, Syd Schwartz, Ian Goldberg, Joe Hettinga, Patrick Gorman, Micah Gordon, and Thierry Arsenault for their contributions, directly or indirectly.

To my behind-the-scenes Umphrey's McGee home and road crew past and present: Robbie Williams (my keyboard tech!), Bob Ston, Drew Queen, Jefferson Waful, Chris Mitchell, Bobby Haight, Aaron "Louie" Meyette, Steve Britz, Sam Sutton, Rachel Simmon, Matt Heller, Mary Welch Fox Stasik, Manny Sanchez, Greg Magers, Shane Hendrickson, Don Richards, Adam Budney, Wade Wilby, Armand Sadlier, Henry Farag, and many, many unnamed others who lent a hand along the way.

To my agents Aaron Pinkus and Jonathan Levine of Paradigm Agency.

To my musical teachers and inspirations: Kathi Best, Robert A. Boyd, Connie Lyda, Daniel Stowe, Donald Doig, Walter Ginter, Sheree Wesenberg, and Frank Caruso.

To our fearless editor, Patrick Price.

And special thanks to my coauthor, Matt DeCoursey, for believing in me and this project from the very beginning.

MATT DeCOURSEY

A BIG THANK YOU to following people!

To my loving, patient, and beautiful wife, Jill, and my kids, Dylan and Cayden, who somehow put up with all my "stuff."

To the following people who made a contribution to this project: Jeff Coffin, Victor Wooten, Taylor Hicks, Huey Lewis, Chris Gelbuda, Pete Shapiro, Alicia Karlin, Robbie Williams, Syd Schwartz, Ian Goldberg, Susan Tedeschi, Nikki Glaspie, Roy Scott, Kevin Browning, Vince Iwinski, Chuck Leavell, Ivan Neville, Brelann Lawler, Jonny Cook, Patrick Price, Lauren Forte, and Krista Vossen!

A second thank you to Patrick Price, the greatest editor in the industry and someone who somehow has managed to make it through three books of mine now. Patrick, you are the man!

To the employees at Full Scale and GigaBook who supported me at time when I needed help of any kind!

To all the supporters and listeners of the *Startup Hustle* podcast.

To Roy Scott and everyone who has helped with Healthy Hip-Hop! I'm really looking forward to making a difference with all of you!

To the entire Umphrey's McGee organization, who, without a doubt, run the tightest ship in the music industry. The access, cooperation, friendship, hospitality, and patience that you have shown myself, my family, and my guests over the last twelve years mean so much to me.

To the family, friends, and fans of Umphrey's McGee!

To all my friends who have worked or still work at Roland or Yamaha.

To Joel's wife, Dasha, and daughter, Willa Quinn, for their patience with us and this project.

And to Joel Cummins, who has been an amazing friend, an inspiration, a hero, and someone who has always taken time for me when I asked for it. Writing this book with you and the other contributors has been such an amazing experience. Thank you.

ABOUT THE AUTHORS

JOEL CUMMINS is a keyboardist, vocalist, and songwriter for the progressive, improvisational rock band Umphrey's McGee. His career highlights include playing in front of forty thousand people at Bonnaroo in 2014, recording an album at the iconic Abbey Road Studios, and opening every show of his college cover band with the Rolling Stones's "Beast of Burden." Every. Single. Show.

Joel was born and raised in suburban Chicago, and graduated from the University of Notre Dame in 1998 with a degree in music theory. Over the past thirty years, he's performed more than three thousand concerts and released fifteen albums of original material, mostly with Umphrey's McGee. Joel has shared the stage with Buddy Guy, Mavis Staples, Huey Lewis, Joshua Redman, John Oates, Skrillex, and other legendary musicians. Joel's many musical influences include a wide variety of artists such as Miles Davis, Claude Debussy, and Queen. He's performed at prestigious venues all over the world, including Japan's Fuji Rock Festival, Australia's Byron Bay Bluesfest, and US destinations like Bonnaroo, Austin City Limits Music Festival, Colorado's Red Rocks Amphitheatre, and New York's Beacon Theatre. Joel enjoys world travel, skiing, yoga, golf, baseball, and running. He, his wife Dasha, and daughter, Willa Quinn, make their home in Los Angeles, which means they're actually there about ten days a year. If you'd like to troll him on social media, send a message to @goldlikejoel and ask him when he's going to cover a particular song.

MATT DECOURSEY is the author of *Million Dollar Bedroom* and *Balance Me*, the co-host of the *Startup Hustle* podcast, co-founder and CEO of Full Scale, an international company with hundreds of employees, as well as the founder of GigaBook. He lives in Kansas City with his wife, son, and daughter.